ONE TWO THREE FOUR...

The life and times of a recording studio engineer.

Richard Digby Smith

Noble Legacy Publishing

Copyright © 2025 Richard Digby Smith

reproduced, stored in a retrieval system, or transmitted in any form or by any means, electronic, mechanical, photocopying, recording or otherwise, without the prior written permission of the publisher, except in the case of brief quotations used in critical articles or reviews. This book is a work of non-fiction. While every effort has been made to ensure accuracy, some names and events may have been altered or condensed for clarity or privacy. First edition

ISBN: (978-1-911761-09-9)

Published by Noble Legacy Publishing

To Kim, Kane and Miles.
Always my rhythm section.

Contents

Contents	iv
Foreword	1
Introduction	2
Bakelite Is Best	4
Fish Finds Water	22
Free, At Last	42
Handcuffs At The Ready	60
"You Can Get It …."	73
"Just Hit It Harder!"	84
A Small Amount Of Steam	97
To Be Living A Dream	115
Tea Towels at The Ready	130
The Joyous Recklessness of Youth	142
Back To The Day Job	155
Two Tickets, Please	174
A Christmas Card View of London	181
-Many Millennia Before-	195
A Quarter of an Inch Thick	210
Happy Days	224
Loud And Clear	239
Just Before She Fainted	252

Time Is Money, Mica 263
"Do You Smoke, Mr. Digby?" 279
"You're No Geoff Emerick--." 286
Epilogue 296
Glossary 300
Acknowledgements 305

Foreword

I didn't plan on writing a book. But stories, like music, have a way of pressing themselves to tape whether you're ready or not.

Looking back, it wasn't the fame or the leads that pulled me in. It was the sound. The thump of a kick drum in a dark room. The way a vocal would hit the tape just right. The quiet handshake after a good take. I was never after the spotlight, just the signal path that got you there. I was lucky. Right place, right era, proper studio. London and Los Angeles in the '70s and '80s. Jamaican tape reels, Abbey Road floorboards, the Wailers in one room, Zeppelin in the next. And through it all, the tea runs, the edits, the all-nighters, the "got it" moments, I kept notes, not on paper, but in memory. Sound has a way of storing everything.

This book isn't a technical manual. It's not about gear lists or microphone patterns. It's about people. The ones who showed up, tuned up, and opened up. The ones I learned from, laughed with, and lost. It's about life in the background, the real noise behind the hits.

So here it is. One, Two, Three, Four...
Let the tape roll.

Introduction

My sister Pat was "----just seventeen, you know what I mean" when she came home with her copy of The Beatles' debut album, Please *Please Me*. She would retire to her bedroom, back-combed her hair into a beehive style, lacquered and set rigidly in place, practising her Jive dancing with the wardrobe door, music blasting away. It was the spring of 1963, I was twelve years of age and taking an early interest in Rock 'n' Roll. As the sound of the voice of Paul McCartney shouting out the "One, Two, Three, Four ---" count-in to the first track, *I Saw Her Standing There*, on the first side of the first Beatles' album came leaping out of the speaker in the lid of my sister's Regentone mono record player, I stood listening outside her bedroom door, goose-bumps down my neck and a joyous feeling in the pit of my stomach. My life's path was determined there and then. I had received my calling. I had to be a part of what I was listening to. I dreamt of being the recording engineer in the recording studio listed in the credits on that glorious vinyl album sleeve.

The 1960s, 70s, and 80s were to be the decades of unique and spectacular explosions of musical talent, accompanying a socially and technologically changing backdrop of unprecedented pace and depth. I was not to start my career as a recording engineer until some years later, in 1970, aged nineteen. Unbeknownst to me at the time, I was, for the next couple of decades and beyond, to be on the inside as a privileged participating witness to possibly the most significant period in the history of the recording of popular music.

As for my dream calling, well, it was to be an almost thirty-five year wait, not until 1998, that I was to be engineering an album for Sony Records in, for the first time, Studio Two at Abbey

Road. The studio where Paul McCartney had shouted out the count-in to the Beatles song that had sparked my enthusiasm.

Dreams can, eventually, come true.

Bakelite Is Best

I was born in Birmingham, England, on November 1st 1950.

Before that, I would have no recollections, although the occasional sense of déjà-vu experienced since might suggest otherwise. There had been yet another World War some few years earlier, and Aunts and Uncles, Mom and Dad, would refer to this period often in conversations that invariably went over my young head. Still, I got the general idea: ration books, food shortages, a bombed-out Cathedral, babies with American names and soldiers who never came home.

Up until the age of seven, I had enjoyed a relatively normal baby boomer childhood. Mom looked after the home, working part-time at a printer, cleaning jobs, whatever it took to bring in extra money. She kept us all clean and fed, whilst my Father, like all my friends' Fathers, always worked. There was plenty of work for all the men at that time, rebuilding the broken world.

And although I saw little of him (he would be out of the house so early in the mornings and out gigging most nights), Dad was the alpha male who loved his wife and children and kept the roof over all our heads. So I felt the love, support, and security of a warm family home from both my parents. And how important is that?

Much later on in life, as I struggled, far from home, with near drug addiction, borderline alcoholism and a completely broken marriage, it would be the bedrock that kept me focused and grounded, whilst many around me fell away. My love, respect and fear of disappointing my family undoubtedly saved me from ruin, and I will always be eternally grateful to my parents for the solid start in life they gave me.

I had two sisters, Janice, who was two years older than me and Pat, who is four years my senior. Janice had health complications, a hole in the heart, and in 1957, there was no cure. So, in that unfortunate year, Pat and I lost a sister. More tragically for them, my Mom and Dad lost one of their children. There is no sadness in all the world greater and more undeserved than that.

Music had always been a backdrop to our lives. Dad played saxophone in various big bands on the Birmingham scene, as well as holding down the day job as a senior planning engineer for Birmingham Small Arms, B.S.A. We had a radio in the kitchen which was always switched on and tuned in to the BBC Radio Light Program. These were the days before Radio One, Radio Four, Classic F.M, Jazz F.M, etc. Until the advent of pirate radio stations such as Radio Caroline in 1964, transmitting from ships in the English Channel, moored outside the jurisdiction of British broadcasting laws, only one radio station played music. In an hour or two listening to the Light Program, you would have been treated to the widest imaginable variety of music: Mantovani, followed by Frank Sinatra, followed by The Beatles. Some Acker Bilk, Petula Clark, a blast of Big Band, Ella Fitzgerald, more Frank and more, yes please, even more Beatles. Mom had done a bit of dancing in her time: tap, ballroom, and even a bit of early Jive. She would be dancing in the kitchen, radio turned up high, whilst at the same time preparing the family meal. An early example of multi-tasking!

So we would be listening to music morning, noon and night. The exception was Sunday afternoons, when all of the Aunts and Uncles would gather together, either in their homes or at our house. Aunty Betty sang all the lyrics to old vaudeville tunes. She knew them all. Uncle Arthur performed magic tricks with cards, disappearing coins, pencils and banknotes. Aunty Ethel and Uncle Len, always the perfect hosts, had a son, Donald, who was obsessed with Jazz. Cousin Donald had dozens of 78s, including artists such as John Coltrane, Johnny Dankworth and Cleo Lane, Miles Davis and Dave Brubeck, all of them played on a beautiful piece of audio furniture, the radiogram.

As we gradually added many of the creature comforts of post-war Britain to our home, such as a washing machine, a refrigerator, a car (with a radio!) and, most significantly, a television, the intensity of our family's consumption of music grew exponentially. Television and radio shows most watched and listened to were invariably the great British classics of musical variety. For example:

Sunday Night at the London Palladium, Friday Night is Music Night, Songs of Praise, Housewives' Choice, Music While You Work.

With the advent in the 1960s of more TV and radio channels, the cultural landscape of musical provision expanded further, including: Juke Box Jury, Cilla Black and Top of the Pops. It was Dad's choice of music whenever we were in the car, as he would be the driver and therefore entirely in charge of entertainment, so the sounds of big band music would accompany us on any journey. I must confess to being an early fan of some big band music, especially Glen Miller.

Once my sister Pat had discovered Rock 'n' Roll, at about the same time as she found boys, then the musical menu was updated to include the likes of The Everly Brothers, Chuck Berry, Elvis Presley, Cliff Richard and, most significantly for me, The Beatles. It was upon hearing the Fab Four that I became inexorably chained to my sole pursuit in life, namely the desire to be part of that music scene.

I bought my first guitar, which cost eight pounds, thanks to a paper round. I learned all the basic chords, courtesy of English guitar-playing hero Burt Weedon's classic manual, *Play in a Day*. Chords like C major, A minor, G7, and here's a tricky one, F. You've gotta hold down two strings with one finger for this. You knew you were learning to play guitar when you could do a bar chord.

So that was pretty much enough chords to know a lot of Beatles tunes. I started writing songs and set up a basic recording studio in my bedroom. I was destined to be the next Paul McCartney!

I remember the joy that music brought to all our family's lives. Even more so after Janice's death, it would seem to me that music somehow helped mask the awful sadness that undoubtedly existed within the family at that time.

Our family was typical of the period: making do and mending during a post-war period of austerity. We had the first telephone on our street, a massive, big black Bakelite object with fabric-covered curly wire. The distance from the giant megaphone of a mouthpiece receiver to the dial was only about twelve inches, so you could never move too far away from the 'phone itself. The metal dial had letters as well as numbers, and with a sliding compartment at its base, used for storing numbers, names and addresses, the whole phone weighed half a ton! The neighbours would come around and ask to use it. I'm sure they thought we were a bit posh, but the main reason we had a phone installed was so that Dad would be able to take bookings for the dance bands he played in. The band booking system in those days was an informal affair. Dad would get a call from one of the gig fixers for a dinner and dance in six months at, say, The Palace Ballroom, Erdington—7 p.m. Black Tie. A note would be made in his diary, and that would be it: no contract, and no further reminders. Six months down the line, my Dad would put on his dickey-bow and dinner suit, pack his sax, reeds and strap it into the well-worn case, jump on a bus and do the gig.

I remember him telling me once that if you didn't have a gig on a Saturday night and you needed the work, you would just go along to The Swan public house in Yardley, south Birmingham. Take your instrument, sit around with dozens of fellow musicians having a couple of pints until someone announces they are short of an alto sax player for such and such venue, and, lo and behold, you have work for the night. Such was the band scene in Brum back in the Fifties and Sixties, and my Dad was a big part of it. We have pictures of him on various bandstands, including one very treasured shot of him in a sax section alongside Larry Winwood, the father of Steve and Muff Winwood. I showed this picture to Muff many years later. We both smiled as broadly as only two very proud sons could.

But back to the big Bakelite thing.

The telephone had other occasional uses. The General Post Office, or G-P-O, as well as handling posted mail in those days, also controlled telecommunications. Every Xmas, my Dad's brother and his wife, Uncle Arthur and Aunty Betty, would book a call week in advance through the G-P-O, to speak to their son, my cousin Arty, in Scotland. He worked at the Dounreay Nuclear Plant in Thurso, in those days a million miles from Birmingham. This would be the only time of year when they would speak with him in person. On Christmas Day, we would all sit patiently by the phone, waiting for the ring and the matronly voice of the telephone operator confirming that the reserved telephone call was being connected. Then my Uncle, full of nervous pride, voice and hand shaking, would speak to his son at length as his wife looked on, waiting for her turn to speak, tears of joyous expectation filling her eyes.

That black Bakelite telephone, with the fabric-covered curly wire, the gig lifeline, the one which brought so much joy at Xmas, was the same telephone that rang on that painful April day in 1957 with the worst news from the hospital where Janice had been for her last few weeks. Dad picked up the phone. He turned grey and went quiet. Mom knew.

In 1960, we bought our very first record player! In that same year, Mom and Dad presented me and Pat with a new baby sister, Jayne, so life was renewed as the World entered one of its most exciting and turbulent decades. Before its end, there would be a man on the moon, a civil rights movement and a dead President.

When I remember them now, these events, both within the family and globally, were all accompanied by their soundtrack. It meant that by the time I was 13 years of age, I was delightfully drowning in music and have never, to this day, had any desire to resurface.

My sister Pat had been buying all the latest albums and singles of the day, including The Everly Brothers, Chuck Berry, Bobby Vee, Cliff Richard and of course, The Beatles. In a few years, as a staff engineer for Island Records, I would find myself in the studio recording three of the Beatles on various sessions at Island's Basing Street studios: Ringo Starr on a session for Joe Cocker, George Harrison on the Phil Spector production for his wife, Ronnie, of the song *Try Some, Buy Some* and Paul McCartney, with his talented and friendly wife Linda, on a track for his older brother Mike McGear, whose album *Woman*, was recorded for Island. I would get to meet George Harrison again and other Beatles people a few years later when I was living and working in Los Angeles.

Back to Birmingham and 1969.

Egg boxes do not make for very effective soundproofing. They may help disperse and absorb some sound, but that's about all. However, they do help give the appearance of a recording studio environment, especially in a music-mad, Beatle-crazy, Abbey Road-obsessed eighteen-year-old's bedroom in Birmingham.

Go round to all the local grocery stores, ask about the availability of any empty or damaged egg boxes, and come home with hundreds of them. Bemuse and slightly annoy your parents by sticking them to the recently redecorated bedroom walls, Dad's patience is challenged yet again. Paint them blue, a rather hideous blue, hang some cheap purple fabric across the window, covering the clean white net curtains—mom's patience by now exhausted. Construct floor-to-ceiling shelves with any old bits of unmatched timber you can find, slightly pleasing Dad because he had shown me how to use a drill, a screwdriver, a saw and a spirit level; boys were taught this stuff by their Dads back in the nineteen fifties and sixties. Encourage Dad to look into buying a Philips Elizabethan reel-to-reel tape recorder, with the multi-sound audio attachment, complete with crystal microphone and desk stand. He did agree to buy it, but only if I complied with his suggested arrangement that I contribute half of the monthly hire purchase payments, about fifteen shillings. This was an attempt to teach me the responsibilities of personal finance and money management. It didn't work then, and it has never worked for me since. I defaulted on the arrangement after a couple of months - just forgot - in a world of my own as usual.

Looking back, I can see how selfish I was. The pursuit of my musical dream was to be at the exclusion of everything and everybody. For example, a few years later, after moving to London, my Dad asked me what I thought I was doing, boxing up the Elizabethan tape machine and loading it into my car. I was caught off guard. "I'm taking it down to London, to my bedsit, where I am going to do some recording" I didn't see what the problem was. But Dad knew exactly how he felt and told me in no uncertain terms that the tape machine was not mine to do with as I pleased. He had pretty much paid for it by himself, I was reminded. We argued. (the only time we ever did). Raised voices. A son, now nearly a man, or at least arrogantly thinking he was, confronting the Alpha Male of the household. Mom was in floods of tears, begging us to stop. Dad just gave me the look that said it all. He pulled rank. His position was indisputable, and I knew he was right. Then he did what all good men do. And if you are lucky enough to have one such good man as your Father, then this is the time and the place where you learn about all good men. He simply said, "Take the tape machine with you, look after it, and bring it back next time you come up to Brum." But then I will need to keep it here for a while because I have some recordings of my own I wish to make. Next time, ask first. I thanked him. We made up. Mom stopped crying.

At the same time as I had been experimenting with stereo sound-on-sound recording, songwriting and music production in my egg-box-lined, garishly purply blue bedroom studio, a young drummer friend of mine, Rob Moore, was introducing me to the professional Birmingham music scene. Rob had been a pro drummer in various local bands since the age of thirteen! Consequently, he was reasonably well connected and by the time we were in our late teens we, that is, myself and long-time close friends Phil Brown and Pete "Beefy" Collins, had visited (often with Rob playing the gig) most of the music venues in and around Brum, such as The Queens Head and The Palace Theatre in Erdington. The Dirty Duck in Walsall and the Locarno Ballroom in the city Centre. The Elbow Room, Aston. The Golden Eagle, Hill Street, is home to Brum's folk scene. This pub was famously where Chris Blackwell, Island Records' chief, first saw and heard The Spencer Davis Group and signed them, right there and then! I had been a massive Spencer Davis fan in my last years at school, with the names of all the band members heavily inked all over my battered leather school briefcase. I wasn't to know then that, two years later I would be assisting with engineering duties on Traffic sessions, making tea and chatting with Steve Winwood about why he had left The Spencer Davis Group, talking football with Jim Capaldi the drummer, being introduced to his beautiful girlfriend, Anna, who like me came from the Pype Hayes area of Birmingham. Her father had been my scoutmaster. I told Chris Wood, the saxophonist, that my Dad also played sax. Then, a few months later, I was sitting at a recording console as a studio engineer, alongside Muff Winwood, the producer, recording albums with The Sutherland Brothers and Quiver, Patto, and Sparks. And later still, engineering alongside Spencer Davis, the man himself, producing. The artist, Paul Korda, led the male cast in the London West End production of the musical "Hair". The studio, Village Recorders, was in Santa Monica, California. Studio two. Next door, at the same time in studio one, were Supertramp, recording their iconic album *Breakfast in America*.

But I am getting ahead of myself again.

Without a doubt, the most famous of all the Birmingham venues was Mothers, again in Erdington, on the High Street above a furniture shop. Formerly known as The Carlton Ballroom, any band of significance in the mid to late sixties played this place:

Pink Floyd recorded live for their album *Ummagumma*;

The Who performed, for the first time in public, *Tommy*, their classic and arguably the first "Rock Opera".

Chicago Transit Authority (later to be simply known as Chicago) played one of only two gigs in the U.K. for their launch, the other being The Albert Hall.

Traffic performed their World debut at Mothers.

All this, right on our doorstep! We could walk there, pay three quid to get in, consume gallons of scrumpy cider at a pound a pint, listen to the likes of Joe Cocker one weekend, Fleetwood Mac the next, Black Sabbath, T. Rex, Elton John and each time walk (or occasionally stagger) home.

This modest-sized club in a small Birmingham suburb was later to be voted the number-one rock venue in the World by Billboard magazine. A blue plaque was placed on the building in 2013.

How blessed we were.

Drummer Rob Moore also introduced me to his close friend and excellent young guitarist Jeff Commander. Jeff lived in a relatively posh part of town, Sutton Coldfield. He had a studio in his bedroom, too. A few egg boxes, as I recall, but more importantly, he was enviably in possession of the Rolls-Royce of domestic tape machines, a Bang and Olufsen Beocord 2000. This was THE machine to have if you were at all serious about home recording: sound-on-sound overdubbing, mixer with tone controls, in-built amplification, echo, the works! He had guitars, keyboards and microphones galore. And Jeff could play. All the instruments. Serious musician. Put me to shame. To say I was jealous of his studio set-up would have been an understatement.

As if that wasn't enough, he would play us some stunning quality demos he had been engineering and co-producing with a nearby friend of his, a guy by the name of Jeff Lynne. These tracks came out of the speakers sounding like finished records: harmonies, double-tracked guitars and vocals, reverbs, and delays. Wow, I remember thinking, who is this guy Jeff Lynne? How does Jeff Commander do this? How come my home recordings sound like, well, home recordings? If I wasn't already hooked on the idea of becoming a record producer, then those visits to Sutton Coldfield hearing Jeff Lynne's recordings nailed it for me. So inspiring, so much to learn.

Rob introduced me to Jeff Lynne at The Queens Head in Erdington. Jeff was playing guitar and singing for one of Birmingham's top bands of the day, The Idle Race. They had a big following and were by miles the most innovative and talented band around the Birmingham music scene at that time. They never quite made it commercially, despite recording sessions at Advision studios in London with the legendary Eddie Offord. The very same Eddie who will have written an article in a magazine that I would pick up and read on my way to work one morning, a couple of years hence. The Road to Damascus, a life-changing magazine moment, more of which later.

Jeff Lyne left the Idle Race and joined forces with Roy Wood in The Move. Then came The Electric Light Orchestra. The rest, as they say----.

I never managed to upgrade to a Bang and Olufsen, but unbeknownst to me at the time, bigger and better tape machines awaited.

Having left Bordesley Green Grammar/Technical School with seven GCE "O" levels, quitting College and finding myself unfulfilled with a career in retail, I messed around in a couple of local bands, pretending to be a guitarist. At one audition, I was asked to play a solo, and I was rightfully exposed as an imposter. This convinced me that although I might know a few chords and could play the guitar, that didn't make me a guitarist. A not too subtle distinction that was reinforced some years later, again at the Island Studios, when I sat next to Eric Clapton as he wrote the lyrics and recorded a couple of solos for a track on his Atco Records debut solo album. It was remarkable how quickly he wrote the lyrics and the ease with which he delivered a couple of stunning guitar solos. The engineer on those sessions was an American, Bill Halverson, who was to be a great mentor for me. He had made his name many years earlier as a staff engineer for Atlantic Records, recording Crosby, Stills, Nash and Young. As an assistant engineer for him, working with Stephen Stills on his second solo album at the Island Basing Street studios, I was to learn much from this great man.

I resigned myself to never being a musician per se, not like Eric. Not like my Dad. But how was I ever going to achieve my goal of working in the recording business?

It is strange, or is it, how specific seemingly insignificant actions can affect the outcome of our lives? A chance meeting, a light bulb of an idea that comes to you out of nowhere. One specific involuntary action, on my way to work one morning, led me along the right path to finding employment in the music industry.

I had been working in a local supermarket as a trainee manager, stacking shelves, serving behind the deli counter, and sweeping out the warehouse. I would take the same short bus ride from home early each morning, get off at the same stop, cross over the road and walk into the supermarket. Same routine every day. Except one day I didn't cross over. I walked down the opposite side of the road and into the newsagent's. Which was odd, because I didn't read newspapers, didn't smoke cigarettes, and had never been in this newsagent's before. I was inexplicably drawn to the magazine rack and perused all the glossy covers until one particular publication begged my attention. It was in the music section, and it caught my eye because there was a picture of a recording studio on the front cover. I took down the magazine and opened it to a random page. On this very page was an article by recording engineer Eddie Offord, and it featured a day in the life at Advision Studios in London, where The Idle Race had recorded. It described every aspect of the studio day, relating the various duties of each member of staff. Of particular interest to me was the role of the tape operator, whose job was to make the tea, set up microphones, music stands, headphones and generally run about assisting the engineer and musicians.

It was as if this newsagent had been on that road to Damascus. The article and its job description of the tape operator's tasks were leaping off the page and saying to me, "This is you, so now go do it". I needed to get that job in a recording studio, but where to start looking? There were only two recording studios in Birmingham that I knew of: one was Hollick and Taylor in Handsworth, where I had already unsuccessfully applied for a job. The other studio was in my bedroom! So in my lunch break, I went to the local library, got a London telephone directory and looked up "Recording Studios". There were thirty-eight of them. I physically wrote down the names, addresses and phone numbers of them all. No printers in those days. No internet!

I wrote to every one of them. The same letter. Thirty-eight times. By hand. No Word Doc! I said, "I will work in your studio doing anything — making tea, washing cars, cleaning shoes — anything" I bought thirty-eight envelopes and thirty-eight stamps. Then I waited for thirty-eight replies.

I received three rejections.

Undeterred, or at least convincing myself, with a great deal of support from Mom and Dad, not to be too disappointed, I decided that I needed to go to London and visit these thirty-eight studios in person and point out to as many of them as possible that they were making a grave mistake not giving me a job and that I would give them a second chance to reconsider their position. I took the train to London and checked into the YMCA in Great Russell Street, off Tottenham Court Road, for three nights. Now they would see sense.

Equipped with an A to Z of London, the Great List of Thirty-Eight and a strong pair of walking shoes, I set off on my travels around that great city. I learnt the location of every tube station, the colours of every tube line, every bus route, every market, all the famous landmarks, bridges, main thoroughfares, side streets and alleyways. After four days of intense, detailed pavement pounding, I could have become a London cab driver.

I had The Knowledge.

I got to know and feel an early affection for a city that would soon become my most cherished Earth Spot. A place where I would live and grow. The place where I would discover the meaning of words like "culture", "ethnic", "background" and "class". Where I would see for myself the difference in living standards between an accountant I got to know who lived in prosperous Golders Green and a family of "hippies" whom I befriended as they squatted in a roofless derelict flat in Ladbroke Grove. What a wealthy politician's house in Holland Park looks like, then see that same politician's son slumming it in a bedsit in Victoria. A place where I was soon to meet and get to know so many famous faces. The beautiful people I had only ever read about and whose music I had listened to on that radio in the kitchen, on our black and white television and out of the grooves from the record player in Pat's bedroom. The city that I would later return to a second time, when my life was in tatters on another Earth Spot, several thousand miles away.

But not until I had worked through my list of thirty-eight.

Number one, in alphabetical order, was, of course, Abbey Road. They had received my letter. Surely they would know who I was? Why did that guy at the main entrance, the one with the uniform, wearing some medals and an embroidered hat, stop me from going in? I had bought some Beatles records. You had my letter. This can't be! (I swear it was the same guy still working security there when I returned as an engineer in 1998).

By Thursday, on a dark, cold and wet October evening, after three days and thirty-seven, yes, thirty-seven studios, thirty-seven dead ends, it was nearly time to go back to Birmingham. Back to the supermarket and my future in retail management. Not that it would have been so bad. I had my family there. Job prospects of a sort. It's not so bad a place. They've got culture and they do ethnic. Somebody is squatting somewhere in Brum. Ah well.

But you know that voice? The one near the back of your head, over by your right shoulder? Maybe you don't ever hear or feel it, but I have and many times since. It said words to the effect that you have tried thirty-seven, but the list has thirty-eight, so you are one short. What is wrong with the number thirty-eight? I answered (as you do when you are talking to that voice) What is the point? It's cold and wet, and I am fed up, and I am going back to Brum tomorrow.

Well, the persistent voice won over, and the next thing I was on a tube train to Elephant and Castle, and I found the bit of the Old Kent Road where number thirty-eight, Maximum Sound Studios, is situated. I ring the doorbell. I walk in. It's tiny and a bit run down, but the guy who lets me in listens patiently to my, by now, well-rehearsed speech about tea and washing cars. I finish. He explains that business is not so hot and there isn't even enough work for him, let alone two, so I thank him, turn to the door, hand on the handle, turning, about to step outside into the dreary, dark October rain. On the other side of this door, when I open it, will be Birmingham.

"Wait a minute!" he suddenly shouts. I let go of the handle.

He says, Island Records is building a studio over by Portobello Road. They might need someone. Here's the guy's name: Frank Owen. Phone number: 229 1229. All on the most beautiful torn scrap of paper I have ever seen. He wishes me luck. I turn the handle. Out onto the street. Still in London!

So, it was number thirty-nine. Not on The List. Didn't need a stamp for this one.

One final round of pavement pounding was swiftly required. What time was it? Five minutes past five, late Thursday afternoon. Someone would still be there over near Portobello, at the studio where I just knew I was going to work!

No mobile phone in those days, so find the nearest telephone box. Do you have loose change? Buy a packet of gum, break into a fiver. The first two phone boxes are out of order. Britain, 1969!

The third one is lucky. Smells like a lavatory, probably used last night by some drunken, disrespectful reveller (Britain 2017). Now, where's that piece of paper....

Dial-tone....... 229 1229.... Ring-tone.... Heart racing.... Patience.... A female voice answers:

"Good evening, Island Records"

Oh my God! Someone just said Island Records! Now what? First impressions will be so important, so don't mumble, speak clearly, sound confident and coherent.

"Hello, can I help you?"

Keep it simple. "Hello, can you tell me where the nearest tube station is to Basing Street?"

"Yes, either Ladbroke Grove or Westbourne Park"

"What time are you open 'til?"

"Someone will be here for another 45 minutes. Why? Who is calling?"

"I'm on my way".

Hang up.

Why did I do that? They must have thought it was some lunatic on the phone. I messed up, didn't I? No matter. Too late now. Get skates on.

It should be about a twenty-five-minute walk from where I was, along the Old, then the New Kent Road to Elephant and Castle tube station. But by achieving my only ever sub-four-minute mile (unofficial, of course), I was on a Bakerloo Line train, heading north, in less than ten. Change at Baker Street onto the Hammersmith and City line, eastbound. I knew this tube system like the back of my hand and was speed-walking out of Westbourne Park station with about four minutes to spare. It was still absolutely chucking it down, so I was completely drenched to the skin as I swam down Westbourne Park Road. Turn fifth right.

Basing Street. Number eight. Through the door with the round window, dripping onto the black, stippled rubber-tiled floor into the reception area. Sit on a plush sofa. The same sofa that a couple of other studio engineers and I would sit on, some two or three years later, in conversation with Chris Blackwell, the founder of Island Records. It would have been about four in the morning. He must have been unable to sleep. Chris wrestled with and shared with us his torment over a decision whether or not to sell the label to the American giants, Warner Brothers. He asked us what we thought. We said unanimously that he shouldn't --- and he didn't.

But it wasn't Chris who would be the first Island person I would meet. It was Muff Winwood, head of the label's A&R department, who came spinning down the spiral staircase from the first-floor office. He stopped, took one look at the soaking wet, pathetic figure, me, then shouted back up the stairs that the minicab was here. Now, I knew who this man was (the school leather briefcase, for example) and was very soon to engineer many sessions with this legendary producer, but this was not the auspicious start I was hoping for. Did I look like a mini-cab driver?! I must have done. Who was it once told me, "Dress like a roadie and people will treat you like a roadie." No disrespect to all the wonderful, hard-working roadies it has been my pleasure to meet over the years, nor to mini-cab drivers in general, but I must have presented a far-from-perfect picture of myself.

I explained. The job thing. Come back in the morning and speak to Penny, he suggested.

So, one last night at the YMCA.

I made more effort in terms of the sartorial presentation for that Friday morning meeting with Penny Hanson, the general manager. And it was short, sweet, and straightforward. Like I said, I knew I would get a gig here. Just knew. That voice again. And I wouldn't have to wash cars or polish boots, but be prepared to make an enormous amount of tea!

Penny asked if I could drive. Gulp. Of course, I could. (Amazing how economical with the truth you can be when determination sets in). Could I ride a motorbike? Er, well (more economy). Did I know my way around London? No question here of selective response. I had just spent the last four days doing The Knowledge and had one pair of worn-out boots to prove it. Besides, I had recently been accused of impersonating a mini-cab driver, so I could look the part if required.

In all seriousness, I fell in love with the place, with Penny, Muff, the spiral staircase, the hard, black rubber floor, the sofa- it all felt like home, instantly. Penny told me they would need a junior as general run-around, probably not until January, when the studios were due to open. Still, if I leave my details, she will give me a call in a couple of days with her decision.

One early October evening, 1969, back in Birmingham, three very long days later, that old Bakelite telephone delivered its familiar ring. Dad answered, as he always did, alpha male and all that stuff. "Erdington 2317", he said, in his best telephone voice. This time he didn't turn grey. His face was almost glowing with a shared excitement and anticipation.

It's Penny Hanson for you, Richard," he smiled proudly, handing me the phone.

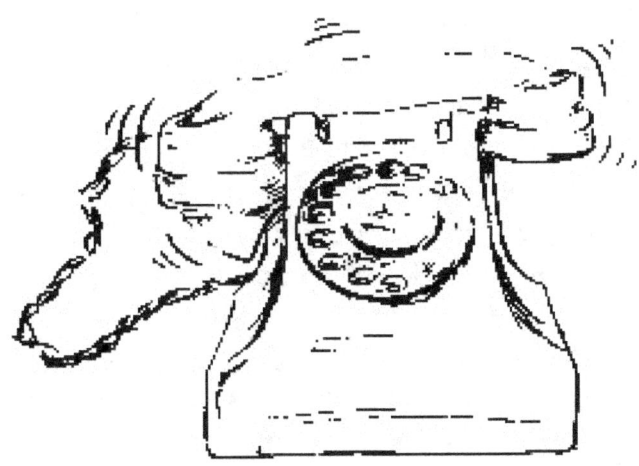

The big Bakelite thing---.

Fish Finds Water

December 31st, 1969, and I was saying goodbye to my Mom. As she stood on the steps waving me off, all smiles, I had no thought for her. Not for anyone but myself. I was off to London to start my life in the music industry, leaving behind all my family and friends. Train ticket in hand, one bag full of clothes and my registration for a two-week stay at the YMCA. I turned for one last look at my home, my street, my old life and my Mom.

Many years later, she would confess to me how, once she had closed the door and gone back inside, she had burst into tears, overwhelmed by a deep sense of sadness that she was losing her son to The Big Smoke- London. Her only comfort, she said, was that, unlike the daughter who could never return, this son would be coming back from time to time.

Penny Hanson, the general manager, Sally Wightman, the studio manager, along with Denise Mills, had been with the label since the late 60s and were Island Records' founder Chris Blackwell's "Girl Fridays". Chris Blackwell was born in London but grew up in Jamaica. Related to the wealthy Crosse and Blackwell food giant's founding father, Thomas Blackwell, Chris was educated at Harrow, an independent boarding school for boys in north London, where the motto is: *Donorum Dei Dispensatio Fidelis*, or, *The Faithful Dispensation of the Gifts of God*. He most certainly would have considered music as one of those gifts when he formed Island Records in 1959, establishing the label in London in 1962, whilst selling Jamaican music from the back of his car. He had astutely recognised the growing market in Caribbean music and culture, post the 1950s *Windrush* immigration into the U.K. The label's name was inspired by the Harry Belafonte song *Island in the Sun* and Blackwell explained in 2009 that "I loved music so much, I just wanted to get into it, or be as close to it as I could." (Pierre Perrone, Independent, April 2009).

My sentiments exactly, Chris.

It was Denise who greeted me on my first day of employment on New Year's Day, 1970. I had arrived early at the record company offices bright-eyed and bushy-tailed, ready for work, which in itself was remarkable because I had been awake since 1 am. From my room in the YMCA, I had awoken to the sound of traffic and noise. Thinking it was the activity of the morning rush hour, without checking my watch, I panicked. I will be late for work on my first day! So, quickly dressed, I rushed down the stairs and out onto Tottenham Court Road, jumped down the steps of the tube station and onto the busy platform. There seemed to be an awful lot of balloons and drunk people with party hats on. I looked up at the platform clock. 12.45 am. New Year's Day. Perhaps you could say I was somewhat overly keen to start work in the music business.

A deconsecrated church on Basing Street housed the Island Records headquarters. It dominated the skyline of this small residential street in west London, just one block north of the bustling street markets of Portobello Road. Inside were four small offices, one on the ground floor next to the reception area, two on the first floor and a box-sized room on the top floor. The two recording studios took up the leading share of the internal space, with the compact studio two being in the basement and the enormous orchestral-sized studio one located up on the first floor in what would have once been the central worship and pulpit area of the original church.

Denise was the only person in the building that morning and knew nothing of my employment, reminding me that it was, after all, January 1st, so that no one would be showing up too early after the previous evening's revelry. "Just hang out and wait for Penny to arrive" was her advice. So I busied myself looking around the smart, trendy offices: telephones at every desk, white plastic ones with masses of buttons on them, and curly, plastic-coated wire --- no black Bakelite here. There was a large, white round table in the middle of the main office on the first floor. This represented the Island round-table philosophy: no one sits at the head of the table; therefore, everyone is equally important. I would later meet, gathered around this table, all the key players: Tom Hayes, international director, Muff Winwood, head of A+R, Brian Humphries and Frank Owen, senior engineers and, of course, Chris Blackwell himself. It was a small team running Island, so it didn't take long to meet everyone and get a close-up understanding of how the record label was run. There were John Slattery and John Leftly, the accountants, and three other individuals, John Glover, Alex Lesley, and Mick Cater, who ran the artist management side. They all occupied the office on the ground floor and were the most likeable, down-to-earth people you could ever hope to meet. Everyone made me feel extremely welcome in this, for me, larger-than-life world. Posters on the walls of all the label's artists, each in themselves mirroring Chris's eclectic musical tastes. From Reggae to Bluesy Rock, Folk, Country Rock and Pop. A variety of musical genres never before assembled under one record company roof: Free, Traffic, John Martyn, Fairport Convention, Cat Stevens, Nick Drake, Mott the Hoople, Spooky Tooth, and Jimmy Cliff. Many of these artists' albums had been in my record collection back in Brum, and I was soon to be in the studio recording all of them and more in the months and years ahead, except for Nick Drake. He had always recorded with the engineer John Wood at his Sound Techniques Studios with American producer Joe Boyd. I would later engineer for Joe, in 1984, on a posthumous Sandy Denny compilation album, *Who Knows Where the Time Goes*, so more about Joe later.

Behind Denise's desk on the first floor was an Aladdin's Cave, disguised as an ordinary cupboard. Inside, as well as records on the Mango, Trojan and Tuff Gong labels, the Jamaican recordings that were licensed to Island were promotional copies of all the latest Island albums, including Nick Drake's *Five Leaves Left*. Many artists have covered one song in particular from that album, titled The Riverman and was even re-released as a posthumous single for Nick in 2004. Nick Drake was to record two more albums for Island before his early death, aged twenty-six, in November 1974.

Over the decades, the music business has accrued a significant body count. In the coming years, Island was to lose many musical friends, often as a result of drug and/or alcohol abuse, or simply depression. Nick Drake was the first.

There were still some last-minute details to attend to before the studios went fully on stream. Perfect for me! I got to see the tail end of the studio being constructed, fitted out, wired and connected up and also the tape store being designed and built. I helped put up the shelving and, with Penny's guidance, developed a Rolodex coloured card system for all the different tape formats: white for mono, green for stereo, and other colours for 8-track and 16-track multi-track tapes. I was given the keys to a rather dilapidated, pre-health and safety death trap, ex-Wimpey Builders Ford Anglia van and sent off around London, mainly to the Edgware and Tottenham Court roads, to pick up cabling, electrical equipment, headphones, music stands, and all manner of studio accessories. Much of the knowledge I gained from seeing these studios being brought to life would prove useful many years later, in 1997, when I was to build my studios in West Weston.

After numerous trips up and down the M1 in this bone-shaking wreck to visit family and friends back in Birmingham, the Ford was eventually unceremoniously towed away to some unpleasant place and given the indecent burial it so richly deserved. It was a miracle I wasn't buried first. Over the coming months, as I became more involved with studio life as a trainee tape operator, the longing for life back in Birmingham began to recede. After all, I was in the most exciting capital city in the world, working for the most innovative record label on the planet, in the most up-to-date, prestigious recording studio in London.

Very early on, I was given much support settling into this unfamiliar new world by the friendship shown to me by senior engineer Brian Humphries. Brian had been cherry-picked from Pye studios near Marble Arch, having recorded Traffic, The Spencer Davis Group, Petula Clark and the original Nirvana. In his early days at Pye, Brian had also engineered sessions with Burt Bacharach and Dionne Warwick, so he was a seasoned veteran of the studio process. He was also, like me, from Brum! He invited me one evening to Pye Studios to sit in on a recording session with the band Blind Faith. It was an induction into the world I was to become part of. Here was Steve Winwood, the guitarist and keyboard player, Ric Grech, the bassist and Ginger Baker on drums, arguing a track, going over detailed aspects of a song's arrangement. Checking guitar tuning, chord inversions, choice of amps and guitar sounds. Engineers are considering microphone selection and placement—test recordings to confirm that drum sounds and headphone mixes were satisfactory. Musicians and engineers talking about and recording music. Then Eric Clapton drops in to play lead guitar on the track! It was heaven to me.

I'm sorry, Phil, Beefy. I love Birmingham, but you should see me now.

Brian also introduced me to the Island Records' football team. As part of a music industry football league, Island were placed somewhere mid-table. There was to be a game on Saturday, on the desolate, wind-swept Wormwood Scrubs, against Mercury Records. I had humbly suggested that I would be available to play, if needed, just to make up the numbers. I turned up and was given a painfully tight green and white Island Records' jersey, probably the last one from the bottom of the bag that nobody else could fit into. Typically, it had been pouring with rain for the whole of the match, and I made my grand entrance early in the waterlogged second half. It was nil-nil with four minutes to go. Brian crossed a low ball at speed from the right wing into the box. I was there. I saw it coming. Like all good strikers, I knew, even before I had made contact, that I was going to score. I flew through the air, van-Persie style and headed the ball into the net. I landed face down in the gooey mud. Brian and Muff came over to me, and as we celebrated the goal, Brian said, "You've played this game before, haven't you? "I made a lot of friends that day.

The studios were not yet officially open for business, so there were some initial trial sessions in studio two with the Island band Traffic, Brian Humphries at the controls and later that week a twenty-piece orchestral session with engineer Frank Owen at the helm. These early sessions were primarily to check out if the studio was wired up correctly and good to go. Even though my initial duties at Island did not require me to be on sessions, I lingered and loitered with intent at every opportunity, soaking up the atmosphere and observing the procedures taking place. After all, I knew what to expect, having worked in my own egg-box lined studio! So by creating a new role for myself (there we go again, selfish and single minded as always) I managed to become an unauthorized assistant to the tape-operators, Clive and Roger. Grabbing cables, headphones, mics, stands, anything. Made a complete nuisance of myself. I insisted on making tea for ALL the sessions that were booked in, morning, noon or night. Within a few weeks, sessions were taking place full time, with both studios fully functioning. Downstairs, studio two, the smaller room with a palm treed Caribbean theme painted on the walls, then up and down the spiral staircase with reel after reel of 2-inch tape into the enormous studio one. This would be where I would later sit alongside legendary engineer/producer Andy Johns on Led Zeppelin sessions, including the night *Stairway to Heaven* was recorded.

Tray after tray of tea, in thin, white plastic beakers, doubled up for safety's sake because the boiling water tended to make them melt! Countless trips to Portobello Road for sandwiches, tobacco and Rizla cigarette papers. Back down the Edgware Road for more cables and headphones. Seven days a week, day and night, both studios were constantly in use, mainly for the Island label artists, but also, as the studio's reputation spread, outside clients too. Most of the evening sessions would go on into the morning hours. No time, no need or desire to go home, just crash out on one of the studio sofas, up early for breakfast at Mike's café on Blenheim Crescent, ready for the daytime shift. I practically lived at the studio and was relishing every moment.

I loved, and still do some forty-seven years later, the sight of microphone cables running across a studio floor. The process of selecting the microphones, of finding the right adaptors and mic stands. Headphones lying across a music stand or chair in anticipation of the sounds that will shortly be passing through them. A new day in the creative environment of the recording studio. A new song to discover, explore and capture.

Chris Blackwell had assembled an illustrious team of studio engineers. He shamelessly poached these key industry figures by not only offering extremely attractive terms and conditions of employment but also by selling them his unique Island dream, that of an independent record label with its own recording studios. As well as Brian Humphries, he recruited Clive Franks from Dick James' studio/publishing company, who had been involved with

The Beatles and Elton John. Chris also cast enquiring eyes and ears towards Olympic, the world-famous, south-west London studio where the Rolling Stones, Led Zeppelin and Jimi Hendrix had all recorded. The Beatles worked at the Olympics and recorded *All You Need is Love* there. They re-created the song at Abbey Road studios on 25th June 1967, as part of the B.B.C. *Our World* television programme, which historically became the first ever global television link-up. From this most prestigious of facilities, Chris hijacked world-class engineer Frank Owen. (Frank also worked briefly for Dick James Music, but was essentially an Olympic protégé). Frank's expertise was in recording orchestral works and film scores, so he was an integral addition to the Basing Street roster of engineering expertise. It was also beneficial to me as a trainee engineer to be in the company of such experienced professionals as Brian and Frank.

Olympic's technical guru, Dick Swettenham, designed and built the Helios desks installed in the Basing Street facility. There was immense interest in this innovative sixteen-track, twenty-four-channel console, amongst not only the engineers who had helped with the ergonomics of the design, but also producers from around the world. The major studio console designers in the U.K. at the time were Rupert Neve, Malcolm Toft (the Trident series) and Electrical Musical Industries (E.M.I.), but Swettenham's desk was different. Cleverly designed with a wrap-around format that meant all the controls for the audio signals were within hands reach, as opposed to the usual lengthy, time consuming journeys traveled, usually on a plush leather chair with wheels, from one end of the desk to the other! The sound engineers of the day were impressed with and keen to try out this new generation of consoles. That was another smart move by Chris Blackwell. As well as being utilised by the in-house roster of Island's own recording artists, these studios were also to be booked by many illustrious outside clients. And the first of many came along, literally, out of the blue of night.

As we all arrived one morning for the start of the day shift, we were greeted by the extremely excited Clive Franks, who had been at the studio on an overnight session. Clive had great news. During the night, a lone musician had wandered in off the streets of West London, asking if he could have a look around the studios. Clive had readily obliged and given him the guided tour. The musician was suitably impressed and left his details, record company, and artist name with Clive. Said he wanted to book six weeks of studio time.

Island Records' Basing Street Studios were about to get on the international studio industry map big-time. The label was Atlantic Records, New York. The artist was Stephen Stills.

Island Records' Basing Street Studios did not have egg boxes on any walls. Here was a newly built professional recording studio, installed within a huge old church, professionally designed and built by qualified experts. Floating floors, non-parallel surfaces to reduce standing waves and acoustic/industrial hard rubber floor tiles. Microphone and headphone tie-line wall sockets everywhere. A comprehensive collection of valve, ribbon, dynamic and condenser microphones: AKG, Neuman, Sennheiser, Sure, Electro-Voice, and at least four of everything. Double-glazed control room to live room windows. Deep, plush leather sofas beneath the elevated wrap-around custom-built 24-channel Helios recording console. In the far right corner, one of the very first 16-track 3M 2-inch multi-track tape machines in the world. Engineers Brian and Frank were like kids in a toy shop, blissfully considering the advances in technology that would allow for the snare drum to be recorded on its own separate track! Tannoy speakers in four huge orange Lockwood cabinets suspended from the ceiling. Silent air-conditioning units and lights on noiseless dimmers. There were two studios like this with Steinway grand pianos and Hammond organs in both. A Mellotron in studio one. Awesome!

And what is more, all the timber matched!

Just a brief word about the Mellotron. It was a tape/sample-based keyboard and quite complicated to operate and play. Not many musicians who used it at Basing Street found it useful, except for the string/orchestral sounds, which is probably why over time the tapes were looted from it and used as tape loops on the reel-to-reel stereo tape machines in the control rooms. The Mellotron fell into disrepair, but not before the only time I ever heard it being played convincingly. I was climbing the spiral staircase towards studio one when I heard the sound of a band playing. Drums, bass guitar, a splash of woodwind, then some violins. Didn't think there was a band booked in that day, let alone an orchestra. Curious as to who was performing this music, I walked into the giant space that was Studio One. In the far corner, a guy with long, very thick grey hair had his back to me whilst he was playing the Mellotron. After a couple of minutes, he must have gotten bored, but I was mesmerized. He stopped and turned around. It was top American session keyboard player Leon Russell and I'm guessing that he had come to put keyboard overdubs on a Joe Cocker track that producer Denny Cordell, a regular visitor to the studio was recording, but I can't be sure. Anyhow, there he was and didn't it sound sweet. So next time you listen to *Nights in White Satin* by The Moody Blues or the introduction to The Beatles *Strawberry Fields*, listen out for that Mellotron.

It would be remiss of me not to mention my first mentor, the Island man who was assigned to give me a crash course on how to set up a studio ready for a session. Any session. Whether it be a four-piece rock band or a sixty-piece orchestra, Kevin (and I apologise immediately for not remembering his second name--maybe I never knew it) had worked at Olympic Studios with Frank Owen. Chris Blackwell had cherry-picked yet another of the best to work at his Basing Street studios.

Kevin was a short, almost midget of an Irishman, with longish, wavy hair and a perfectly manicured, greying goatee beard. He had some difficulties with his gait and even further problems remaining sober for an entire day! But you know what? He wouldn't have minded this description of himself by me because he was such a kind and clever man who took me under his wing and showed me the ropes. He would have known how much respect I had for his knowledge and his predicaments. He showed me how to mic up a drum kit. Why should the bass player be positioned to be able to make eye contact with the drummer? Why everyone should be able to make eye contact with each other easily. Where to best position different instruments in the studio in such a way as to reduce leakage and increase separation. He told me that classical musicians prefer one-sided headphones or even speaker playback. Where to place music stands for first and second violins, violas and celli, when some like to share the manuscript and others do not. How to lay and wrap cables correctly. How to arrange the chairs and set up the studio for a sixty-piece orchestra and not have any wires to trip over, thereby reducing the likelihood of a mic and stand falling over and smashing into someone's priceless instrument. Which microphones, what patterns, and where to place them. Attenuation, high-pass filters, and the whole technical thing were taught to me by this one guy in just a few weeks. It was an intense and thoroughly wonderful, magical period of learning. Skills that junior engineers at other studios would have taken a couple of years to be formally trained in.

But most important of all, Kevin taught me studio etiquette. How to welcome people to the studio? Make musicians, engineers and producers feel at home and relaxed in an environment where unencumbered creativity can flourish. That recording studios are magical places. That they are *Temples of Sound* (Clark, Cogan, Jones, Chronicle Books)

And to put things back when you have finished with them! Zero the desk, ready for the next engineer, out of professional respect. Be tidy, be organised and be on time!

Kevin lived on his own in a small flat in Roehampton, southwest London and outside of the studio kept himself to himself. The more I got to know him, the more I sensed a quiet sadness in his heart. Not sure why. He was always outwardly jovial and pleasant, and I know, as sure as you know with certain people, that he liked me. We got on really well. He was another good man.

So that's what made it all the more puzzling and hard to take when, one ordinary day, after he had wandered off for his usual lunchtime pint or three, he didn't come back. No one ever saw him again. He just disappeared.

Must just say, if it's never too late, take care and thank you Kevin.

Basing Street and the surrounding areas of Portobello Road, Ladbroke Grove and Notting Hill were to become my new home, a new Earth Spot where I would experience so much of life and learn most of the growing up stuff. After a brief period of sharing a double bedsit in Ealing, west London, I moved into a room in a house-share in Ladbroke Square, nearer the studios. I became ensconced, not only in Islands' record label and recording studio life but in the wider, extremely chic and hip, 1970's West London culture: Up and down market antique stores; chaotic and colourful fruit and veg markets, with an abundance of exotic Caribbean and continental foods, the likes of which would never have been seen in my Mom's kitchen back in Birmingham.

The Electric Cinema on Portobello Road is renowned for its unmatched presentation of groundbreaking, alternative, independent avant-garde movies. Kensington Market for affordable floral shirts, colourful scarves, large, showy hats and Edwardian-style leather jackets. The extravagant sartorial landscape displayed on the streets, complemented by the likes of Andy's the shoemaker on Goldhawk Road, Shepherd Bush, famous for his hand-made leather boots. This is where bands like Mott the Hoople and Marc Bolan's T-Rex bought their glam-rock, multi-coloured leather boots with the ridiculously tall platform heels. The trendy chain of Finches' Pubs, one on Portobello, one up in Notting Hill Gate. A myriad of patchouli-oiled, invariably long-haired, bearded and beaded characters. This was Woodstock, London Style.

Caribbean record shops blasting out thunderous bass frequencies; T-shirt and head shops; the Apollo pub, where little old ladies drinking stout would sit opposite a couple of long-hairs discreetly skinning up, hands under the table—Jamaican restaurants like The Mangrove on All Saints Road. Very few white folks would even consider walking past this place, let alone dine in there. Still, many of the artists and staff from Island would frequently indulge in the fine food on offer, especially the studio engineers and bands working the late shift around the corner on Basing Street. We were always made most welcome there, I think in part because we were music people and because Island was, as the local West Indian community knew, owned by a very special Anglo/Jamaican guy. Even before Bob Marley and The Wailers arrived, we were recording with Jimmy Cliff, Toots and the Maytals and other Jamaican musicians who Chris Blackwell had inspired to come to London and be part of his unique label experience; so we were well respected and indeed cool enough to be allowed in.

Many of the Island artists, staff and friends lived in this cosmopolitan and uniquely Bohemian-esque part of west London, including members of the Island band Quintessence, Paul Kossoff

(Free), Carol Grimes (Uncle Dog) and Trevor Burton (The Move). Paul Bennet was one of the Island maintenance engineers and a wonderfully gifted guitarist and songwriter who, along with his beautiful, gentle wife Carla lived in a mystical flat near to the studios on Blenheim Crescent. Pictures on the walls of all the Indian deities; Shiva, Brahma, Vishnu .... Persian carpeted, stripped wooden floors; psychedelic wall tapestries and bejewelled leather sandals everywhere! Scrumpled-up bean bags, where everybody sat cross-kneed on the floor, passing around the endless flow of "joints". You could enjoy the company of many beautiful friends almost any evening around their home, with music, Carla's inimitable home-made authentic Indian food, wine, incense and plenty of hashish. The creativity that abounded was intoxicatingly magical. We played guitars and tablas, wrote songs and sang in harmony. Relationships were forged that were unlike anything I had experienced before. It was blissful and I was in my element.

My Mom, back in the late sixties, when I was a bit of a lost soul working in retail had once gone along with a neighbour of hers to meet with a medium. Amongst many astonishing observations that came from this extraordinary clairvoyant was a reference, addressed to my Mom of a young man, a son perhaps, who was at that time unsettled, living his life like "a fish out of water."

In west London, working at the Island/Basing Street studios, I had found my lake.

Working life for me had changed beyond recognition. No longer the somewhat mundane routine of the number eleven bus along Bromford Lane every morning, ready for an eight o'clock start behind the deli-counter at the Maypole supermarket. Now it was the luxury of a black or mini cab, paid for on account by Island, to get me into the studios for an evening session, or to get me home in the early hours of the morning. Sun-up and a brand-new day for the working people of London --- the sleepy end to a fifteen-hour session for me. I applied the same work ethic that had been forged into me by my parents and reinforced by Kevin. Be punctual, polite, presentable, and work hard. Although it was more often than not incredibly long hours spent listening to the same song over and over and over again, with intricate attention to the details of sound, pitch, tonality and performance, it was by no means the sort of hard work I had been accustomed to back home. The hard work of my Dad and Mom, sisters, family and friends would identify with back in Brum. The hours would fly by, almost effortlessly. I was quickly progressing up the career ladder here at Island, thanks in no small part to the trust and opportunity afforded to me and other young trainee engineers at the studio by Chris Blackwell and his team at the label.

Chris was a visionary, in the sense that he had spotted musical talents that no other record company would engage with, gave them a record deal, and put them in the studios with a team of enthusiastic engineers and producers, confident that our combined talents would thrive and grow in this excellent creative environment, Island's Basing Street Studios. And grow it did. By the summer of that first year, I had gone from tea-boy, gofer, van-driver to engineering and co-producing my first album. In less than six months! The album was *Ace of Sunlight* by the Island band Bronco. Kidderminster-born Jess Roden was the lead singer, and we would go on to record together many times, including a solo album for Jess, produced by New Orleans legend Alan Toussaint. This was one of the producers who had made the records that Phil, Beefy and I had all grown up listening to back in Birmingham: The Meters, Dr. John, Art and Aaron Neville and Lee Dorsey, to name but a few. Although I never actually got to meet him --- his work on the record was all done in New Orleans --- I had now worked on an album with the credits on the sleeve notes showing my name alongside an established, world-renowned record producer.

This was not hard work!

The career path I was on at Island was not the usual route taken by aspiring engineers at other studios. For example, back at Pye Studios on the Blind Faith session I attended with Brian, I had been talking to the assistant engineer, Len. He was sitting dutifully by the tape machines, doing what all good tape-ops do, making sure there was always plenty of tape for the recordings, moving mike stands and headphones and making gallons of tea. Len explained to me that he had worked at the studios for a couple of years before he was even allowed in the control room as an assistant. He had spent his first twelve months just filing tapes and working in the copy rooms. Then there was another year spent learning the dark arts of tape splicing and editing. A further two years as an assistant on actual recording sessions, before you would be placed in charge as a first engineer on your very own session. An extremely disciplined and structured apprenticeship, typical of the set-up at most of the professional studios at that time. Len and I became good friends, and he informed me that he was about to move out of the family home into a bedsit in Ealing, west London. I was desperate to move out of the YMCA and so became his flatmate. About a year later, I moved into my place in Ladbroke Square, nearer the Island studios. I had several albums under my belt by then. Len was still sitting by the tape machines.

Back at Basing Street, it has to be noted that Penny, Sally and Denise were, in my eyes, the most gorgeous females I had ever seen! But this was, after all, London post swinging sixties, and the industry I had joined was full of the beautiful people. The various band members' girlfriends, such as the Guinness Girls (heiresses?) as they were known, and Errol Flynn's daughter, Rory, frequented the studios daily. All the men in the office were handsome, well-dressed and coiffured. The artists with their fashionable long hair and stylish clothing. The classic cars: Chris's Mercedes, Rolls Royce, Pontiac Firebird and his Camero; Steve Winwood's Masserati; and Muff Winwood's pink 12-litre Jaguar. In time, I would add my own Mercedes to that bespoke forecourt. But before I owned my car, on one Friday evening, Penny threw me the keys to her trendy Volkswagen Beetle. She was away for the weekend and didn't need her car, so she lent it to me on the condition that I pick her up for work from her Grosvenor Mews flat in London's prestigious Mayfair. After a weekend with wheels, I arrived at her stylish residence early Monday morning, probably about 9.30 am, which in the music business is early! Another change to my working life. The exclusive secluded mews, just off Hyde Park Corner, were the kind of place I had only seen on TV and in the movies, maybe starring Michael Caine or Alex Guiness in some sixties gangster film. The cobbled street and the large converted stable doors. Colourful hanging baskets and windows with ornate, leaded stained glass. Inside were oil paintings and Tiffany lamps, crystal glasses in the enamelled sink, still wine-stained from the night before. On the floor, an empty bottle of Chateau Laffite Rothschild and in one corner, an acoustic guitar. Whilst Penny was upstairs dressing, getting ready to leave, I picked up the guitar and strummed a couple of chords. "That's o.k. Go ahead and play," she shouted down. "It's horribly out of tune. Whoever tuned this guitar doesn't have a clue," I yelled back up. I should have noticed there were two glasses in the sink, because later that day at the studio, I was to meet for the first time Mike Harrison, who was the lead singer with the Island band Spooky Tooth. (I had repurchased a couple of their albums in Birmingham. I could pick up their latest one for free now that I worked for the label, from the Aladdin's Cave cupboard behind Denise. Mike introduced himself. He had long, thick, wavy, black hair. Another bloody movie star! I overheard him say to Penny, "Is that the cheeky git that played my guitar this morning?" Yet even after such a shaky start, I was to spend many wonderful hours in the studio engineering for Mike on his solo album and later with his band The Junkyard Angels. I had assisted on a few of the Spooky Tooth sessions, towards the end of their last album together, aptly named *The Last Puff*. The engineers were Brian Humphries and Roger Beale, and this was a continuation of my working relationship with Brian. He struck me as being a lot less showbiz than some of the other engineers and producers. He was very matter-of-fact and down-to-earth, with a razor-sharp dry wit that was always useful in the sometimes stressful environment of the studio. Being a fellow Brummy added much to our friendship and working relationship.

It was with Brian that I assisted on my very first professional project for Island, the Michael Giles and Ian McDonald album. These two ex-King Crimson musicians were to be my introduction, not only to the complexities and patient attention to detail required in the making of a record, but also to the magical nature of the creative process. Brian's stoic humour, equally matched by Ian's and Mike's splendid repartee, made light of some of the more tedious and sometimes frustrating aspects of the making of an album. After several months, the record was complete, and I went to Aladdin's Cave and pulled out a copy. Sure enough, there was my name listed on the credits. My first album. And I still have that copy, and whenever I refer to it or, as I type this, referencing it on Google, I still get a massive buzz of pride and achievement when I see my name on the album sleeve. What absolute joy!

Brian also engineered the Bronco sessions for their *Country Home* album, and I was to assist Brian on these recordings. The band was Jess Roden on vocals, formerly in The Alan Bown Set, Kevyn Gammond, and Robbie Blunt on guitars, with John Pasternack on bass. John and Kevyn had connections with Robert

Plant and his Band of Joy, as did Robbie, later, in the early eighties, so there was an early West Midlands Zeppelin connection developing here for me. I was soon to work with Robert Plant on Zep stuff, with engineer Andy Johns, not to mention playing football a few times out in Los Angeles with Robert, but those tales must wait.

Every evening on those Bronco sessions, Brian would receive a telephone call from his wife, enquiring as to how late he might be working. These calls would come through at about ten or eleven o'clock and invariably resulted in Brian either wishing to leave or having to leave at about midnight. So he would leave me at the desk with one channel fader set up for maybe a vocal or guitar overdub, with instructions to complete that particular task, switch off the desk and equipment, fill out the session worksheet and send the band home. Umm. The band was not too happy with that. Umm. I knew how to run the desk, change faders, and adjust tracks and headphone mixes. I was familiar with EQ and the reverb settings. I had studied Brian's work so carefully that I could see myself as an engineer already. So the band and I worked on it into the night with more guitar overdubs, more vocal takes, and a quick rough mix. I was good at this!! The band noticed. They asked me to do their next record, *Ace of Sunlight*, which I engineered and co-produced. Remember, just about six months, and Len is still an engineer in waiting.

I never did get a chance to thank Brian's wife.

The secluded mews, just off Hyde Park Corner-----

Free, At Last

The Americans arrived and set up camp in Studio Two. There was the usual assortment of road and technical crew, who packed the studio with guitars, amps, more guitars, cases and cases of Coca-Cola and Marlborough cigarettes. In attendance were a couple of photographers, most worthy of note being Henry Diltz, who had been the official photographer for the 1969 Woodstock festival. A pleasant, relaxed laid-back Californian who I was to get to know better the following year when the whole entourage would return to record Stephens Stills' second solo album. But this was to be Stephen's first solo album and Basing Street's most prestigious client to date. It was spring of 1970 and as yet I hadn't quite obtained the necessary experience to be an assistant on this level of sessions, so the task was shared between Roger Beale and Clive Franks. However, I made my presence felt by generally helping set up the studio, making tea and assisting the assistants! I wasn't going to miss this for the world and watched and listened in amazement as the record progressed. Stephen had brought along his own engineer from the States, Bill Halverson, the Atlantic Records engineer/producer who had recorded most of the Crosby, Stills and Nash records, not to mention many of the other Atlantic greats. When he came back the following year to record Stephen's second solo album I was to be his assistant for a three-week project and I would get to know him well. So I will hold back on any further observations about Bill until later.

Now I was to see and hear what the big time was all about. The musicians who turned up to play were the legends: Ringo Starr, Eric Clapton, Jimi Hendrix (to whom the album was dedicated, as he had died shortly before its release), Graham Nash, David Crosby ------. I made tea for all of them! I was soon to record

Ringo myself as an engineer on some forthcoming Joe Cocker sessions.

Somebody else would make the tea.

Stephen Stills was staying at a top London hotel on Park Lane and always took a guitar with him back to his hotel room when he left the studio. The sessions were late-nighters, so no one turned up much before six o'clock in the evening. One night, as the musicians were assembling, Stephen came rushing into the control room, guitar in hand. He was extremely excited. He summoned everyone to gather around and said "This is the song we are going to record tonight" He played the guitar and sang the song that he had written in his hotel room the previous night. What a great guitar player. What a great vocal hook — "If you can't be with the one you love, love the one you're with" Magic. First public performance of a classic and I was standing right next to him. The recording features a Hammond organ solo using the Basing Street studio two Hammond. Same one Steve Winwood played on all the Traffic stuff. Same one Bob Marley and the Wailers used with legendary Texan keyboardist John "Rabbit" Bundrick on *Burning* and *Catch a Fire*, Johnny Nash's *Stir it Up*, *I can see Clearly* and *More Questions than Answers*.

Amongst all this joy, there unfortunately also came one horror story. I relate this tale of woe, if only to stress to any would-be young, up-and-coming recording engineer the importance of utmost concentration at all times, particularly when you are operating up in these dizzy heights of a major label, major artist, and significant budget. A black felt-tip pen had boldly written the uppercase words that sealed the assistant engineer's fate and very nearly ruined the newly formed reputation of the studios. Left in full view on Sally's desk, that morning after the fateful night before, it said:

PLEASE INSTRUCT YOUR ASSISTANT ENGINEERS IN THE SKILL OF TAPE SPLICING. I DON'T WANT THIS ASSISTANT ANYWHERE NEAR MY TAPES AGAIN. REPLACE HIM.
Signed: **STEPHEN**

When you consider the dangers inherent in crudely cutting through magnetic recording tape with a razor blade, it has always amazed me that there have not been more disasters like the one about to be described here. The assistant engineer would be responsible for extracting the Master takes from the work reels onto a Master Reel. Saves having to carry dozens of reels around, searching for the best take --- just cut them out and join them all together on one reel. I have always thought this practice had the potential for catastrophic damage, and I was to be proved right. Blank leader tape, usually green at the beginning of a reel, white in the middle and red after the last track, would be used to separate song titles. The join between the leader tape and the magnetic tape would be made with very thin, very adhesive splicing tape. The whole operation (and it is akin to a surgical procedure, sweat usually dripping off the forehead, hands shaking) is performed around a large metal editing block, which is designed to align the various sections/widths of tape, ensuring a smooth, hopefully seamless edit. The slightest snag or microscopic misalignment is most undesirable, especially when you put the Master reel on at the start of the evening work, tail out first, hit rewind and watch and hear tape travelling through guides, rollers, past pinch wheels and head blocks at what seems like a hundred miles an hour. Watch what happens when the ever-so-slightly proud bit of splicing tape catches on one of the nasty, sharp edges of the tape guides. Stare in mortified horror as a wafer-thin tear extends down through the tape, ever-widening, going deeper and deeper. The unmistakable smell of burning flesh as the palms of the engineer's hands act as additional brakes to slow and bring to a halt the spinning metal spools. Then survey the damage.

What happened next was to be one of the most remarkable analogue tape repair and salvage exercises I have ever witnessed. Bill Halverson, the engineer, cleared the studio control room and the live room. He took the damaged tape, which had left the sanctuary of the spool and was lying in a tangled, coiled heap on the floor, gathered it all in his arms and cleared a large area of floor space in the live room. He laid out the tape, end to end, on the floor. By all accounts, there was something in the order of 150 feet of torn 2-inch tape, starting at one end as a hairline tear, continuing along the length, gradually increasing to a slice of about 1 inch. Armed with quarter-inch splicing tape, a razor blade, steady hands, a keen eye and interminable amounts of patience and concentration, Bill cut the splicing tape into little one-inch lengths and, along the back of the tape, proceeded to stick it all back together. It took about four hours to complete the surgery, after which the repaired tape was sent away to be copied, and all was well. Stephen thanked Bill and suggested that we all thank Bill, because the rest of the sessions could so understandably have been cancelled.

In those often precarious days of analogue multi-track tape machines, V.U meters, test tone tape alignment procedures, hiss and splicing tape, there was very little scope for combining different takes of a song's performance, other than, for the most part, relying on the capabilities of the musicians to get it right in one take. No digital cut, copy or paste. You could physically splice between, say, take one (good intro, first verse and chorus) and take four (good middle eight onward) and hope that the tempos and pitch all matched. If the splice didn't work, you would have to remember how to reassemble the tape back to square one. Reels of tape everywhere, bits of tape stuck to the side of the multi-track machine, endless chinagraph pencil marks.

Invariably, a piece of tape would be spliced back together the wrong way around, resulting in whoops of laughter and gasps of amazement as the playback of the re-inserted piece of tape was in reverse! But as is the inventiveness of the creative human mind, we soon learned that tape in reverse was a pretty cool effect, so it was sometimes used intentionally. Next time you listen to Paul Simon's *You Can Call Me Al* check out the bass guitar solo. The second half is the same as the first, only in reverse. Genius.

Bill Halverson took the art of splicing together different takes to a whole new level. He and Stephen would listen through to various takes of the same song and, if they preferred one particular chorus section to another, would make multi-track tape copies of that chosen chorus, as many as the song required and splice them together to make one complete take. Same with the verses, solos, etc. This would only be possible if the tempos and tuning between the different takes did match, which, with the quality of musicians being employed on the record, nearly always did. All you need are the likes of Dallas Taylor, Conrad Isedor and Ringo Starr on drums and Calvin "Fuzzy" Samuels on bass. Simples.

I remember my very first professional edit—a minor affair by comparison, but traumatic enough for me at the time. The edit in question was on a two-track stereo mix of a song called *Freedom Rider* by Traffic. It was to appear on their *John Barleycorn Must Die* album. Again, Brian had been the engineer, had finished the mix with Chris Blackwell as producer and left me, as the assistant engineer, to make whatever tape copies were required, label up the boxes and worksheets and finish the session. Chris was listening to the mix. Something was troubling him. There is a one-bar break that occurs twice in the song; one of the gaps featured a snare beat, the other a hi-hat. Chris wanted a snare beat both times. Brian had left the studio, so Chris asked if I could remedy the situation. Had I ever done editing before? (I was beginning to wish Len was at hand). "Yeah", I said confidently. (I had spliced and edited tape before, at home in Birmingham on the little Philips Elizabethan tape machine, using sellotape and scissors! But this wasn't the time and place to let Chris know that. It required making a copy of the snare beat onto another piece of tape and replacing the hi-hat beat with this copy. I made the copy and, with Chris hovering over my every move, proceeded to do the tape splicing. With beads of sweat dripping from my forehead and hands shaking like a needy alcoholic, I was in a serious state of quiet panic. Chris was convinced I was doing it incorrectly. "Why are you measuring the tape? Isn't that the wrong place to cut? Are you sure you know what you are doing?"

I made my stand. Here was the boss of the company giving me a bit of a grilling, suggesting that the consequences of my actions might result in the ruination of the mix. I thought of the consequences of the ruination of my short-lived career. I humbly suggested that I knew what I was doing (Gulp! Help! Len, where are you?) and that if I did the edit his way and it was wrong, then I would probably still get the blame, so if I do it my way and it is a mess-up then I will at least feel a sense of justice as I collect my P45.

Chris mumbled his indignation and left the room. I completed the edit, rewound the tape and had a momentary flashback to a supermarket in Birmingham near a number eleven bus stop. I pressed play. The edit worked. Thanks in no small part, it has to be said, to the excellent timekeeping of Jim Capaldi, the drummer. I played it to Chris. "Give the tape to Sally for filing", was all he said. No appreciation. No praise. The first thankless moments in the life of a studio engineer. However, I did detect a wry smile from him as he left the room, and my P45 remained in the drawer of the wages clerk.

There it remained for the next two years, until the summer of 1972. That was when I was offered a chance to go to America and do the front of house sound for the Island band Head, Hands and Feet. It was to be a two-month tour with the band's itinerary reading like a Google Earth map of the U.S.A. Every major city, and some not-so-major ones as well. Forty-eight shows in fifty-two days. More on my first American experiences later, but suffice at this point simply to say that Island couldn't give me that much time away, so I handed in my notice and turned freelance, did the tour, came back and just carried on as if I hadn't been away. I found out later that it was Chris who had recommended me to the band. He was encouraging me to progress and must have known that an experience of this kind would be of great benefit to me. Once, Chris even sent me to Los Angeles for the day to deliver a Jim Capaldi solo single master tape to Capitol Records! Chris knew I had a girlfriend, Janet, who worked for Capitol out in Hollywood. I had met her that summer, during the band's tour, because Head, Hands and Feet, as well as Jim Capaldi, were signed to Capitol for the U.S.A. Chris could easily have simply couriered the tape, so how mischievously kind of him. I had been in session the Saturday night before, until about four in the morning and after no more than three or four hours' sleep, the phone rang. It was Chris. Had I any plans for the day? Other than sleep, no. Meet me at the studio in an hour with your passport and an overnight bag. We sped along the M4 in his little Mini Cooper towards Heathrow, and at the TWA ticket counter, he enquired as to the next flight to Los Angeles. None until tomorrow. So it was London to New York, New York to Philadelphia and then connect on to L.A. Fifteen hours. I wouldn't have minded if I had been twice as long. I was off to California. Yippee! Chris gave me a couple of hundred dollars cash and I flew out on that Sunday, checked into a motel in Hollywood, close to the Capitol. I wanted to surprise Janet the next day. I walked into the office where she worked on the Monday morning, dropped off the tape, took a very surprised young lady to lunch, got a flight back the same afternoon and was on a session at Basing Street Tuesday evening. How cool was that. A twenty-one-year-old jet-setter from Birmingham.

After the Stephen Stills solo album sessions came to an end, Bill Halverson booked one more day in the studio. He was taking advantage of being in the U.K. to put a few additional touches on another record he was working on with another solo artist. To my surprise, Sally posted me up as his assistant and I got my first chance to work behind the desk alongside the great man. Perhaps my renowned editing skills had come to Bill's attention. On the booking sheet, it listed the label as being Polydor/ATCO. The artist was Eric Clapton. It was to be a short four or five-hour session and consisted of Eric adding some additional guitar parts to a couple of tunes and a vocal on one track, titled *Bottle of Red Wine*. I watched and listened in awe as one of my guitar heroes, sitting right next to me, wrote out the lyrics to the tune there and then. He was chewing on the end of the pencil as the lyrics came to him, pausing occasionally, gazing upwards, scribbling away. Then he grabbed the pieces of paper and dashed into the studio. I followed. A Neuman U.87 was what Bill wanted for the vocal mic, so I obliged, gave Eric the headphones and went back into the control room. Was it two takes? No more than that. Incredible. Then the guitar solo, rough mix and home. Done. Just like that. Bill thanked me and flew back to the States. I would see him again the following year.

The band Free had already recorded two albums for Island: *Tons of Sobs* and *Free*. You couldn't imagine that happening today. A record label prepared to stick with an artist over several years, in the belief that eventually the record-buying public would catch up with and recognise the talent on offer. So Chris engaged Roy Thomas Baker, an engineer at Morgan Studios in Willesden, northwest London, to start work on their third album. A hit was surely due soon. Roy Baker was later to become the engineer/producer for Queen, and *Bohemian Rhapsody* would be his most outstanding achievement. But back in 1970, along with producer John Kelly, additional sessions at Trident studios and also at Island, the third Free album, *Fire and Water*, were in the can. Free were in desperate need of a hit, and so too, no doubt, Island. The title contender from the album was the track *All Right Now* but the problem was with the length of the song. At 5m 32s, it was far too long for radio airplay. Three and a half minutes was the norm, with the possible exception of the Animals' House of the Rising Sun at almost four and a half minutes; radio stations simply wouldn't give the air-time. So, out with the razor blades and the splicing tape and enter Andy Johns. Having already worked with the band on their debut album, *Tons of Sobs* he was best placed to work alongside label boss Chris Blackwell, in studio two.

That was the first time I met Andy. Peering into the smoky control room, I saw him behind the console, sitting next to C.B., cigarette conveniently stuck onto one of the silver insert switches of the Helios desk, with his head rocking back and forth as the track was played over and over. He looked the epitome of cool. I took orders for tea. Another bloke with luscious long hair! Lots of smiling and laughter, Chris enjoying his company and, more importantly, respecting his judgement. Andy had in his head the perfect edit: take out the second verse and shorten the guitar solo. Just a smidgen over 4mins. Done. A few weeks later, I remember all the band members walking into the Island Records' reception, heads held high and a victorious swagger in their steps. The guys were on top of the world. The island's belief and support had paid off. The single reached number two in the U.K and was number one in about twenty territories around the world. It was a big record for Island and the band, so it was no surprise that

Andy Johns would be recruited to record Free's next album, Highway, later that year, in September. I assisted Andy in these sessions, along with Bob Potter, Islands' latest recruit as a trainee engineer. I had been introduced to Bob through Len, from Pye Studios. Bob later engineered sessions, along with senior, ex-Olympic legend Phil Brown, at Basing Street with Sly and the Family Stone and also with Leon Russell. Between us, Bob and I would handle most of the assistant engineering duties for Andy Johns on many forthcoming sessions carried out at Basing Street, not least of all with Free, Mott The Hoople and Led Zeppelin. Meanwhile, the Highway album, despite the critical acclaim of tracks like *Stealer* and *My Brother Jake*, was not as big a success as hoped, and the band began to fragment.

Even back in the Birmingham days, I had been a massive Free fan and had bought both of their early albums, whereas my copies of *Fire and Water* and *Highway* came gratis courtesy of Aladdin. The next album to be recorded by Free was to be their penultimate and would have my name on it as an engineer. But not before two of the band members decided to engage in a temporary musical side-step.

Because of the lack of widespread success of the *Highway* album, an inevitable, albeit brief separation occurred. The band had, after all, been together for over four years, joined at the musical hip as teenagers. Time to explore other musical possibilities. Drummer Simon Kirke and guitarist Paul Kossoff combined forces with Texan keyboard player John "Rabbit" Bundrick and Japanese bass player Tetsu Yamauchi to record the *Kossoff, Kirke, Tetsu, Rabbit* album, released on Island Records in 1972. Having worked as an engineer with Rabbit as the keyboard player on several Johnny Nash sessions (*I can sey*, *stir it Up*, *More Questions than Answers*) and working as an assistant engineer on Free sessions for *Highway*, I was the first choice, along with some additional engineering from fellow Island staff engineer Tony Platt, to engineer this hybrid album. Vocal duties were shared out between Simon and Rabbit, with one contribution from Paul Kossoff on the wistfully hypnotic track *Colours*. This was an altogether thoroughly enjoyable album to record. Gone, for Simon and Paul, were the pressures of trying to repeat and better the previous glories of Free. A creative opportunity for them to exchange musical freedoms with the additional writing and playing skills of Rabbit and Tetsu, outside the restrictive confines of the blues/rock style of Free.

When musical and political differences between Free's vocalist Paul Rodgers and bass player Andy Fraser were eventually set to one side, and along with the hope that Paul Kossoff's drug dependency problems could be resolved, the original Free line-up got back together in the studio. This was to record the *Free At Last* album. To now be sitting in the engineer's chair, about to commence the recording of Free's fifth studio album, was to me a dream come true. During the *Highway* and *KKTR* sessions, I had established a solid relationship with the band members. I remember one time going to Andy Fraser's house, listening with him to his record collection: Aretha Franklin, James Brown, Wilson Pickett. This was the kind of music these guys grew up on. Same as me. Looking back now, I can understand Chris Blackwell's ideology when it came to putting certain engineers together with the different Island artists. He must have noticed a synergy between me and the band members, with my affinity for the band and perhaps even my youthful enthusiasm and energy that were to be in seemingly endless demand during the coming weeks and months., I was to learn of the extreme highs and lows of the recording process; of the sometimes deeply intense personal relationships that form within a band; and the occasionally fractious nature of studio life that starkly contrasts with the overwhelming sense of joy and satisfaction of seeing an album through from conception to completion. In this case, of being in a studio listening to and recording one of the greatest British blues/rock vocalists, guitar solos of exquisite passion and soul, combined with the tightest of drums and bass, to the extent that even to this day, I am still a massive fan of Free.

The *Free at Last* album was to be an expression of the band's further progressive development away from their original blues roots. However, the single release of *Little Bit of Love* was never to recapture the success of *All Right Now*, and there would be only one more album to follow.

The swan-song album by Free, *Heartbreaker*, was to be their most mature and sophisticated. With additional musical contributions and co-writes from Rabbit on keyboards, "Snuffy" Walden's complimentary additional guitar (he would later go on to enjoy success as writer of the music for the American political drama series *The West Wing*) and the replacement of Andy Fraser on bass by Tetsu, it was to result in an album of considerable musical depth, so completely removed from the blues/rock simplicity of their debut album, *Tons of Sobs* some four years earlier. As an engineer, I was to be tested beyond anything I had experienced before in terms of intensity, emotionally fuelled artistic expression and pressure. The heat was on for this record to be a success, and everyone in the band and at the label knew. The issues surrounding Kossoff's drug problems and friction amongst band members were at a high. On completion of the album and despite the success of the single *Wishing Well*, it was glaringly apparent that this particular group of individuals would never again record together in the same studio. This iconic band were to split up into many disparate groups, the most successful of which was to feature the vocalist and drummer teaming up with Mott the Hoople's guitarist, Mick Ralphs and King Crimson bass player Boz Burrell. Bad Company, under the same Led Zeppelin management heavyweight of Peter Grant, would take the world by storm.

And whilst I have the chance, if I may indulge myself, I would like to put the record straight regarding the production of the *Heartbreaker* album. The production credit on the album is given to Andy Johns. The label decided to bring Andy in to do the final mixdown. After all, he had the reputation and the skill and could get his magic touch to the project. However, many of the mixes used are mine. Andy re-eq'd and compressed some of them, undoubtedly making them louder and sonically improved. However, he was not present at the recording sessions and didn't produce the album. No hard feelings, Andy. It's a cruel business, and I still think you are one of the greatest.

Besides, Morris the studio cat was in attendance the whole time we were mixing the album, so we all knew the mixes were fine. If they hadn't been, then Morris would have made you aware. He would sit across the top of the desk right in front of the massive Tannoy speakers, ears twitching with every snare beat, his chest heaving on every bass drum. He was very fond of music, especially reggae, blues and rock, but if he disapproved of what he was listening to, then he would jump down and simply exit the control room. Invariably, you would need to address the mix, so to speak, from scratch; start all over again and await Morris's return. As soon as he was ensconced back in front of the speaker, the confidence amongst the crew was restored. Having been one of the label's senior A+R executives, his paws on approach to production was directly responsible for several hits that came out of the studios.

But one of my most lasting memories of this project was an incident involving myself, Paul Rodgers and Kossy. Paul was in the studio on his own with headphones on, preparing to overdub a vocal on one of the tracks. I was adjusting reverb to the headphone mix and obviously overdid it, because Paul threw down the headphones, stormed into the control room and verbally attacked me, along the lines of "--- don't EVER and I mean EVER put

F*!#+*ing reverb in my headphones when I'm singing---"Oops! I was shaking and quite visibly upset. Kossy literally stepped between me and Paul and, waving his finger at Rodgers, came to my defense. "Don't EVER and I mean EVER talk to Digby like that again.!! He is our engineer and the most important person in the room. Without him, our music would never be captured, not the way he does it. He is the best and we should all show him the greatest of respect!"

There was a long, silent pause. We were all sort of welling up. It had been a long day. Paul Rodgers reached out his hand and apologized profusely. I said no worries. We were all so emotionally wrapped up in this record and a lot of stress and tension had been bubbling under the surface. This cleared the air. We were all too close to let anything break us up so we got back to work. Paul delivered yet another breath-taking vocal performance and Kossoff and I became as close as mates can get. I loved that guy, not just for sticking up for me, but because of his great sense of humour, his almost overwhelming modesty and most importantly, his unique mastery of the guitar. Nobody before or since could make an electric guitar sound like the complete uninterrupted extension of the human soul as he could.

Later, in 1976 (by that time living in Los Angeles), I recorded an album with Paul's newly formed band, Back Street Crawler, with sessions in L. A and New York. This was to be that band's second album, entitled *2nd Street* and was released on Rhino/Atlantic records. On drums and bass were the top Texan duet of Tony Braunagel and Terry Wilson, musical partners of John "Rabbit" Bundrick, who handled keyboards, with vocal duties provided by Geordie blues legend Terry Slesser. Paul was in a pretty bad way. John Glover, the band's manager, had put me and Paul in the same New York hotel room, John's logic being that if anyone could keep an eye on Paul it would be me! But I was in no position to mentor and one evening Paul went off out into the Manhattan nightlife returning in the wee hours with an entourage of adoring hangers-on. I was abruptly awoken and snapped at Paul to get rid of these people and get some sleep, as we were due in the studio the next morning, early. And not just any old studio.

Most of the New York sessions were at Atlantic's famous recording studios on Broadway. Founded in 1947, these groundbreaking facilities had been home since the 60s to top American producers such as Tom Dowd and Arif Mardin. The artists who they recorded at these facilities are too numerous to list here in full, but let us narrow it down to these: Aretha Franklin, Otis Redding, Bobby Darin, John Coltrane, Charlie Parker, Ray Charles and Eric Clapton. During the whole of my time there, about a week all told, I felt an immense sense of wonder and awe that my journey from an egg-box-lined bedroom studio in Birmingham had led me to such a palace of musical grandeur. I was provided with a highly likeable and knowledgeable assistant on my first day there, Gene, a young guy who gathered microphones and headphones for me, showed me the idiosyncrasies of the studio equipment, fetched me lunch from the nearby deli and brought me coffee by the mug-full. When I later asked him his full name I was as humbled as I was astonished. He was Grammy Award-winning Atlantic engineer Gene Paul, son of studio guru/guitar maker Les Paul. Trust the New Yorkers to lay it on in style for a visiting young English engineer.

Back in Los Angeles, there were only a few guitar overdubs left to complete the recordings, before the tapes were to be shipped back to London for the producer Glyn Johns to mix. I was left alone in the studio with Paul on that last night, and we worked into the early hours nailing the previous bits of guitar. Paul, with one headphone on, one off, was listening to me, sitting at the piano, shouting out the chord changes as they arrived. It was painful and slow. Paul was very stoned and could hardly stand. It was almost too much to take, watching and listening to the sluggish, inept fingering on the frets, struggling to make the changes. Note by agonising note, we completed the task, unplugged his guitar, switched off the amp and put the tapes away. I said goodbye to the assistant engineer, who had fallen asleep many hours earlier! This was to be the last time. The last session. The last overdub. The last notes.

Paul, John Glover and Rabbit all flew back to London. I arrived back at my Hollywood apartment in the early hours of Saturday morning. Later that day the 'phone rang. It was Rabbit. Had I heard the news? Kossoff was dead. Had died on the 'plane.

What a sorrowful end. So sad for his family. So young. So gifted. This was the body count I referred to earlier, growing in numbers.

Back in 1973, we had managed to accumulate enough unreleased material of Paul's, featuring many of Island's artists who had jammed in the studio with him: Jess Roden, John Martyn, as well as guest appearances by Alan White (drummer from Yes), Trevor Burton (bass player with The Move) and many others. We put together Paul's first and only solo album, and it was called *Back Street Crawler*. Just as a quick aside, it is worth mentioning this little anecdote regarding Paul's unique guitar sound. As was often the case, Paul had been overdubbing some lead guitar on one of the tracks, using his legendary gold Les Paul through his Marshall amp. This was the sound only he could achieve; deep, rich, powerful legato: economic use of long, single sustained notes, with lyrical vibrato at the end of every phrase. We paused for a break, and the amp was left on standby, tone controls set, volumes set, ready to recommence when required, to finish recording the part. Some curious would-be guitarist was passing the studio door and looked in, noticing Paul's guitar leaning on a stand next to the Marshall. Before I could stop him, he had picked up Paul's guitar and was about to play. "Don't touch", I yelled out. "We are right in the middle of an overdub and don't want to lose the sound!!" But it was too late. He had the guitar in his hands. He switched off the standby. The guitar began to feed back through the amp. It was deafening. The feedback, the distortion. It was uncontrollable! What a racket. Couldn't even get one single note out of it. He put the guitar down, switched on the standby and walked away in bemused disgust. "How can anyone play this pile of sh*t!" he grumbled as I led him away from the scene. Enter Paul. Suitably refreshed and ready to continue with his guitar playing, he switches off the standby and like a well-trained dog, the guitar and amp are back on their best behaviour. Beautiful sweeping melodies, controlled sustain, back in the hands of its rightful master. Standard service is resumed.

On a photo shoot for the album cover, Paul took his Fender Stratocaster out into the side alley next to the Basing Street studios. He took the guitar lead and "plugged" it into a dustbin!! That photo of Paul plugged into a dustbin was to be the album cover and was to signify the defiant nature of the man in a most humorous way, which was typical of him. The alley cat, rebel of a guitar player. He sounded like no other and wanted an image to match.

I am so glad I had a chance to work with one of my all-time guitar heroes. All that vinyl back in Birmingham during the late '60s. Walking around the dark streets of Erdington, with my mate Pete "Beefy" Collins, late at night, listening to *Tons of Sobs* and *Free* on an old mono cassette machine. Me, from Birmingham to New York. Paul, from London to New York.

A couple of Back Street Crawlers.

We all knew the mixes were fine.

Handcuffs At The Ready

In David Sinclair's book celebrating the fiftieth anniversary of the founding of Island Records, *A History of Cool* (Guardian 2009), music journalist Paul Morley sums up perfectly the beautifully organised chaos of success that was Island Records in the early seventies:

"I eventually grew to appreciate how Chris Blackwell, and therefore Island Records, was not about one thing, or one style, or one system, or one way of doing things--- (I began) reflecting how the world functions and reinvents itself precisely because it is a fluid, sometimes dangerous, always exhilarating union of systems and beliefs and the best way of allowing the world to progress is to mix up and place in glorious conflict these various systems and beliefs"

On any one day at Island, you would find yourself in the mildly chaotic company of, say, Steve Winwood, a Wailer or two, Rebop Kwaku Baah (the Ghanaian conga player with Traffic), John Martyn, maybe Paul Kossoff. Everybody is ready and waiting to go into one of the studios to record. As one of the extremely overworked and fatigued staff engineers, you would be forgiven for being somewhat confused and not knowing whose session/album you were recording that day. Was it a John Martyn session that Paul had come along to overdub some guitar, or was Steve doing some Hammond on one of Kossy's tracks? Rebop would play congas for anyone, anytime, anywhere! Was it me or Tony with the Wailers today? Best check with Sally or Penny. There were now two studios fully operational, 24/7, 365 days a year. One session out, another in. This conveyor belt of record production was to be my life for the next five years.

The creative advantages of working for a record label with recording studios meant that there was a constant interactive synergy between all of the artists; a close interest and co-operation with each other's work. Same with all the engineers. How was John Burns getting on with that Jethro Tull *Aqualung* album upstairs in studio one? Is Frank Owen standing up well with that New York producer, Lew Futterman, in studio two, on the *If* album (Island's equivalent of the American band Chicago)? Will engineers Phil Brown and Bob Potter recover in time for tonight, after last night's over-indulgent session with Sly and the Family?

As in-house studio engineers with hectic, usually around-the-clock schedules, we would often find ourselves taking over from one another on album projects. So consequently, we younger, up-and-coming junior engineers were in increasing demand. Tony Platt, Bob Potter, Phil Ault, Rhett Davies, Howard Kilgour and I collaborated on many of the studio projects: Sutherland Brothers and Quiver, Patto, The Wailers, Roxy Music, Sparks, Fairport Convention, and John Martyn. It was as if Chris Blackwell was checking out the chemistry, to see which engineers worked best within specific musical genres. Tony's laid-back, relaxed style found him completely at home with both the slow, measured pace of Bob Marley and his fellow Rastafarians, as well as the almost matter-of-fact methodology of Muff Winwood's daytime sessions. Bob Potter's high-energy, rock'n'roll approach saw him network well with bands like Hatfield and The North (formerly Joe Cocker's Grease Band), Carol Grimes' Uncle Dog, and Sly and The Family. Myself? I gravitated predominantly to the likes of Free, John Martyn and John "Rabbit" Bundrick, as well as the always friendly, sensible, easy-going sessions with Muff. Looking back, I can see myself as being one of those utility players; reasonably versatile, flexible, and into lots of different types of music, so at one time or another I managed to find myself in the studio with just about every artist/band on the label, as either assistant or first engineer, sometimes both! For example, on the Uncle Dog sessions, featuring the soulful, sultry vocals of Carol

Grimes, John Porter producing (he had made and played bass for Bryan Ferry and Roxy Music and was to later work with The Smiths) it would sometimes be me engineering with Bob Potter assisting and at other times, Bob was booked in as engineer. I would step in to replace an assistant engineer who had telephoned in as "missing in action". We often swapped roles during the same session. We both made tea!

Every Monday morning, from ten 'till one pm, studio two was exclusively booked out to Muff Winwood for his A+R audition sessions. This time slot was reserved for the further exploration of the most promising of the dozens of demo tapes submitted to the label every week from young hopefuls wanting to break into the industry. Muff, to his credit, listened to all of them, if only for a few seconds each. You can usually tell quite quickly if there is anything of merit. Remember this, all of you who seek musical recognition: the first fifteen seconds of your song will determine your chances of a second listen. And even then -------.

If you passed the initial test, you would be invited to spend three hours in the studio with Muff and me, or one of the other staff engineers, to be put through your paces in the open glare of a real-time studio experience. Some showed promise, but insufficient desire. Occasionally, a decent song, but a woefully lacking vocal interpretation. Sorry, can't play your instruments --- who played on the demo? Most amounted to little and have more than likely never been heard of since.

So close.

But one particular Monday morning heralded the arrival of a very talented young songwriting duo who were about to break into the industry big time. Gavin and Iain Sutherland were a folk duo of Scottish descent and came down for their invited day in the studio by train from their home in Stoke-on-Trent. Equipped with brand new guitars (I think bought for them by Island), a most productive few hours in the studio followed. Their harmonious, well-rehearsed vocals showed great talent and led to their signing with the label. Their debut album, *The Sutherland Brothers Band*, was produced by Muff and engineered by Tony Platt and me, and it was a moderate success with the first single, *The Pie*. The same recording and production crew worked on the second album, *Lifeboat*, which was released later that same year. I remember recording one particular track that Gavin insisted needed a large, military band-style bass drum to be overdubbed. We didn't have such an instrument in the studio, and we could have hired one from one of the many instrument hire companies. In any event, we broke for lunch and Gavin went for a walk down to Portobello. He returned some twenty minutes later and had with him a rather large, slightly dilapidated but fully functioning military-style bass drum! He explained that he had found the drum in a nearby skip. Serendipity or what? The front skin was torn, but it sounded explosive, especially when struck with some force out in the reverberant reception area. So that's where we placed the microphones, two of them, Neumann U.87's, one close to the main door where Gavin stood holding the drum, the other halfway down the stairs—sounded great! The track was called *Sailing*, and despite vigorous radio airplay, it received no commercial success. Not, that is, as a Sutherland Brothers release.

    I remember hearing the news a few months later after Island had sent a copy out to Lionel Conway, head of Island Music Publishing, in their Los Angeles office. Lionel was mates with, playing football in an ex-pats football team out in L.A with a certain successful British vocalist who had taken up residence out on that glorious west coast. I wasn't to know this at the time but before too long I would be playing up front, alongside Lionel and his mate in the same football team. So it was Lionel on the phone to Muff. Yes, Lionel's "mate" liked the song and was going to record his own version.

The success of Rod Stewart's version of *Sailing* meant that, once the airplay and PRS royalties began pouring in, the Sutherland brothers would, from now on and for always, be buying their guitars.

In 1973, the brothers joined forces with the band Quiver, featuring Bruce Thomas on bass, who later went on to work with Elvis Costello, drummer Willie Wilson (David Gilmour, Pink Floyd), keyboardist Peter Wood (Cyndi Lauper, Al Stewart, with whom he co-wrote *Year of the Cat*) and guitarist Tim Renwick. Tim had played with Elton John and also Al Stewart. (Listen to the beautifully evocative, lyrical guitar solos on *Year of the Cat*. That's Tim.) The first album with the new lineup was *Dream Kid* in 1973. No chart success. Then followed *Beat of the Street* in 1974, similarly lacking in commercial glory. The band left Island Records and signed to CBS. September 1975 saw the release of the first album on the new label *Reach for the Sky* and the second single from the album, released in April 1976 was *Arms of Mary*. This single charted top ten in the U.K and number one in Ireland and the Netherlands. It has become the song for which the band is to be most remembered by, still being played on the radio today at not infrequent intervals.

But back to the earlier days on the Island. There was one other piece of exciting news for the brothers and the band that came, again by phone, to the studio two control room during a session with Muff and me. Up until the summer of 1973, the boys had been gigging mostly around the U.K., promoting the first two albums. They had supported some very influential acts in the process: Ten Years After, David Bowie (as Ziggy Stardust), Status Quo, The Beach Boys, The Doors and Roxy Music. Muff took the call. Just nodded his head a few times. Iain and Gavin looked on quizzically and then gasped at the news that they were all off to America, as The Sutherland Brothers and Quiver, for a nine-week tour supporting Elton John.

Just as well they sent that demo tape to Island.

In the summer of 1970, Spooky Tooth had been recording their *Last Puff* album in Studio Two, with Brian Humphries handling engineering duties. Even though I had by then been engineering myself and even producing (with Bronco), I was still called upon to assist on some of these sessions. Behind Denise's desk, inside Aladdin's Cave, I had seen copies of Spooky's previous 1969 album, *Ceremony*, with its stunningly brutal album sleeve artwork by John Holmes.

This was typical of the innovative Island Records album format of the day: album sleeves like Mott the Hoople's 1969 album of the same name, with artwork from M. C. Escher's lithograph: *Reptiles*. John Martyn's use of Schlieren photography for *Solid Air*. The iconic artwork of Tony Wright featured on, amongst others, Traffic's *Low Spark of High Heeled Boys*, Steve Winwood's *Arc of a Diver* and Bob Marley's *Natty Dread* albums. These and many others all had as their front covers exquisite, often controversial artwork, designed to lure you via your visual senses into the musical journeys that awaited inside, within the grooves of those magical vinyl scrolls.

Spooky Tooth were in the studio again, artwork no doubt already in the can. Mike Kellie, a fellow Brummie with the longest legs ever seen on a drummer! Luther Grosvenor, guitarist from Evesham, Worcestershire, the land of Zeppelin's John Bonham. Gary Wright, an American from New Jersey on keyboards and vocals (who would later go on to pursue his solo career and have a massive hit with his song *Dream Weaver* released in 1975 on Warner Brothers Records), Greg Ridley, bass guitar and Mike Harrison, lead vocals, both from Carlisle, Cumbria. I had already gotten to know Mike Harrison as a consequence of my earlier disparaging remarks concerning the questionable tuning of a particular acoustic guitar I had come across at Penny's mews flat that morning, some months before. This acute attention to tuning and pitch would come in handy over the years to come, not least of all with Mike, as before too long, I was to be sitting in the engineers' chair recording Mike's first solo album. His almost forensic attention to detail, especially with regard to vocal tuning, was to be an enormous challenge to my patience and studio tenacity. So after the final break-up of Spooky Tooth, Mike joined forces with musician friends from back in his home town, Carlisle. The Junkyard Angels, as they were to be known, were Frank Kenyon (guitar), Ian Herbert (guitar), Kevin Iverson (drums) and Peter Batey (bass). A more motley, dishevelled and immensely likeable group of seasoned northern musical grit would be hard to find—the perfect accompaniment for the rough, passionate, gravelly vocals of Mike.

And so, into the cathedral-sized studio one at Basing Street we did enter, to commence recording Mike's first solo album, little knowing what horrors were about to unfold.

Mike's band members would travel down from Carlisle, suitcases and guitars in hand and muster up whatever makeshift accommodation arrangements they could on a shoestring budget: cheap hotels and B+B's, or, sofas and floor space at Mike's. An image of one suitcase in particular, belonging to Pete the bass player, has stayed in my mind to this day—specifically, the moment when the police officer asked Pete to open it.

We were a couple of weeks into the album and had recorded most of the backing tracks, i.e. drums, bass, guide guitars and guide vocals upstairs in studio one. The most memorable moments from these sessions were the sight and sound of Pete playing bass for the whole of the album with his broken arm in a sling, with only the very tips of the fingers on his right hand protruding out of the plaster cast! This feat of musical instrument mastery was the brunt of many a jibe, but you had to admire the man's strength, tenacity, dexterity and will power.

They build people like that in Carlisle.

The first signs of doom appeared over the Notting Hill horizon one late afternoon. One of the roadies, I forget who (just as well; he wouldn't take too kindly to my mentioning this), had been out and about looking to score some puff. Now, for those too innocent or naive not to know the meaning of the words "score" and "puff", well, you probably wouldn't be reading this anyway, so I will continue in the knowledge that you are entirely on board with what I am about to describe. The roadie, let's call him Alan, came back to the studio with a rather grubby, somewhat wasted-looking character, let's call him Brian, who assured us all that he could supply a sizable amount of hashish (Red Leb' I seem to recall) at a below-market rate, depending on quantity. Therein followed a whip-round amongst band members and crew, followed by Alan and Brian disappearing out into the streets. About an hour later, they returned. Alan had in his hand a lump of foil-wrapped hash, the size of a house brick. The foil was torn away, and the bounty examined. Finger nails and car keys scraped away at the moist but firm surface of the block, and several joints were quickly rolled in succession. The sweet, alluring smell suggested this was the real thing, so a lot of money changed hands. Brian was hurriedly stuffing the assorted crumpled bank notes into his pockets as he waved goodbye, never to be seen again.

It was only later, the next day, that the true scale of the crime was revealed.

I seem to recall that it was Frank who screamed out loud the first tirade of verbal expletives, which was then followed by a huge collective groan. The house brick-sized piece of hash had by now been scraped away sufficiently to reveal its innermost secret. The outer veneer of hash was merely the surround to disguise a lump of potter's clay. I would say about seventy-five percent of the brick was clay. We had been done. Everyone turned and glared at Alan. He was pale and slightly clammy. For his safety, he was sent out of the room, back onto the streets of Notting Hill to look for Brian—fat chance.

And just when you think things can't get any worse -------.

We were downstairs in studio two by now. Guitar overdubs, vocals, repairing bass parts, Pete's arm still in a sling. His grey, well-worn suitcase was parked innocently on the floor near the door. As we worked on through the night, well into the early hours of the morning, no one had noticed Alan's absence. He had been gone all day. We were later to learn that he had been stopped and searched by police earlier in the evening, near Notting Hill tube station. In his possession, police had found tablets, downers (sedatives), I think, about a hundred of them! Where was he going? he was asked. To Island Studios in Basing Street, he helpfully replied. To take these drugs to the musicians? No need, he told them. They have their own, he fatefully added.

Back at the studio, it was by now about four in the morning. Mike and I were sitting at the console playing back vocal takes. Jerry, my American assistant engineer, was, in the finest tradition of all Island assistants, doing an excellent job keeping the tea flowing. The control room was dimly lit, smelly and smoky. We were all exhausted and about to call it a day, so one last round of tea, please, Jerry. Mike and I were both face down, staring at the faders on the desk, switching between different vocal takes, listening intensely to phrasing and pitch. Suddenly, the control room was illuminated as bright as a floodlit football ground! We both looked up at the same time, stunned and speechless, into the glare of the police flashlights. There before us stood the mass array of bobbies with helmets, flat-topped embroidered hats, female officers, plain clothes detectives and very large, aggressively excited dogs. We were being busted.

Jerry impressed me with his American coolness, as he walked into this chaotic foray with a tray of hot tea, handed one to a nice, thankful policeman, swiftly turned 180 degrees as effortlessly and gracefully as a ballerina, glided upstairs and left the building. He didn't spill a drop. The rest of us, however, were subjected to something a little less polite. One policeman appeared beneath my feet as I stood, shocked and frozen to the spot. As he crawled from under the console, his helmet was knocked off his head. He looked ridiculous, like something out of a *Carry On* movie. He had a plastic bag of marijuana in his hand. He looked up at me with his somewhat sadly apologetic face. "I saw you drop this", he lied. "You are under arrest".

Everyone was searched. As we were being led outside to the awaiting mass of assembled police vehicles I saw Pete, tightly clutching his suitcase. An officer cornered him and demanded he open it. Pete, sling, plaster-cast fingered and all, unclipped the two fasteners and reluctantly lifted the lid. The memory of the look on that policeman's face as the large assortment of pharmaceutical contraband inside Pete's suitcase were revealed will stay with me forever. It was the most grimaced, lascivious evil smile I have ever witnessed. As if in an episode of the television detective series *The Sweeney*, the officer turned to Pete, handcuffs at the ready, glowered and said "You're nicked".

We were all taken to Notting Hill police station and individually questioned at length. My interrogation took place in a large, freezing-cold room near the front of the building. I was made to stand next to an open window, the cold night air combining with my state of shock and tiredness, resulting in my shivering uncontrollably. We were led downstairs and thrown into individual cells. Everyone was laughing and shouting their protests in a defiant and oddly humorous way. I felt surprisingly upbeat and reassured in the company of such northern camaraderie as displayed by Mike and The Junkyard Angels.

The next day we were taken to Marylebone Magistrates Court and formally charged. Island had sent along a solicitor and we were all out on bail and back at the studio by lunchtime. Everyone at the label, including studio staff rallied around us offering support and condolences. Mike was at pains to point out that nobody had died and that we were all o.k., just a bit shocked and tired, but what an adventure! We explained the course of the previous day's events and it was agreed that security measures at the studio, especially at night, would need to be reviewed. The solution was as follows:

On the ground floor was the main reception area, which at night had a security chap in attendance. There was already an intercom system in place, so no one could just walk in, but how to alert engineers, producers, and musicians in the two studios to any, err, shall we say, official danger? Well, that was addressed by the addition of a red light inside each control room, activated by a button behind the security guy's seat. If the red light flashed, it was time to clean the place up. Never anything too heavy it must be said. Cocaine wasn't as yet fashionable so that it would be mostly hash or grass, small amounts for personal use. Some chose pills, usually just to keep awake. The most prevalent would be alcohol, not remotely illegal, but arguably the most dangerous of all.

It was during a session with Mike and The Junkyard Angels that the first test of the efficiency of the new security measures was to be conducted. It was a few months later, upstairs in studio one. There was just Mike and me in the studio; everyone else had left. We were recording more vocals. It was again, coincidentally, about four in the morning. No, Jerry, this time to make tea, just me and Mike scanning the faders again, listening, adjusting, heads down in the dark. I was experiencing an extremely strong sense of déjà vu. Then it happened. The red light flashed. EMERGENCY!!! QUICK!!! Hide everything, clean the place up. There wasn't much for me to hide as I was still a fairly clean-living young man in those early days, but Mike moved swiftly into action. His small silver pill tin was the first thing to go, so into the headphone amp it flew. These amps were rack-mounted and easy to access for maintenance purposes. You just grabbed the handle and pulled them out. But this amp was still switched on and live! As Mike pushed the amp, now with his silver tin inside, back into place, the whole rack started to spark and blew all the fuses in the room—total darkness, apart from the rapidly flashing, extremely bright red light. My heart was racing. It was only a matter of time before we would, once again, be surrounded by police. Mike also had in his possession a small amount of hash, about the size of half an Oxo cube. I didn't see where this went, but it seemed to disappear. Then we waited. And waited some more. The tension was too much. I was going to go downstairs and confront the situation, so I left Mike in the control room and made my way down the spiral staircase. I thought of Muff Winwood coming down those same stairs on that October evening back in '69, and was beginning to wish I had chosen mini-cab driving as an albeit less exciting but hugely safer profession. Coming up the stairs was Bill, the maintenance man. He seemed very calm, saying he was going to look at the fuse box. Tony, the security guy, was sitting relaxed at the reception desk, feet up, leaning back in the chair, reading a newspaper.

"Everything all right Diggers" he enquired, very nonchalantly. It most certainly was not, I told him. Then I noticed that the back of Tony's big leather chair was in contact with, yes, you've guessed it, the emergency button. False alarm.

I went back upstairs to tell Mike about the situation. We sighed in huge relief. I suggested we call it a night, but that we should have one little smoke for the road before we leave. Not possible said Mike. Can't remember where you put the puff? No. I've swallowed it, he said.

It took about a year before the jury trial at Marylebone. My case was thrown out because two police officers contradicted each other, both saying that they had been the one to see me drop the plastic bag on the floor. I was extremely relieved it was all over. A couple of the band members got suspended sentences, but no more.

After these recent tumultuous events, I sensed there was a feeling throughout the label and amongst the studio staff in particular of the need for a period of calm. A more philosophical sense of harmony and oneness was required.

And then along came Bob.

...a fully functioning military style drum.

"You Can Get It …."

I was introduced to Johnny Nash by John "Rabbit" Bundrick, Texan keyboardist, songwriter and producer. I had first worked with Rabbit on the *Kossoff, Kirke, Tetsu, Rabbit* album, a most delightfully easy and pleasurable record to make, coming out of the initially painful break-up of Free. At the same time, we were laying down tracks for Rabbit's first solo album, *Broken Arrows*. Chris Blackwell had signed Rabbit to Island and gave us carte blanche studio time. We were both so busy on other projects that we usually had to record during studio downtime, late at night after the close of play, and whenever the studio was free on a weekend. Working with Rabbit on his album was the first opportunity I had to show my more musically creative production skills. For the most part, it was just Rabbit and me in the studio, layering pianos, Hammonds, synthesizers, Moogs -----. Then experimenting with vocal sounds and harmonies, recording the vocals sometimes through the Hammond's Leslie cabinet or Marshal amps, creating an echo chamber in the heavily tiled and many mirrored ladies' toilet! Lots of creative exploration for a young engineer/producer such as myself to get his teeth into. And good fun too.

As Rabbit's record progressed we began to bring in additional musicians: Jim Capaldi, Conrad Isadore, Randy Reader and Simon Kirke on drums; Gerry Masters and Tetsu Yamauchi on bass: Junior Marvin, Pete Carr, Richard Reeve and W.G "Snuffy" Walden on guitars: Reebop Kwaku Baah from Traffic on congas (who else?!) and horn sections *Sons of the Jungle* and *The Dundee Horns* (later to be re-named The Average White Band). Such was the faith Chris Blackwell had in this record that some tracks were sent off to the famous Muscle Shoals studio in Alabama to be mixed.

Rabbit had known and worked with Johnny Nash previously, so it was no surprise when Johnny booked Island Studios and employed Rabbit to take care of keyboard overdubs on his 1972 I Can See Now album for CBS Records, which Rabbit requested me as an engineer. The easy-going chemistry that existed between Johnny and Rabbit, based on their years of playing together, meant that Rabbit almost instinctively knew what was required on the tracks. And what classics they were to become: *More Questions Than Answers*, the title track *I Can See Now*, along with *Stir It Up* and *Guava Jelly*, both written by Bob Marley. So here was an early connection for me and Island with the great reggae man himself.

Rabbit had met Bob Marley whilst in Sweden, working on the soundtrack to the Swedish film *Vill sa garna tro* (Want so much to Believe) directed by Gunnar Hoglund. Marley, Bundrick, and Nash became roommates during their stay together. Sometime after returning to London, Bundrick was brought in to collaborate on arrangements for Marley's *Catch a Fire* album, adding keyboards to the original Jamaican recordings to make the record sound more contemporary.

But back to the sessions with Johnny.

On a number of occasions, we would all go back to Johnny's house in Bayswater, west London, to listen, probably off a cassette, to the day's recordings. At all times, both in and out of the studio, we would be in the company of his manager, Danny Simms. Danny had been a music publisher, promoter, producer, club owner, and head of JAD Records, which was the first label to sign Bob Marley. He was also, how can I put it, the biggest man I have ever seen!

One evening at the house, listening to the studio's daily rushes, Danny emerged from one of the bedrooms, totally and unashamedly naked, his immense manhood on full, flowing display. I found it difficult not to stare. Rabbit and Johnny on the other hand had probably seen it all before and weren't distracted in the slightest. Danny went over to the fridge, grabbed a couple of beers, and went back into the bedroom. Didn't blink, didn't say a word. Here was a man on a mission. I could hear the faint girly giggles as the door closed behind him.

Danny Simms had managed Johnny Nash since the mid-sixties, and both had first heard Bob Marley back in Jamaica at a Rastafarian ceremony, around 1968. Danny promptly signed Marley to his first international publishing and recording contracts and so can be credited as, if you like discovering Bob Marley and setting him on the road to becoming the first and biggest global reggae superstar.

It was on one of the sessions with Rabbit and Johnny Nash at Basing Street, studio two, that Johnny turned up for work with this friend of his. A not too tall, very handsome young man with short dreadlocks surrounding a warm, friendly smiling face. "This is my friend Bob" Johnny said, very matter of factly, as if this was some school mate or drinking buddy. "He's a reggae singer". Pleased to meet you, I said, shaking his warm hand, feeling that special glow that comes when you meet someone you instantly take a liking to. But I had no idea who he was and even less of an inkling as to who he would become. I don't think any of us did, except possibly Danny. We took Bob into the control room and played him some of the music we were working on. Very few words were spoken, but lots of nodding of his head in approval and always that warm, infectious smile. You could just tell. Here was a man who knew what this was all about --- making music --- bringing joy to the World through peaceful and loving harmony. He was soon to be delivering that himself on a significant, global scale.

Danny and Bob left the studio and went upstairs to one of the offices whilst we carried on with the keyboard overdubs. I don't know for sure, but I suspect that was the day the deal was done between Danny Simms and his JAD label, CBS (who had initially signed Bob Marley), and Chris Blackwell's Island label. Because before too long myself, Tony Platt and other staff engineers would find ourselves in studio two, complete with the painted palm trees on the walls, plugging up mics and headphones for Peter Tosh, Bunny Wailer, Aston "Family Man" Barrett, Carlton Barrett and Mr. Marley himself.

It must be said that Tony Platt was more involved as an engineer with the *Catch A Fire* album than I or any of the other Island staff engineers, but I did my share. In later conversations with Tony, we both agreed that it was not always easy to tell who was who in the dark, smoky control room during those early sessions. Musicians seemed to come and go, depending on what overdubs were taking place. For me, at least, there wasn't the familiarity of recognising each band member as easily as with, say, Free or Traffic. At times, there seemed to be more of Bob's friends than official Wailers. You could, however, easily identify Rabbit, who was providing additional keyboard overdubs. He was the loud, tall Texan, the only one without dreads! I remember vividly the afternoon when one of the musicians arrived with a Tesco plastic carrier bag full of marijuana --- stems, seeds, twigs --- as rough and ready as you like. A page from a red-top daily newspaper was ripped away, filled with handfuls from the contents of the carrier bag, seeds, twigs, and all, rolled into a conical-shaped spliff about fourteen inches long and set fire to!! This was passed around the room with both hands and enjoyed by all. All that was except me and Tony, because neither Tony nor myself smoked in those early days. But boy! Did you get stoned, just being in the room! And this was a different experience being in the company of Rastafarians as opposed to, if you like, white musicians who tended to smoke hash, drink vast amounts of alcohol, get loud and leery and fall over. The Rastafarians had it down to a much more sophisticated, spiritual fine art. The idea wasn't to get wasted and lie about being stoned, doing nothing. Quite the opposite. It was genuinely about making contact with a higher order and being inspired. It was about tuning in, not out and switching on, not off. There was no rushing anything; a slow and measured, timely approach to everything most definitely worked. Just listen to the music and tell me I'm not wrong.

The other fond memories I have from working with the Rastas (and I still feel the same about them today as then) are the peaceful, kind, and generous nature of their souls. I got to play football with them all a couple of times outside the studio in All Saints Mews, as we would often take a break and kick a ball around. Bob Marley played on a couple of occasions with us in the Island football team, most usually over on Homefield Recreation ground in Hammersmith at our regular team practice meetings on Wednesday evenings. He was an intuitive, naturally gifted quality player. A selfless, accurate passer of the ball and most notably a player who would put the team as a whole above his own individual glory. The best kind of player to play alongside, both as a footballer and as a musician. You would see the same smiling face, full of pleasure, when he was playing football as you did off the pitch, in the studio.

What a lovely man to be around.

The tapes that arrived from Jamaica were mostly eight-track, inch. Rarely would there be any accompanying notes or track sheets. So the first thing as an engineer would be to transfer the whole thing over to sixteen-track, two-inch, probably with Dolby noise reduction to minimise any additional tape hiss. Signal-to-noise ratio was the name of the game in those days. Then you would listen through to the whole reel, making notes, creating track sheets, identifying which instruments are playing where, and choosing the master takes. These were usually the takes that might have an overdub or two, additional vocals perhaps. Typically, on track one would be drums and bass, combined, already balanced. Track two might be piano and guitar, lots of reverb on the guitar, but none on the piano. Track three, perhaps overdubbed guitar solo, backing vocals, and tambourine. All on the same track! Vocals could be found anywhere and everywhere, often quite distorted. How the hell were you supposed to mix this lot? Fortunately, with a twenty-four-channel console, you could afford to split each track onto several faders, using paralleling strips on the patch bay. So, for example, the track that had piano and guitar recorded together would be split into two separate channels, one equalised to bring out the best frequency qualities for the guitar and the second channel likewise for the piano. It would never give you the same amount of control as you would have had if the instruments had been recorded on separate tracks, but small miracles could be achieved. If you were fortunate that the guitar and piano were playing within individual parts of the arrangement, then you simply muted out each fader as required, or transferred each instrument onto different tracks of the sixteen-track transfer. Not as complicated as it may sound. In terms of a learning process for a studio engineer, it was an invaluable way of learning about equalization, compression, and filtering. In the old days, this process would have to be achieved using the analogue hardware available on the desk or with free-standing outboard gear. Today, in the digital world of software plug-ins, you also get the bonus of a visual representation of what is happening to the sound. In both instances, you learn what is and what isn't achievable, and invariably, that least done, soonest mended. I struggle today when I work with engineers who have a complete digital toolbox of software signal processors at their disposal and insist on using as many of them as possible, at all times! Take note, all students of the art. In the world of audio, less is most definitely more.

With the original dishevelled contents of the master eight-track recording suitably cleaned up and transferred to a sixteen-track, you would now have the option to add more overdubs, such as percussion, extra guitar parts, double-track backing vocals, replace lead vocals, and perhaps even get someone to overdub some Hammond organ. Enter Rabbit! Or Steve Winwood?! We were spoiled for choice. These sessions, recording with Bob Marley and his Wailers, were some of the most relaxed and even soothing sessions I have ever attended. I had never heard, in such detail, this wonderfully hypnotic style of music. The cool, laid-back feel of Carlton Barrett's drumming; the deep, measured pulse of Aston Barrett's bass; guitar, percussion, keyboards, and vocals from the most talented Peter Tosh. The soulful depth of what was to become the unmistakable vocal sound of Bob Marley.

Most certainly, those slightly imperfect and very basic, almost primitive original recordings were spruced up and made to sound more current, polished, and commercially acceptable. However, what you didn't want to do, although the technical temptation was available to you, was to lose the "feel" of the original recordings. Again, it's a question of balance. How much should you do or not do? That tambourine hit is slightly behind the beat --- does it matter if that guitar is ever so slightly sharp in pitch? The vocal sound is not the cleanest, but it is such a soulful performance --- put more reverb on it, and see if it masks the distortion. Some would argue, quite rightly, that it is the human imperfections in art that separate us from machines. These imperfections are manifest throughout the natural world, extending to the depths of the Universe. They are what make us strong and unique. That is why machines, even programmed to the highest levels of artificial intelligence, will never take over the World. They will be the ultimate victims of their O.C.D.

I must say that I am pleased today to have digital control at my fingertips. I was never a fan of tape hiss. Or waiting on the maintenance engineers to complete the time-consuming process of test tone tape alignment. Lugging big, heavy spools about, threading them through the cumbersome tape guides, splicing leader tape between takes. Running out of tracks. The fear of running out of tape! The great recordings of those days were made possible despite, not because of, tape. But notwithstanding all of that, many of my favourite and most treasured records are on vinyl and were recorded around that time and with that state-of-the-art analogue technology.

Not least of all, my Bob Marley and The Wailers albums.

Another of Island's reggae artists I was fortunate enough to record was Jimmy Cliff. Here was another enormously likeable, slightly shy, modest Jamaican guy who was destined to become a legend. When I had first arrived on the Island in 1970, Jimmy had already released his successful singles Wonderful World, a Cat Stevens composition, and *Vietnam*, the latter being described by no less than Bob Dylan as being "his favourite protest song".

Just a brief remembrance of my first time in the studio with Cat Stevens. Whilst assisting engineer Phil Brown on the session in studio two, a request came from the artist for daffodils, as many as would fit in the studio. (Obviously not impressed with the Palm tree decor). I was given twenty out of petty cash and went down to Portobello. Spent a lot. Came back with armfuls. We dug out milk bottles, beakers, mugs, buckets, bowls, and any vessel that could hold water and filled them all with daffodils. Studio two was suitably adorned with what must have been a hundred daffs. Very bright. Very, very yellow! Fragrant, bordering on smelly. Ambience suitably installed, the creative process could begin.

I was to work again with Cat Stevens some years later as a senior engineer, when he was producing tracks for English singer/songwriter Linda Lewis. On a third occasion, many, many years later, I composed some music for him to use on a song he had written. We had a common publishing company involved, and he provided me with a melody and lyrics, and I wrote and produced the musical accompaniment. It was called *The Little One's*, and Yusef, as he was now called since his conversion to Islam, had written these tender words and haunting melody as a response to the terrible shootings of school kids in Dunblane Primary School, Scotland, in 1996.

To this day, whenever I hear a Cat Stevens song, I hear little children and can smell daffodils.

Chris Blackwell had already decided to break into the world of movie-making, and Jimmy Cliff was to star in Island's debut picture. Joining production forces with Jamaican-born film director Perry Henzell, *The Harder They Come* was to be described as "possibly the most influential of Jamaican films and one of the most important films from the Caribbean". (Barbara Mennel, *Cities and Cinema*, Routledge, 2008.)

The soundtrack to the movie was an album of the same title and featured Jimmy on four self-penned tracks: *You Can Get It If You Want It*, *Many Rivers to Cross*, *The Harder They Come*, and *Sitting in Limbo*. I recorded the lead vocals to all these tracks with Jimmy, upstairs in Studio One, throughout three or four sessions, usually and quite oddly for most vocalists, reasonably early in the mornings, at about eleven. Looking back, I am convinced that the reason I was given these important vocal sessions was in no small part thanks to Jess Roden. Jess was signed to Island as lead vocalist with his band, Bronco, and it was during sessions with him and his band that Jess and I had recorded many lead vocals. Jess was always very complimentary about my work, especially (here we go again!) my attention to phrasing and pitch. I know that, thanks to Jess, word had filtered through to the boss, Mr. Blackwell. So I found myself as the first-choice vocal engineer for these Jimmy Cliff sessions.

Jimmy was so easy to work with; an engineer's dream. No diva moments here, just polished, professional studio performances. Maybe two or three takes, compile the best lines, and most would probably come from one take. And again, those self-same "positive vibrations" coming from this man, as from the Rastas. An effortless, relaxed style and approach to not only studio work but life in general. Because you don't just go into a recording studio, push buttons, record somebody, rattle off a mix and go home. You have conversations in between takes. There is always banter. During playbacks is when you get to know your artist: do they notice the out-of-tune "pitchy" bits? The timing/phrasing issues? The enunciation difficulties? If they do, then you are on a fruitful and worthwhile joint venture to achieve optimal performance. You are in business. If these factors pass by unnoticed, then disappointingly, mediocrity is imminent. In the relatively confined, intimate environment of the recording studio, you get to know one another very well. It's not just about twiddling knobs! All young students of the game take note --- you have to develop highly tuned people skills, be considerate and concerned for your artists' needs and identify with them a common purpose. With people like Jimmy Cliff, it was mission accomplished.

Even today, I love listening to those tracks from that album. Whenever I hear them on the radio, I can picture Jimmy in the studio, as if it were happening as I listen. I was in the large spaceship-like control room, looking down into the studio below, Jimmy standing over to the right, near the wall, facing towards me, occasionally looking up, awaiting some words of encouragement through the talkback. Neumann U.87 microphone, "pop" shield, cardioid pattern, no attenuation, Urei 1176 compressor/limiter. Beyer DT100 headphones. Helios desk. Tannoy speakers in giant Lockwood cabinets. Top studio. Great songs, great music, great guy. Absolute heaven.

I want to run back down the Old Kent Road, back to number thirty-eight on The List. Thank the guy at Maximum Sound for giving me Frank Owen's name and the Island telephone number. I'm in the best studio on the planet, working for the coolest, most important record label of the day, recording some of the best music ever written. As I hear Jimmy singing, I'm beginning to believe it: "You Can Get It If You Want It".

Whenever I hear a Cat Stevens song ------

"Just Hit It Harder!"

Island's Basing Street Studios facility was becoming one of the most prestigious recording studios in London, outshining at least another thirty-eight competitors in town. But not all could compete at this highest level, save for perhaps four or five others offering similar high-end, state-of-the-art recording provision: Trident in the West End, Abbey Road in St. John's Wood, George Martin's Air Studios on Oxford Circus, Morgan Studios in Willesden and Olympic in Barnes, south-west London. Yes, there were other top professional studios in abundance: CBS on Whitfield Street, IBC on Portland Place, De Lane Lea, Pye, Advision. Many, indeed, most of these studios had history and international reputations, but none had the same artistic, trendy caché that was quickly being attached to Island. The nearest, it seemed to me, would have been Olympic, simply because absolutely everyone who was anyone in the world of modern popular music had recorded there: Jimmy Hendrix, The Rolling Stones, The Beatles, The Yardbirds, Dusty Springfield ----- In the slightly more high-brow atmosphere of classical and film score recording, then undoubtedly Abbey Road would and will always be the place to work. The technical support, the versatility of the engineering staff and the sheer size of its main studio have always been a draw, particularly for large orchestral sessions. If Jazz were your thing, then it would most likely be Lansdowne, just off Ladbroke Grove. But undoubtedly, Olympic was always seen as "the musician's studio", especially amongst the sixties style of blues and rock bands. No surprise then that Chris Blackwell hijacked Olympic staff members Dick Swettenham, for his groundbreaking Helios-designed consoles, Joe Yu as his studio technical guru, Frank Owen and later Phil Brown, along with Brian Humphries from Pye studios as senior engineers. These were the men who not only helped design and construct the Basing Street studios, but because of their immense knowledge and experience, gave Island the internal industry respect that it was about to build on.

That growing respect and high status within the business would be strengthened and consolidated by the arrival at the studios of two of the top independent, freelance engineers/producers of the day.

Glyn Johns and his younger brother Andy were globally recognised as the two major players in the recording industry during the period when it came to making hit records. Glyn's resume would read as the who's who of artists of the day: The Rolling Stones, The Beatles, Eric Clapton, The Eagles, The Who. Andy's also has credits such as Led Zeppelin, The Rolling Stones, Rod Stewart.

Myself, along with other young assistant engineers at Basing Street, were about to be taken on a journey of audio excellence in the presence of these two studio giants. I had already been treated to an invaluable amount of specialised studio knowhow working alongside Frank and Brian. Let's also not forget my first mentor, Kevin. Now I was to be placed on sessions with both Glyn and Andy, learning "the ropes" from these Great Masters.

Without access to any timings of specific studio bookings data, it is difficult to recall the first sessions I worked on with Glyn, but it was quite probably when he was commissioned by Capitol Records in the U.S.A to mix tracks from The Band's *Stage Fright* album. Studio manager Sally Wightman took the booking in the early summer of 1970. Studio two, for about a week. I was assigned assistant engineer duties, and I remember quite vividly the first time I laid eyes on Glyn! Nothing romantic, it has to be said, but the feeling of being totally awestruck at the sight of this extremely handsome, sun-tanned, gold bejewelled man, with a Rolls Royce to boot parked on the bespoke forecourt. He came waltzing into the studio reception area like a Hollywood movie star. This man exuded a confidence and certainty of self that I had only witnessed to any similar extent in the demeanour and aura of Chris Blackwell. These were a different kind of men to those I had known before, back in Birmingham. The same striking features, coiffured hair and fashion chic attire I had seen with the likes of Steve Winwood, Mike Harrison and all the other "beautiful people" of the day. But with Glyn, as with Chris, this was taken to a completely higher level. Here was a man at the top of his game, the world's most successful freelance recording engineer/producer of the day. Glyn told me once (and I have no reason to doubt him) that he was the FIRST modern freelance engineer. During the late sixties, in an industry of in-house studio staff engineers who were, for the most part, more technicians than producers, Glyn broke the mould and started the trend that would lead to so many of us wanting to pursue the same path; be world travelling, freelance, independent recording engineer/producers, become incredibly successful, wealthy and famous and maybe even drive a Rolls!

I've been trying my best ever since.

Having been recorded at the Woodstock Playhouse in New York during the late spring of 1970, the sixteen-track copy masters of The Band's *Stage Fright* album were delivered to Island studios and preciously placed into the tape store, under lock and key. Day one of the mixing sessions and the tapes were taken into the downstairs control room of studio two. I opened up all the boxes, and removed the aluminium foil wrappings, unrealistically and unscientifically used to protect tapes from x-rays at airport customs and gamma-rays from outer space when placed onboard an aeroplane. It was a common practice also when travelling with tapes on the underground, which of course, you were NEVER supposed to, taking extra special care NOT to sit on a seat in a carriage above one of the powerful electric motors! I have travelled on the Tube with quarter-inch master tapes and cassettes, to no detriment, but would have been reluctant to take any multi-track, two-inch tapes, so I never did. Strange really, because magnetism shows no favouritism or scientific respect to specific tape formats, so all would be equally doomed. But it never happened to me. Maybe I was just lucky. You most certainly would remove all tapes from the control room whenever the maintenance engineers Bill, Paul or Joe came in to de-magnetise the head blocks on the tape machines. This was a procedure that would take place maybe once a week, in order to stabilise the magnetic environment around the tape machine head blocks, rollers and guides. Apparently, this was done to help improve recording quality in this rather fragile analogue world of oxide coated magnetic tape. Improve signal to noise ratios, reduce hiss? No idea!

Far too technical for me.

I have a sneaking suspicion that all this technical stuff didn't particularly interest Glyn or Andy either. No more so than would have been of basic necessity. They were both at the vanguard of a new type of studio production, where the engineers and producers were increasingly seen as part of the creative process, as equal to the musicians themselves, even as honorary band members. The expanding capabilities of the consoles, the introduction of sophisticated signal processing and outboard equipment, and the flexibility of multi-tracking capabilities; these were all impacting the methodology of making records.

The new breed of producers were increasingly being recruited from the schools of engineering. First and foremost of these would have been Norman Smith and Geoff Emerick, engineers at E.M.I studios in north-west London (later to be re-named Abbey Road Studios after a certain album recorded there by a popular beat-combo of the day). They had been encouraged by The

Beatles and their producer, George Martin to stretch the studio technology beyond what previously would have been considered normal practice: intentional over compression; alarming amounts of distortion; unconventional use of tape delay and reverb to create often bizarre vocal sounds; bouncing and combining tracks between multiple multi-track tape machines; audio reversal; tape phasing. Ground breaking recordings that were to change the sound of the world of music forever. The beginnings of the long playing, thirty-three and a third r.p.m record being seen and heard as significantly more than just a collection of song recordings. The birth of the album as a concept.

These engineers knew the basics of sound recording technology, as per the theoretical handbooks, but were pushing on forward with a whole new bunch of toys to play with. To watch Glyn or Andy behind the controls was to watch artisan craftsmen at work. They were slick, confident, innovative and decisive. The studio was their theatre, the musicians their audience and every recording, each overdub and mix was akin to a performance. The console was their musical instrument and my word, how well they could play.

But back to studio two and the *Stage Fright* mixing sessions with Glyn.

I immediately noticed that something was different here. These were tracks that had been recorded elsewhere, never before heard by Glyn, or myself. No familiarity with how the recordings had taken place, which overdubs to use, which lead vocal, guitar solo and backing vocals were to be the correct ones. These would be Glyn's decisions to make. After all, that's why he had been chosen. No doubt the band, along with the record's American producer Todd Rundgren, had already attempted to complete final mixes back in New York. There may well have been reservations as to the quality achieved. Perhaps the record label had suggested that maybe a fresh pair of ears are required to bring out the best from these tapes. This is often the case. Having been on both sides of this creative equation numerous times myself since those early days of my career, I know first-hand that it makes sense to engage the services of another engineer/producer to complete the final mixdowns. Imagine the levels of concentration involved over the weeks and sometimes months of being in the studio, day after day, with the same musicians, listening over and over again to the same dozen or so songs. Adding numerous overdubs, with seemingly endless microscopic adjustments to the song arrangements. The various layers of audio that are experimented with, sometimes to the benefit of the track, other times, despite hours and hours of trial and error, to be cruelly discarded. It becomes almost impossible to see the musical wood from the audio trees. The tracks start to sound stale and unimaginative. Then come the woefully pathetic cries of despair from all involved, not least of all the record label. Why is this record taking so long to make? Why does it not sound "right"? Bring on the fresh ears. Give Glyn a call.

Glyn would always start a mix with the drums. Common practice is to begin, so to speak, at the bottom as Glyn used to say, down in the engine room. I would sit next to Glyn at the console, with the tape machine remote controls as I watched, listened, and learnt. Don't spend too much time soloing the different drums. After all, no one is going to listen to the bass drum at home on its own. Different parts of the bass drum sound come from the mics on the tom-toms, the overheads and the snare. Equalise to a minimum and, in context, fine-tune the whole of the drum kit as a single unit. Check phase relationships between microphones. Most importantly, be quick, assertive and decisive. Don't dwell too long on any one thing. Move on swiftly to the bass. We are still in the engine room. Make the drums and bass powerful and punchy, not too much reverb, not yet. Then listen through to the guitar takes, maybe make a bounce onto one track of the best bits of the rhythm guitar(s). Same with the lead guitar(s). For my own part, I will never forget how the quality of the musicianship on every track fader that was auditioned, was so utterly amazing. These musicians were simply the best. The keyboards of Richard Manuel and Garth Hudson (who I would work with many years later in a Hollywood studio). Robbie Robertson's guitar playing. The incredibly tight bass and drums, courtesy of Rick Danko and Levon Helm. I was privileged to be listening to this.

Keyboards next. Begin to consider stereo placement and audio imagery. Guitars to the left, keyboards to the right? That guitar level is difficult to secure, too many level changes. No automation yet, not in the '70's, so prudent use of compression is required. Which compressor? What ratio? Fast attack, slow release? Doesn't matter. Forget the rule books, just experiment, and make a decision. Whatever sounds right. Move on. Vocals next. Track nine is by far the best. Maybe not quite in tune in a couple of places, but it has by far the most emotion and sounds like a heartfelt performance. Guarantee you this was the first take! The later takes are more accurate, and more controlled, but just ain't got it. They had it, then lost it. They couldn't hear it anymore.

But Glyn could.

After several days, Todd Rundgren himself made an appearance. He had engineered the original recordings back at The Woodstock Playhouse. He was and still is an American songwriter, multi-instrumentalist, engineer and producer, with a list of credits that put him up there into super-star status: Grand Funk Railroad, Bad Finger, Meatloaf and The New York Dolls amongst them. He was also a successful artist in his own right and I recognised his face from magazine articles I had seen. I knew

I was in the presence of yet another studio legend. He sat behind the Helios desk next to Glyn. They rocked back on forth in the large leather chairs, both as cool as you like, listening to the mixes Glyn had done. I had catalogued all the correct versions and assembled a Master Reel, so the playback was just like listening to the album. Intros and endings are edited tight with two or three-second gaps between tracks. Glyn was pleased with my work because I was mindful and attentive to the detail he expected from his assistant engineer. Good running order. Sounded great. You could hear everything, clear as a bell. Punchy and tight. Todd nodded respectfully. Smiles all round. I made some tea.

I was to work with Glyn on a number of other occasions after this first project together. Basing Street Studios had impressed him enough for him to return on a frequent basis and next up was to be recording with him on some Humble Pie sessions, upstairs in studio one. By way of a brief background to these sessions, I must be forgiven for modestly sticking a small feather in my cap.

On a session some days before, starting on a Friday I recall, but having extended on into the wee hours of Saturday morning, I had tidied up the studio, put away tapes, headphones, mics and cables, zeroed the desk ready for the next session shift. By which point it was approaching five a.m and I was wide awake. I was not expected at the studio until the following Tuesday, to be in attendance with Glyn on further Humble Pie sessions. I jumped into my beloved red mini, which was parked on Basing Street, squeezed in between the Camero and the Firebird and, witnessing a beautiful sunrise, was spontaneously inspired to immediately drive up to Birmingham and visit my family. They would be pleasantly surprised to see me arrive unannounced and I would enjoy a couple of days of Mom's homemade cooking, a nice warm luxurious bath and some much needed chill time away from the hectic pace of London life.

I nearly didn't get there.

I had decided, due in no small part to the beauty of the unfolding sunrise, to take the scenic route via the trunk roads, away from the motorway madness. There would be little traffic at that time, and I would enjoy the drive through the countryside. There was indeed very little traffic, but it doesn't require too many vehicles for an accident to occur. It only takes one other to be coming towards you on the opposite side of the road, approaching a single lane hump-back bridge over a canal on a blind corner. Combine this with me experimenting with a double-declutching technique shown to me by my motor racing enthusiast cousin Donald (he had a Mini too), and me thinking I was some sort of top rally driver. I wasn't paying enough attention to the tight bends in the road, and with an absence of much daylight along these tree-lined roads so early on this beautiful morning, it was an accident waiting to happen. I was messing with the clutch and the gear stick, pausing in neutral to release the clutch, then seamlessly down into second. Very cool, I thought. Except that, I hit the apex on the top of the hump-back bridge at precisely the same time as a minivan full of American airmen from a nearby air base. The resulting head-on collision left a considerable amount of crushed metal and bodies lying on the road. I was still in my Mini, life-saving seat belt attached, suspended over the bridge parapet, dangling above the canal some fifteen feet below. I wrestled my way out and limped over to the other, upturned mini. Three or four guys were walking around dazed and confused. I was apologising to them for not paying attention to the road, and they were apologising to me for driving too fast. But no matter. We could see one other person trapped inside. There was petrol running everywhere. Another guy and I ripped open the upside-down passenger side door and dragged the person out and away from the cars and the stream of fuel.

Flashing blue lights, and I am in the hospital. Not too serious. The seat belt did its job. Bruised and battered, a deep hole in my right arm where some small shard of windscreen glass had decided to live for a while, and no serious injuries to any of the Americans. A miracle, methinks. Dad and I revisited the accident scene the next day with a Brownie camera, a tape measure, and a notebook and pencil to make measurements and take some pictures, ready for the inevitable court appearance. The Americans were already there! Spotlights, laser measuring machines, wide-angle cameras, like a movie set. We put our modest equipment away and quietly left. Six months later, I received a ticking off from the judge, with a charge of careless driving—a big lesson learnt. I never drove like a rally driver again, and to this day, I continue to drive like a chauffeur.

So I am in Birmingham and on the Bakelite telephone to Sally telling her that I will be unable to do the session with Glyn on Tuesday, because I have one arm in a sling. She says not to worry and to get well soon, she will get someone else to do the session and come back when you are ready.

Five minutes later, the telephone rings. It's Sally. She says Glyn said he would rather have me with one arm than have anyone else assist him.

I'm so flattered. Pretty big feather really.

Not sure whether Glyn thought he had made the right decision though, when he saw me struggling to pick up heavy boxes of two-inch tape, threading tape onto the machine with one hand whilst holding mike cables with my teeth!

The Humble Pie sessions, for their second album, *Rock On*, were mostly recorded at Olympic, but did include a few sessions at

Basing Street. This was to be the time and place where I learnt another invaluable lesson from the great man. In the studio were several rather large egos, to put it mildly. You had Peter Frampton, formerly from The Herd on guitar, ex-Spooky Tooth bass player Greg Ridley, a seventeen-year-old drummer, Jerry Shirley and formidable guitarist and vocalist from The Small Faces, Steve Marriot. It was the way Glyn handled and managed this huge amount of explosive talent that made me aware that to be a successful engineer and producer required high-octane people skills. The sophisticated art of being respectful of the artist's talents and skills, accommodating of the sensitivity of their expectations yet, on the other hand, expressing your own seniority and experience in a commanding, sometimes forceful, but always irrefutable way.

A perfect example of this can be illustrated in one brief exchange between Glyn and Jerry, the drummer. Whilst back in the control room listening to a playback of a take, Jerry asked Glyn if he could make the snare drum louder. Glyn abruptly stopped the tape. He turned to Jerry and simply said, "If you want the snare drum louder, then just hit it harder." He pressed the play button and we continued listening. Jerry pushed his luck. "Can you turn down the cymbals?" he timidly asked. Glyn stopped the tape again. "If you don't want the cymbals to be so loud," he said through slightly gritted teeth, "then don't hit them so bloody hard!"

That exchange very much sums up Glyn's no-nonsense approach to recording. You are the drummer; come to the studio with the right sounding kit; play your drums the way you want them to sound. Same for the guitar; make sure your instrument and your amplifier both provide the sound quality you are looking for. Vocalists? Well, you are very much on your own. Suppose you can't sing in tune and deliver a performance on the microphone, with powerful emotion and expression, providing a strong melody and interesting lyrics. In that case, you've no business being in the studio with me. No amount of equalisation, compression, or reverb is going to turn a mediocre sounding song and performance into a masterpiece. That's not the job of the engineer or the producer. We can only capture the musical landscape as it appears before us. We are photographers of soundscapes and, as always, the camera never lies.

As a side note, I will just add a personal reflection on the famous Glyn Johns' Drum Miking Technique. I am often called upon to illustrate this when I am with young students of the game, who always ask me to demonstrate this legendary piece of studio folklore. Unfortunately, I can't! Because every time I worked with Glyn on a tracking session he never once used this approach to recording drums. He may well have at Olympic and elsewhere, but never with me at Basing Street. The usual approach was two overheads, left and right behind the drummer, snare (top only) and bass drum. Rarely would Glyn mic up individual toms or cymbals. He would, as Jerry Shirley will have learned, expect the drums to be tuned and balanced within themselves. Economy was always his way. The fewer mics the better.

I consider myself extremely privileged and fortunate to have had the opportunity to work alongside such a Grand Master of the trade. Priceless skills that were passed on to me from watching and listening first hand and close up. And if one genius child in a family is as much as any parent can wish for, lo and behold, Mr and Mrs Johns produced two! Andy Johns was already making a name for himself as being an exceptionally talented engineer/producer. On one session, in studio two, I started the days' session (Humble Pie again) by assisting for Glyn. He had to leave early in the evening, but the session continued with a half-time substitution of the engineer in the shape of his younger brother, Andy. How blessed were the band and I to spend a day in the studio with Glyn and the night shift with Andy.

Andy had also become a regular visitor to Basing Street. They were pretty different in their studio styles and techniques. Glyn was the almost father-like elder statesman who employed a staid, disciplined approach to his work. Andy, more of a fun-loving boyish charmer, with a cheeky smile and an almost unstoppable ability to rock'n'roll with the best of them! But there was one thing they both had in common: excellent results. More than one thing. Both were fast and decisive, exuded confidence and made the studio come alive like no other engineers I had worked with. My first experience of how incredible Andy's sound could be was during mixing sessions in studio two. It was the summer of 1970. The band was Led Zeppelin.

Smiles all round. I made some tea.

A Small Amount Of Steam

Andy Johns had begun his career at Olympic Studios under the guidance of legendary studio engineer Eddie Kramer, assisting him on numerous Jimi Hendrix sessions. Kramer's career dates back to the 1960s and is arguably one of the most prolific resumes of anyone in the business. Credits include: The Beatles, David Bowie, Led Zeppelin, The Rolling Stones, Jimi Hendrix, The Small Faces, Dionne Warwick, and Santana. To top it all, he and his crew had recorded the entire iconic Woodstock Festival in the summer of 1969, so Andy's pedigree, through the work of his older brother Glyn and his association with Kramer Olympic, was established very early on.

In between the *All Right Now* editing session and the forthcoming recording of the *Highway* album, Bob Potter and I would be treated to the almost immeasurable benefit of working with Andy, in Basing Street's studio two, on mixing sessions for Led Zeppelin's third album.

So, where do you start when writing about your recollections with regard to being party to the privileged inside the World of Led Zeppelin?

Unlike the sessions with Bob Marley and his beloved Wailers, this band was already a hugely successful, internationally acclaimed phenomenon. Mr. Marley and Co. were a relatively unknown collection of local musicians, signed to their first major record deal, trying simply to make a living, ever hopeful that their music would one day be heard. Their global domination was lying in wait. Led Zeppelin, on the other hand, had been strategically assembled, and individually, their creative pedigrees stood up as justification for the creation of the term "supergroup". However, it is not my place here to fully document the historical lineage of this band of musical heroes. There have been many books written by others more qualified, so suffice for me to just briefly outline what little I know about the origins of one of the most successful U.K. bands of all time.

Jimmy Page had been in much demand as a studio session guitarist for many years, appearing on records for, amongst others, The Who, Marianne Faithfull, The Rolling Stones, Brenda Lee, and Petula Clark. After the departure of bass player Paul Samwell-Smith from The Yardbirds, Jimmy Page joined the band. Robert Plant had previously played with drummer John Bonham in the group Band of Joy, and both joined forces with Page in what would initially be called The New Yardbirds. John Paul Jones had also, like Page, been a prodigious session musician, appearing on records for The Rolling Stones, Dusty Springfield, Rod Stewart, and many more. Knowing one another from the London studio session scene, he had once asked Page if he should ever be thinking of putting a band together, could he perhaps be considered as a bass player.

But I, like many music fans of my age at the time, knew little or nothing of the background of Led Zeppelin. To me, they were quite simply the biggest band on the planet, Rock Gods of incomparable size and the benchmark of all that was possible in the world of rock music. So imagine my excitement as they stood there, all four of them, in studio two with Andy Johns as engineer and me as his assistant. Robert Plant, tall and slim, with his beautiful wavy, flowing locks (I promise not to refer anymore beyond this point to "hair", the abundance of it, or my general lack of it!). Jimmy Page, constantly pacing slowly, thoughtfully around the control room. John Bonham, large and powerfully mischievous, and John Paul Jones, the quiet one. There was an incredible, collective presence about them that made me once again aware of the uniquely magical place I was now inhabiting.

But no time for gloating or gobsmacking incredulity. We were there to work, and Andy wasted no time in getting me to start sifting through the multi-tracks in search of the first song to explore. As best as I can recall, the sessions were mainly for the final mixes of Led Zeppelin III. There were a few overdubs, but most of the tracks had already been laid down by Andy out at Headley Grange, their mansion retreat in East Hampshire, and at Olympic Studios in Barnes, south west London. When I look at the sleeve notes for the record, it refers to Ardent Studios in Memphis with Eddie Kramer at the controls as the mix-down facility. Still, indeed, mixes were made at Basing Street, and who knows which ones appear on the final album, other than Jimmy, Andy, Eddie, and Atlantic Records. In any event, Andy Johns' masterful handiwork was written all over these recordings. The size and shape of the sounds that came out of those Tannoy speakers in their Lockwood cabinets were beyond excellent! The power and depth of it all --- drum sounds that were huge and clear --- guitar playing of epic sonic proportions --- the tight, emphatic bass lines --- the melodic and dynamic, emotional sincerity of the vocal range, with the blissfully evocative lyrics. I had been in attendance by then on many sessions in these Island studios, hearing some pretty fantastic music over the months. Still, nothing would have prepared me for the quality of this audio assault. I watched every move that Andy made at the desk; how much EQ, what type of reverb for the vocal, drum compression ratios, stereo placement, etc. I watched the interplay between Andy and the band members, particularly with Jimmy. I could sense an absolute trust and respect between them all, both with each other and with Andy. I felt an immediate "click" with Robert Plant. Knowing that he was a fellow Midlander might have helped—such a cool, relaxed, gentle soul, so modest, just short of shy. Jimmy was always smiling, but by far the most focused on the production side of things. With all who were present, including, I might say, myself, there was, as would be expected, a professional, cohesive thread that wove itself throughout the sessions. Once again, I was struck by the honest devotion to the job in hand displayed by all. Yes, there were occasional stress points, and slight disagreements over which vocal take was best, how loud the guitar solo should be, and how much reverb on the drums ---. But never with any hint of friction or animosity, simply knuckling down to the work required for this particular creative process to succeed.

Imagine listening to just the drums on *Immigrant Song*. Then the guitars go into solo. And Robert's vocals without any music! Same with *Celebration Day* and *Gallows Pole*. Just a brief pat on my own back about *Celebration Day*: In a previous session with another artist, I had experimented with reverse reverb, something I had picked up from one of the other engineers. An extension of the common practice of recording, with a tape being played back in reverse. To reverse the tape, turn the reel of tape upside down, so that track sixteen becomes track one, track fifteen becomes track two, and so on. The music then starts from the end of the song and ends at the beginning. What you hear is the music being played backwards. If you put reverb on, say, the reversed drums, then record that reverb on an empty track (remembering that the track order for recording is also reversed, so if the available track is track nine, then in reverse, you would need to arm the record head for track eight). Concentrate now! So I humbly suggested to Andy and Jimmy that the drum intro on *Celebration Day* would sound quite interesting if it were introduced with some backwards reverb. So we went through the process as described, returned the tape to normal playback conditions and hit the play button. Jimmy was impressed. Andy probably thought "young upstart!" or something like that, but he liked it too and thanked me for the idea. So, at approximately twenty-three seconds into the song, you can hear the reversed drum reverb pre-empt the actual drums—my idea. Well chuffed.

But back to the mixing. Back to The Master at work. Watching and listening as Andy creates the perfect vocal sound for a particular song; tape-delayed reverb, compressing the reverb returns, feeding vocal delays back on themselves. The enormous, complete sonic clarity that I was bearing witness to.

One evening stands out for me above all others, as far as this album is concerned (there would be an even more monumental evening to come, working again with Andy Johns, on Zeppelin four) and my favourite Led Zeppelin song of all time, *Since I've Been Loving You*. I cannot be sure where the rhythm/backing track was recorded, as by the time I was involved, Zeppelin were at the vocal overdub stage. I have subsequently read that Ardent Studios in Memphis, with engineer Terry Manning, was one of the studios involved, possibly for the lead guitar overdubs and the mixing. Headley Grange, Olympic or even Basing Street may have been the location for the recording of the backing track; I simply don't know. All I know is that the multi-track tape of this classic recording was in my hands that night as Andy Johns instructed me to load up the master take of *Since I've Been Lovin' You*. We had moved upstairs to the larger studio one, and Robert was in the mood for vocalising.

From the space-ship-like control room of studio one, with its three-sided glass windows and elevated, wrap-around Helios console, you would be looking down into the vast live room, some ten feet below. I had already assisted on some orchestral sessions in this studio, with my mentor Kevin showing me how to set up for the classical musicians. I remember counting sixty-eight on one occasion; a complete orchestra, from percussion, brass, woodwind, double basses, violas, and celli, through to first and second strings. The conductor, baton in hand, is standing at the lectern with their individual talk-back microphone and headphone link to the control room. Frank Owen at the helm, sheets of manuscript all over the desk. It was definitely to your advantage as an engineer on orchestral sessions to be able to follow a musical score at least, even if you couldn't sight-read or play an instrument. I have both my Dad and my "O" Level music teacher at Bordesley Green Technical School, Mr. Birkin, to thank for my having some extremely useful, albeit limited ability in this regard. This particular session that I am describing --- not forgetting that I have left Robert waiting patiently in the wings ready to sing --- was for a Kellogg's Cornflakes advertisement! A specifically written piece of music, recorded three times; version one, a minute and a half long; version two, forty-five seconds; and a third version, lasting only twenty seconds or so, the full-on orchestration used throughout. Advertising executives, arranger, composer, and producer were all present in the crowded control room to witness Frank, Kevin, and me capture the opulent, musical extravaganza as it unfolded. The massive sound of a full Symphonic Orchestra, three hours in the studio, no expense spared, simply to help sell a breakfast cereal.

I remember being back in Brum some months later with my family, sitting in front of the television one night, when an advertisement for Kellogg's came on, complete with orchestral music. I recognised it. All seven seconds of it, very quiet in the background, drowned out by some mind-numbingly bland American voice-over talking about "sunshine", "mornings", and "vitamins". You could barely hear the music, and what's more, it wasn't even faded out sympathetically. It just stopped suddenly, in a place of no musical cadence or of any melodically satisfying conclusion; it just stopped dead in the middle of musical nowhere. What a waste.

I wonder if Frank or Kevin ever heard it?

So Robert makes his way down the steps from the control room, out into the vastness that was studio one. Andy asked me to set up a few sound-absorbency screens in a semicircle behind Robert, just to deaden the acoustics a little. A Neumann U.87 microphone and a pair of Beyer DT-100 headphones, quick headphone balance and mic level check, and we are good to go. Andy was nothing if not fast, especially when you know you have a vocalist who is all keen to go. You don't want to lose the mood.

Anyone who knows Zeppelin's music will be more than familiar with the song that Robert Plant was about to sing. But for those who aren't, well, you should simply stop reading this and immediately find a computer or smart phone somewhere, type in *Since I've Been Loving You*, and listen, from beginning to end to this masterful track. To me, it exemplifies everything that is Led Zeppelin. The authentic, soulful sound of this great singer, the exhilarating energy of the guitar playing, the power of the drums and bass. And not bad keyboards either, courtesy of John Paul Jones. Be sure to listen very carefully to the squeaky bass drum pedal on the intro! I have read since that Jimmy Page thought it was an unfortunate oversight on his part not to try and somehow remove this audio artefact from the recording. However, in actual fact it is this noise that draws you into the music. A sonic close up of John Bonham's foot. I'm convinced to this day that Andy Johns used every engineering trick in the book to make it louder!

We all watched and listened in the control room as Robert delivered his vocal.

One take.

From beginning to end.

The band members were standing up. Andy and I were seated. We were all silent, open mouthed, listening in awe as Robert moved around the microphone, eyes closed, stepping forward for the quieter passages, moving back for the louder phrases. Perfect mic technique, as if the microphone were the listener's ears. We enjoyed the best seats in the house for a live performance of this most incredibly moving song. Not sure about Andy, but I had to remind myself that I was actually at work and should be mindful of any adjustments, or re-takes, or maybe the headphones cutting out, whether or not I might need to stop the tape. But no need.

At the end of the song, as the Hammond organ concluded with its ad-libbed flourish, I stopped the tape. There was a long pause. Everyone was speechless. Andy was sweating, and I was shaking slightly. Bonham, Page and Jones said nothing. We just knew that we had all witnessed something magical. Robert took off the headphones, gently laid them on the floor next to the microphone stand and slowly made his way back up the stairs into the control room. "How was that?" he asked Jimmy with genuine modesty. "I can always sing it again, if you think I can do it better". No need, said Jimmy, rubbing his chin, a twinkle in his eyes. It's fine. We played it back. Robert must have sensed he had delivered the goods because everyone was smiling. So what did Mr. Plant do? Amazingly, he offered to make everyone tea. Hang on, I thought, that's my job! But make the tea he did. He probably won't forgive me for partly destroying here the image of this macho, tight trousered, strutting Rock God performing in front of tens of thousands of worshippers, with this image of him putting the kettle on, but that's what he did. What a guy, I thought. How important it was for him to be inclusive with the other band members, as well as with the crew, after having performed with such passionate intensity at the top of the song's musical pyramid. I saw it then, as I still do today, as the mark of the real quality of the man.

Andy rattled off a quick mix, which sounded simply incredible. The way he adjusted the reverb on the vocal at different parts of the song. The deft use of double tracking sections of the guitar solo. The great drum sound. Wonderful stuff.

I can't say for certain whether that was the vocal or the mix that made it onto the final record. But as I have mentioned before, in this studio game you can usually recognise your own work, or rather that of Andy Johns and the band. Certain musical nuances in the performances and in the mix that you remember from the session never leave you. And even if it wasn't the final version then it doesn't matter anyway, because I was there when Robert Plant sang in front of me and I hit the record button and listened in wonderment, along with the other members of Led Zeppelin, with Andy Johns at the desk and I was in heaven and it sounded the best that it can ever sound in a studio.

And to top it all, I drank a delicious cup of tea made for me by Robert Plant.

Towards the end of 1970, the band were to return to Basing Street, again with Andy, to record Zeppelin Four. By this time, I was betwixt and between being an assistant engineer on some sessions and first engineer on others. It was the same for all of us "up and coming" juniors: Bob Potter, Howard Kilgour, Tony Platt, Phil Ault...... The senior engineers were still Frank Owen, Brian Humphries and newly recruited, ex-Olympic man Phil Brown, closely followed by Clive Franks and Roger Beale, but we knew kids were on the up! It wasn't uncommon for Bob to assist for me for a couple of evenings on, say, an Uncle Dog session with Carol Grimes on vocals, John Porter producing (Roxy Music, The Smiths) and then for us to swap roles, with the same artist, me assisting for Bob. It was that sort of relaxed vibe that made Island such a special place to work. Chris Blackwell was confident enough in us as junior engineers that he encouraged us at every opportunity to progress as quickly as possible up the career ladder, to become full engineers and producers. By the Summer of 1970, I had engineered and produced my first album *Ace of Sunlight* with Midlands band Bronco, whilst my friend Len, back at Pye studios in Stanhope Place, near Marble Arch was still to be assisting on sessions for another two years, because of that studio's more traditional approach to training. Chris, on the other hand, just gave us the keys to the studio, threw us in there with a band and said "Go make a record --- as much time as you need --- come out when it's done." An album would be recorded, then released, and then back into the studio to make another one with another band or artist. You would be working on two or three albums at a time. Bob Marley one week, John Martyn the next, orchestral session in the morning, evening session with Free or Traffic. A record company studio production factory. Not to mention all the outside clients that came through the door to make albums. Like the one I was about to start, in late 1970.

Bob and I shared assistant engineer duties on most of the Zepp sessions that Andy Johns engineered, and Led Zeppelin IV was a continuation of that relationship. If my memory serves me well, by then Bob was working more with Andy than with me, and I seemed to be Glyn's preferred choice, so recollections of specific sessions with Andy on this record are hard to come by. Titles that resonate with me are *Black Dog*, *Misty Mountain Hop* and *When the Levee Breaks*. These sessions were all upstairs in the larger studio one. You could simply get a bigger drum sound up in that room, studio two being much smaller and "deader" sounding. And what a drum sound! Andy's choice would be an AKG D20 dynamic mic on the bass drum, AKG 414, with 10db attenuation on the snare, Sennheiser 421s on the tom-toms, Neuman U87 condenser mics as stereo overheads and finally a Beyer M500 ribbon mic, suspended about three feet above the drums. This last mic would be quite heavily compressed at the desk (a studio technical term for squashing the dynamic range of an audio signal, making it, well, squashed! But cleverly done, can make loud things sound even louder). But of course, you could have recorded John Bonham's drum kit on a cassette recorder with an in-built microphone and it would still sound big and mighty; that's just the way he sounded. If I had a pound for every time drummers in the studio have since asked "can you make me sound like John Bonham?" I would have about thirty of forty quid. The answer is always the same: "No".

Many of the tracks for this fourth album were also recorded, using the Rolling Stones' mobile studio, at Headley Grange, the band's musical retreat in Hampshire. Basically, a studio control room in a truck, linked up to the house with microphone cable looms and CCTV cameras, mobile recording units were becoming very sophisticated ways of recording outside of conventional, fixed base studios. Island built one and I remember recording one particular album for Island in 1977 where we were using all three Island studios (by now an additional facility in Hammersmith had been acquired, The Fallout Shelter in British Grove). The band was Rough Diamond, which featured David Byron, formerly Uriah Heap vocalist, guitarist Clem Clempson (Colosseum/Humble Pie) Willie Bath on bass (Epic band Champion) and ex-Wings/Paul McCartney drummer Geoff Britton. We had a very tight deadline to finish the record and on one winters evening the producer, Steve Smith (from Muscle Shoals studios in Alabama, U.S.A) and myself were recording the guitar overdubs inside at The Fallout Shelter, vocals in the icy cold truck parked outside in the car-park and sending by cab finished tapes to be mixed over at Basing Street. I cannot recall ever being on another recording session that was taking place in three studios at the same time!

As to how many tracks for Led Zeppelin Four were from the Basing Street sessions or Headly Grange, I'm not one to know. Most of the overdubs were at Basing Street and although originally mixed at Sunset Sound in Los Angeles, the album was re-mixed with Andy, Bob and myself, at Basing Street. One of the tracks from the album, on the "Sunset Sound Mix" version that was definitely recorded at Basing Street, upstairs in studio one, with Andy as an engineer and myself as assistant was the iconic *Stairway to Heaven*.

At the time, I don't think anyone present had the faintest idea that this track, probably more than any other Led Zeppelin song would become the legendary, landmark rock classic signature tune of the twentieth century. *Bohemian Rhapsody* and *We are the Champions* from Queen would be contenders for that top spot, but for me (not because I am prejudiced in any way!) it has to be *Stairway*.

As so often happens in life, the fickle finger of fate once again pointed in a unique and peculiar way. After something like an eighteen-day straight working schedule, I was due a night off. A well-deserved break for me considering, like all of us engineers in those heady days, I had typically been working 12 to 18-hour days, non-stop, session after session. Surprisingly, whenever you had a day or two off, you would invariably find yourself turning up at Basing Street regardless, simply because you had nowhere else to go! You had no social life, and no friends outside of the studio, other than the musicians, artists and fellow engineers. Besides which, what could be better entertainment than dropping in unannounced on a Traffic session, where you might go with drummer Jim Capaldi for a pint up at The Apollo pub on All Saints Road and talk football, or chatting to engineer Tony Platt as he was putting final touches to a Bob Marley mix. See how Johnny Burns is getting on upstairs in studio one, still working on the *Aqualung* album!

But a night off was on offer and on this rarest of occasions I was actually at home, in my basement flat in Cumberland Street, Pimlico, watching television, looking forward to an early night. Enter the finger of fate. The 'phone rang. It was Sally. Bob had phoned in sick. You have to come in. I wasn't too pleased. What time? Now. Who with? The Zepp boys.

I'm on my way.

If it had been almost any other band, I think I may have protested and put up a fight. But not for Led Zeppelin. The music is just too good to miss and with Andy? No way. I jumped in a cab and was there in plenty of time for the 7pm start.

Upstairs to studio one I went, and there was Andy, already at the desk, listening to a mix from the night before. Bob had been assisting over the previous couple of nights, and I suspect he had probably overindulged the night before, which was why he couldn't attend. But of all nights, Bob, this was the one you should never have missed.

The studio was pretty much all set up, with Andy's usual drum mics in place, particularly, I noticed, the Beyer M500 ribbon mic hanging over the top of John Bonham's drum kit. As per the norm, I went walk about, checking all mics were secure and in position, headphones were in place and functioning, and generally tidying up ready for the band's imminent arrival.

Jimmy Page briefed everyone as to what he wanted to achieve that evening. It was to record a song they were all reasonably familiar with, as it had already been rehearsed and recorded one time out at Headley Grange. So tonight he wanted to nail this epic of a track, *Stairway to Heaven* and after a brief chat with Andy, I was summoned to create a square shaped booth, made from tall, hessian covered sound screens, just in front of the drums, to the left hand side, looking from the control room, one with a window so that Jimmy could make eye contact with Bonham. This was to enable Jimmy to play acoustic guitar at the same time as Bonham played his drums, with the necessary sound isolation. Jimmy Page sat on a high stool, an AKG 451 pencil condenser mic on the acoustic, always Andy's mic of choice for acoustic guitars, mainly because of its bright frequency response and directional properties. John Paul Jones was playing bass on a keyboard, not sure if it was a Moog or an ARP or similar, but it was plugged into the direct injection box that was always customary for keyboards if you didn't want to play through an amplifier, again, as an assist to sound separation between the instruments.

A quick sound checks for purposes of microphone levels, headphone balance, a clean reel of two-inch tape and away we go. Take one. Bonham counts Jimmy in. "One, two, three, four".

From beginning to end, a faultless performance by all. No mean achievement considering how long and reasonably complex the song is, but there you have it. One take. Masterful. What an incredible piece of music, I thought. Played so well, with such passion and feeling. So the band marched up the steps together into the control room for the playback. I rewind the tape and, on cue from Andy, press play. Andy cranks up the volume. He always did like a loud playback! Robert was quietly singing along to himself, checking for sure that the arrangement was correct, as indeed it was. Bonham and Jones were highly pleased with their performances and turned to Jimmy for confirmation that they had in fact "nailed it". But Jimmy was quiet, hand on chin, reflective. Play it again from the top please, he requested politely. I could sense Bonham's frustration. So play it again we did. It sounded even better the second time!

But not to Jimmy.

I can only paraphrase the conversation that followed, but it went something like this:

Bonham to Page: What's wrong with it?

Page: Nothing.

Bonham: Then why aren't you smiling?

Page: I just think we can play it better.

Bonham: You always do this. Everyone is happy with the take, except you.

Page: Let's give it another go.

Bonham: ------------------------.

He said nothing. Just grabbed his drumsticks and stormed back down the steps into the live room and sat, somewhat seething, behind his drums. I'm sure I noticed a small amount of steam coming from his ears.

From my perspective, I was to witness a unique production technique on an ingenious scale, because what happened next would stay with me forever. To this day, every single time I hear *Stairway to Heaven*, I am reminded that it was take two that made it onto the record.

The tape rolls. I make a note of the numbers on the tape machine counter. I write on the tape box. Jimmy plays through the first part of the song while Bonham waits. Seething slightly less now, because you are concentrating. Drums make their initial, quite sedate entrance. Slight pause. Guitar chords strummed majestically. Big drum entrance. Guitar solo. Last epic verse. Drums exploding everywhere. Bonham is on fire! Next time you listen to this song, picture the scene as I am describing it, and it will double your pleasure! Going through Bonham's mind is, without doubt, the thought that if, Mr. Page, you want another take, if you really want to "nail" this song, then how about this?

Control room for playback of take two. Playback ends and as the tape stops everyone is looking at Jimmy. His hand is back on the chin, but this time he is beaming a wide smile and Bonham goes over to him and gives him a big man-hug.

You see, it's a crazy old game this recording lark. Just when you think it can't get any better, someone comes up with a production technique that isn't in any of the rule books. It goes like this: wind up the drummer, just a little. Get him very slightly annoyed with you for being so demanding, not realising that this is being done to you for a purpose. Just angry enough to not storm out, but to get you behind your drum kit and let all the passion and frustration come out in your playing. That was all that was required. It's how you achieve this that is the clever part and the mark of genius.

By the end of the evening, John Paul Jones had overdubbed the recorders and Jimmy Page had added some extra guitars, including the solo. Fellow engineer Phil Brown, in his detailed and fascinating book *Are We Still Rolling?* (Tape Op 2010) Recalls subsequent sessions with Jimmy Page at Basing Street, overdubbing guitar parts, including the solo, so I can only assume that the solo created that night with Andy and me as engineers was probably replaced with Phil. In any event, on that particular evening, Jimmy set up his amp and guitar, chose playback speakers instead of headphones and, with a cigarette hanging lazily between his lips, rattled off three successive takes of simply stunning lead guitar. On playback, it became apparent how difficult it would be to choose the best one. So, as was and still is the norm, you make a compilation of "the best bits". Andy and Jimmy wrestled with a particular section of the solo, where Jimmy wanted just a couple of guitar licks from one of the takes that simply didn't seem to fit. But I could see how it could work. Should I say anything? What the hell, I stepped! Andy must have thought, "Oh no, not him again!" I suggested, with as much humility as required, that I might have a solution as to where to switch takes. Jimmy, being as encouraging as he could without upsetting Andy, wanted me to show what I had in mind. I sat next to him, in front of the desk. I'm sitting next to Jimmy Page. Andy moved aside, rewound the tape and hit play. Andy Johns was assisting me! With swift fingers, I switched a couple of times between all three guitar takes, managing to include Jimmy's favourite phrase. Do that again, he said. I asked Andy to rewind the tape and play the solo again. Pushing my luck here, I thought. I quickly assigned the playback channels to an empty track and pressed record. I repeated the switching of takes and had the resulting compiled guitar solo ready for playback from one channel instead of three. Done.

Jimmy was impressed. To his credit, Andy was congratulatory also, but I thought it best to move away from the desk and sit back over by the tape machine where I was meant to be.

When I hear *Stairway* I convince myself that I am listening to the solo that I helped create, but it doesn't surprise me that Jimmy Page might have had another stab at it at a later date. Still, it was huge for me to work so closely with the guy, and hey, you never know?! I don't recall Robert recording the vocal that evening, maybe just a guide track for purposes of the arrangement, so the lead vocal was almost certainly recorded on a separate occasion. So no cups of tea from him that night.

I love Led Zeppelin. One of my favourite bands of all time. The Best of British. I still get a thrill every time I hear Stairway, but nothing sends tingling down my spine more than when I hear *Since I've Been Loving You*. I was most definitely in the right place at the right time at least twice with those guys.
Just wish I could have taken a "selfie" with them.

All seven seconds----very quiet in the background.

To Be Living A Dream

I never keep a diary. I attempted one once, for a couple of weeks, when I was about fifteen. But when my mates got hold of it after it fell out of my pocket one afternoon on the way to playing football up at Pype Hayes Park, well, the embarrassment of it all as Colin, Terry and Robert discovered my innermost feelings for Glynis and Sandra.

Never again.

So perhaps I can be forgiven for being unable to assemble my studio recollections in any sort of chronological order. Only now, as I try to retrieve these memories, do I realise they are all assembled in my head as a homogeneous mass. I have sought accuracy from a few ex-employees of Island, but it would appear that all the studio bookings data has been lost. If anyone out there can throw any light on these missing records, then please do NOT get in touch with me because I do not wish to reorganise anything I have written so far! Everything that I am writing is most definitely the right notes, not necessarily, as Eric Morecombe once said, in the correct order.

Before I return to my somewhat disconnected remembrances of studio events, I have thought that this might be a suitable point at which to reflect on other surrounding events of my London life. Such as the time, when living in a damp basement flat in Talbot Road, west London, just a stone's throw from the studios, that I became desperately ill. Not just the usual feelings of exhaustion which were common amongst all the engineers and staff due to the intense work rate and commitment shown by all to the increasing success of the label and the studios.

No, this was different.

Typically, I had been living a rather negligent lifestyle: not eating correctly, relying heavily on takeaways, fish and chips, kebabs, sometimes not eating at all and drinking a lot of London ales. Not exercising, not sleeping, smoking, or rather, "puffing" too much and generally being a little lackadaisical in terms of my approach to personal hygiene. I paid a price. The damp, somewhat unclean state of the basement in question was the tipping point. Now that I begin to recall this rather unpleasant episode, I am reminded that I lived on the ground floor, sharing with another guy from the studio, Ron. He was one of the maintenance engineers for the studios and was an enthusiastic music festival fan. He played guitar, sang a little and wrote some songs, like we all did. He also had a penchant for one of the current drug trends of the day, that of taking acid. Not whilst at work, of course, but over those long 1970s summer weekends at, say, the newly created Glastonbury Festival, it was the done thing to "trip-out". That particular substance abuse was never my forte, and the only time I ever engaged with the psychedelic experience was when I lived at Talbot Road. Some way or another a small "tab" of acid found its way into my stomach, squeezed in between a kebab and a bottle of beer. How did it get there? No idea! There was plenty of the stuff about, people walking around with it in their pockets, showing and comparing products. But swallow some I did, because next thing I was downstairs in the basement with some hippie friends of Ron's, lying down, covered with a threadbare, smelly blanket, on a very worn out damp sofa. All I can remember is looking up at the many strange, blurred, spinning faces of the other occupants, their voices distant and muffled. Everyone seemed quite unconcerned for my well-being and although the tripping eventually stopped, every bone in my body ached. I had a high temperature and was running a fever. Hours turned into days as I lay there, ignored, somewhat confused and extremely disorientated. People came and went, looking down at this rather pathetic figure, me, all rolled up in the blanket on the sofa.

Did I hear someone suggest getting a doctor? I got up a couple of times, when the flat was empty, and dragged myself over to the sink for some water from the tap, which tasted disgusting. The kitchen was a complete tip, with several days' worth of dirty dishes, half eaten cans of mouldy green stuff, greasy pots and pans everywhere. I was weak, sweating profusely, cold and on my last legs.

Euston train station was as busy as ever and in my present wobbly, shaking state of disrepair appeared all the more distant and confusing. But I had managed to drag myself there, knowing that the only place for me to be was back home in Birmingham. It was the child-like cry of a grown adult male: "I want my Mom!!"

The train journey up there was painfully long, all the time spent in between the carriages, next to the toilet as I didn't want to throw-up over any of the other passengers. Then the rickety bus ride from New Street station out to Pype Hayes, taking forever. Drag myself from the bus stop to Mom and Dad's front door. Back home, dehydrated, faint and white as a sheet. Mom opens the front door, takes one look at me and gasps. "Get inside", she says sternly. A hot bath, clean clothes, gallons of tea and a huge, steaming hot plate of home cooked food.

Warm and dry Bed.

Sleep.

By the summer of 1975, when I was to leave England to start a new life in California, I would have lived in several different parts of London, in varying types of accommodation. The rental market at that time was completely different to that which exists today and it was relatively easy to frequently move from one place to another. You simply picked up a copy of The London Evening Standard and scrolled through page after page of affordable bed sits, studio flats or rooms in house shares. Armed with a pocket full of loose change you would go to Victoria Station at 5am in the morning, buy the first edition and commandeer a telephone booth. You could find a private rental property or go through estate agents. All that would be required might be a one-month returnable deposit and a month's rent up front. No bank statements or proof of income, no guarantor or credit checks, just slap down the cash and you were home and dry.

Spoiled for choice really.

I next found myself, thanks to the Evening Standard and Victoria station, renting a room in a house in Fulham. The house was owned by Jane Stonehouse, whose father was John Stonehouse, a Labour MP under Harold Wilson's 1967 prime-ministership. In 1970, he had served as Minister of Posts and Telecommunications and was eventually exposed as being a spy for the Czechoslovak Socialist Republic military intelligence. In 1974, Jane's father unsuccessfully attempted to fake his death on a Miami beach. But I knew nothing of all this political intrigue at the time, only that Jane was a charming and sophisticated lady who helped me settle into my new home, introducing me to the other tenants who included, amongst others, a top Michelin chef, Robert, who disappointingly would never cook for us! An assortment of actors and actresses, politicians' sons and daughters and socialite luminary friends of Jane would pop round most evenings for drinks. These charming and entertaining elite held me in relatively high esteem as the guy who worked in, to their minds, the fabulously exciting music business for an extremely cool record label in that big converted church near Portobello Road. I spent a very entertaining six months with Jane and her interesting friends, in a very busy, well-kept house just off Fulham Road. No damp.

Whenever I am back in London, driving along the Fulham road on my way to Hammersmith or Chiswick, looking along the river at Fulham's Craven Cottage football ground, I think of Jane, her Dad and of course Robert, who I don't think even knew where the kitchen was.

The next port of call was Highgate.

136 metres above sea level at its highest point, Highgate nestles alongside and indeed overlooks Hampstead Heath, with the road down Highgate Hill to Archway being the first cable car route to be built in Europe. There is also a famous cemetery to be visited there. Go see the graves of Karl Marx (philosopher), Douglas Adams (Hitchhikers Guide to the Galaxy), Jeremy Beadle (television presenter) George Eliot (novelist) Ralph Miliband (political theorist and father of Ed and David).

At the very top of Highgate Hill, on the corner of North Road, is an old converted Georgian house and I took rooms at the highest most part of this building, in a loft extension. Therefore, I can make a claim as to being one person who has lived at the very top of London, overlooking everyone else in the City. Except that the events that were to take place there would not rank in my memories as anything like a high point.

I had become the proud owner of a revolutionary new tape machine, a TEAC reel-to-reel four-track recorder. I was busy pursuing my main love and ambition at the time, which was to be a successful songwriter and this piece of kit was the bee's knees when it came to producing home demos. It had come into my possession after a stroke of good fortune. The recording and co-producing of the Island album by the band Free, *Heartbreaker*, had been my overwhelming occupation at the studios for many weeks. It had been a challenging record to make, to say the least, what with personnel conflicts within the band and pressure from the label to come up with another hit. I had received my normal weekly remunerations whilst working on the record and so was pleasantly surprised when John Leftly, Island's chief accountant, walked into studio two control room one afternoon when I was engaged on another session some weeks later and handed me an envelope. Inside was a cheque for one thousand pounds. Now this was late 1972, so this amount would be today's equivalence of maybe ten times that. It was certainly the most money I had ever received, the equivalent of a year's wages for my Dad. But why? There must be some mistake. I have already been paid my wages. John explained that this was a gift from the guys in Free; a royalty advance against a percentage of sales of the forthcoming release, their way of saying a special thank you for all the hard work I had put into the album. I was shocked. So shocked in fact that within a week I had spent the lot! A well-turned-out Japanese sales guy from TEAC walked into the studio one day soon after my windfall, on an international sales pitch, with one of the first ground-breaking four track tape machines from this company in the country. I said how much? He said five hundred quid. I said I'll have it. Sold. Boxed up and straight to my bedsit in Highgate it went. The other five hundred quid went on a second-hand Mercedes 190 SL convertible sports car. White, with red leather interior, very flashy. I had seen one on Park Lane some months before and had determined that if I ever had enough money, then that was the car for me. Frivolous at best and typical of my mind set at the time. A new one would have cost twenty grand, so five hundred was a good deal, or so I thought until I discovered what a rust-bucket it was! But for the short time I had it, when it was parked outside my digs in Highgate and during the day on the forecourt at Basing Street, next to the Pontiac, the Maserati and the pink Jaguar, it looked pretty cool.

In the meantime, I had set up a basic recording studio, with the TEAC at its heart, in my Highgate bedsit. My song writing partner at the time was Richard Reeve. Richard had worked for a short while as an engineer at Island, having learnt his craft at Decca studios in West Hampstead. He was a very accomplished rag-time guitar player and pianist, so our song writing efforts progressed well. However, an early technical problem within the recording environment presented itself. Because of the location, on top of London, Highgate was the place where many mini-cab companies had set up transmitters. We could see one or two from outside the window, across the street. As a consequence, all our recordings were intermittently enhanced with the recorded sound of mini-cab controllers' outgoing messages to their drivers. For example: "Anyone give me Pimlico?" was quite a common one, as was "Two cars for Oxford Street" and "Come in Streatham, over!"

Richard, being a bit of a techy, devised all sorts of earthing loops and transformers to try and eliminate the interference, but the problem was incurable, so we pressed on regardless. Many years later, on listening to our early efforts at song writing and recording, it would be easy to identify which of our songs had been recorded in Highgate.

On the plus side, we did manage to secure a publishing deal with Chappells, a major publishing house in the West End, which paid us both twenty pounds a week each for a year, but no further. Many months later we used the same tape machine to record our friends Chas Hodges and Dave Peacock, not at Highgate, but when I had relocated to a basement flat in Victoria, so no mini-cab chatter. Those three tracks we recorded together were the first recordings of the successful duo Chas and Dave, who later went on to have numerous hits with their "Rockney" style of music.

But no such happiness at Highgate.

One evening, Richard and I were joined for musical company by keyboardist John "Rabbit" Bundrick. We were jamming on guitar and keys well into the night, drinking, puffing, and snorting. Musical party animals, enjoying the creative process as only young, energetic, selfish and inconsiderate people can.

There was a loud bang on the floor. We were upsetting our neighbour below, so we turned down the volume. It was, after all, about three in the morning. Stupidly, we started a pillow fight, collapsing on the floor with a mighty thump, only adding to our neighbour's distress. There was another, even louder bang. We decided it best to call it a day. Maybe this person has to get up early for work. Or have they got an important job interview?

We would never know.

Rabbit had left in the wee hours, and Richard and I just crashed out on the bed. There was a loud knock on the door. It was morning. I opened the door, blurry-eyed and bloodshot, and there stood our landlady. She was hysterical and rightly so. She showed me the man's suicide note, scribbled out in blunt pencil on the cardboard insert you get with a shirt when it comes back from the dry cleaners. As best I could make out, I read the awful words about how he hadn't been able to sleep because of all the noise we had been making above him and that he was at the end of his tether. "Look what you've done!!" she screamed at us. I followed her out onto the landing and saw the most awful sight below, on the ground floor. Layers of bloody newspaper covering a body. He had leapt from the floor below us, the third floor, I think, impaling himself on the lamp standard that stood in the reception hallway at the foot of the stairs.

The two girls who lived in the adjacent room to us were discouraged from looking down the stairwell. We were told the police were on their way. It was all too horrible to take in and still is as I write this. The feelings of guilt run deep. Never knew who he was. Never went to his funeral. Think about him often.

Richard and I cleaned up the mess in my room from the late-night activities: the beer bottles, the hash, cigarette papers. The police came and questioned us, and we told them exactly what we had been doing, in terms of making music and too much noise. Then I noticed the leftover vial of cocaine by the sink. Oh dear, is this going to go from bad to worse? But no matter. The two policemen were almost as upset as we were and treated us very gently. We might just as well have been Peruvian coke dealers for all they cared. It wasn't the point. A man is dead, and it is all so sad.

The landlady came by the next day as I was packing and apologised for being so accusatory. She said that he lived alone and had no family or friends. Can that be so? Everybody has someone, somewhere. I so wanted to be his friend now. Would have invited him up and given him the acoustic guitar to play, or maybe a tambourine. He might well have loved music. I would have recorded him. Could have shared his company. I feel so guilty, so foolishly inconsiderate, and so unbearably sad.

Within a week, everyone who lived there had moved out. In my case, it was as if I needed to run away from that place and pretend it had never happened, but it couldn't be done. You are trying to run away from something that travels with you forever.

R.I.P. Sir.

I do have some happy memories of my time in Highgate. The girls who lived next door used to drop by with their American friend, Greg. We would all sit around singing and listening to music, usually at a respectable time and low volume. There was a vast public house across the road called The Gatehouse, which had once been next to a toll-gate into London, back in the days of Charles Dickens. Upstairs was a large ballroom, complete with glass glitter balls and parquet flooring, an elevated stage with double curtains, footlights and a beautiful baby grand piano. A long, oak-panelled bar with hand pumps and polished brass spirit optics behind the bar. Sumptuous.

But the upstairs was empty and had been for years.

I knew a local drummer who was keen to find a venue for Saturday night live music. He had contacts with plenty of bands who were looking for places to play and for all the members of the public in North London who wanted to hear live music; he was sure he could pack the place out. He approached the manager of the pub. He would cut a deal whereby the manager gets a percentage of the door, plus all the profits from the bar, bands would be paid out of the bulk of tickets sold at the door, and my drummer friend would take his cut. A win-win situation if ever there was one.

The manager was less than enthusiastic. Had he tried this before and failed? I asked my drummer friend. Not at all, replied the pub manager. Last time he had opened up the ballroom on Saturday nights, the place was packed. Full to bursting. So why not again? Can't be bothered, too much hassle. Had to take on extra bar staff, ordering loads more drinks ------.

My drummer friend had always wanted a drum riser, so that he could be in an elevated position on stage, above the other band members. When next I met him at a gig he was playing, he relayed the outcome of the discussion he had had with the pub manager, and we just laughed at how typically negative it was of him to see success as too much hard work. I couldn't help but notice how high his drums were on the stage, perched on beautifully curved, ebony woodwork. Piano-like. Even had wheels.

I wonder what happened to the glitter balls?

The Island owned a property on Cumberland Street, near the Victoria coach and train station. The basement flat became available and I agreed on a price with John Leftly, of eight pounds a week. Millie Small of *My Boy Lollipop* fame had lived there once. Island's first hit record! On the top floor was John Slattery, an Island accountant who lived there with his stunningly beautiful American girlfriend. On the first floor were two elderly ladies whom I never got to meet. The ground floor was occupied by Benjamin Foot, who worked at Island in their new offices at Saint Peter's Square in Hammersmith. His Uncle was Michael Foot, leader of the Labour Party from 1980 to 1983. Benjamin's brother, Oliver, dropped in on me one night. Literally.

I was well ensconced in the basement at Cumberland Street, with an upright piano I was learning to play, a couple of guitars and, of course, the TEAC reel to reel. Richard, my song co-writer, had built an early drum machine, basically just a bass drum, snare and high hat, but enough to keep a beat. It was here that we recorded Chas and Dave.

One night I was there on my own, quietly watching some television when I heard an almighty crash and bang. It was the sound of the metal dustbins which were outside my front door. Dustbins for all occupants of the house. No big plastic wheelie-bins out on the street in those days, just everybody's smelly rubbish outside my flat—the price you paid for living in the basement. I went to the front door to investigate. It was Oliver, Ben's brother. By all accounts, Oliver was a bit of a party animal, and he certainly did present a splendidly humorous spectacle of himself as he lay there, somewhat inebriated, comically half buried in the dustbins, one leg in, one out, covered in rubbish, with a dustbin lid on his head. "Good evening, Digby", he said, nonchalantly unconcerned and in the polite, matter-of-fact way of a perfect English gentleman. "I trust you are well, kind sir", or some such pleasantry. "Do you know if Benjamin is in residence this evening?" Oliver had attempted to enter Benjamin's flat through the ground-floor window by climbing onto the window ledge, with a drop of about twelve feet below him. A drop that was alcoholically cushioned by several dustbins.

He recovered his composure, swaggered away down the street, and I went back in doors. I never saw much more of Oliver after that.

I found out later that Oliver had been working on his autobiography, which detailed his early life as the son of a diplomat, his struggle with addiction, his passionate faith, his immense love for his family and the worldwide adventures of his career. By all accounts, he eventually got his life together, working for, amongst others, Orbis International, the Flying Eye Hospital. Also, charity work supporting Jamaican coffee growers. He died in 2008, and I would have loved to have got to know him better. Must have been devastating for the Foot family. Another unfortunate tick on the body-count list.

One other event took place at Cumberland Street that is worth a quick mention. The basement flat where I was living was dark, cold and damp. Not on the same mega scale as my acid-tripping abode on Talbot Road, but a little like camping indoors. I came home in a cab one morning as the sun came up, after a gruelling week of eighteen-hour-a-day sessions. I didn't even get undressed. My head hit the pillow and I was gone. Out cold. Twelve hours later I awoke. Something was different. It was warm. I looked around and saw that there were radiators everywhere. Under the window, in the kitchen and in the bathroom. There was even a radiator in my bedroom, right next to the bed where my head had been lying! There was running hot water. I had slept through a complete central heating installation, which has to be a first.

By now, my Mom and Dad were frequent visitors to London. I would sometimes drive up to Brum and bring them back with me. Like me, they had fallen for the allure of London on a grand scale. Dad would love it when I took him to the studios, letting him play around with a multi-track recording from one of the sessions. I would record him playing the Hammond organ, sometimes with me on guitar. We put an imaginary band together: Bert Smith and The Wipeouts. I've still got the tapes! He admired and fully understood all the technical wizardry that he saw in the studio. He appreciated the nuances of capturing a good performance on tape and all that it involved in terms of people management skills. He understood the demanding and sometimes insecure nature of creative musicians, as indeed he should, being one himself. Most importantly for me, he showed a growing respect for what I was achieving in my chosen career.

Mom just loved to walk around the streets of London, with all the noise of the traffic, all the people pushing and shoving their way around. This was right up Mom's street because she was a city girl and didn't take too kindly to where they had had to move to in later years. The kind, caring Labour Council of Birmingham had compulsorily purchased the right to buy the council family home they owned and forced my Mom and Dad to have to move, further out, near the countryside. Mom hated it. Too quiet, no shops, no traffic, no people.

No life.

And those visits to London? Ah, the joy. We would get a tube map, gaze at it, look away and just stick a pin in it. "That's where we are going today", I would announce. Might be Farringdon or Whitechapel. The Tower of London, Westminster, Kew Gardens, wherever. Up and down endless escalators between platforms and ticket halls, adorned with posters advertising, amongst other products, glamorous Nelbarden swimwear. I proudly pointed out to my Mom and Dad the ones which featured Chris Blackwell's beautiful girlfriend and model, Marilyn, (who, along with Chris, had been so kind to me when I first arrived at the label.) Dad showed more interest in the posters than Mom. We would exit the tube station and walk for miles, especially along the river, east side near the docks. I think it reminded them both of Birmingham and the canals, before the war.

In later years, Dad became too unsteady on his feet, and Mom was not at her best. They both suffered from the visual impairment of Macular Degeneration, so the trips to London became fewer and fewer. My wife Kim and I would travel up to Birmingham at every opportunity, taking our young family with us to play in their garden, drink their tea and listen to stories told as only elderly folk can; words of the wise. We occasionally went to car boot sales and aircraft displays. I remember Mom covering our young son's ears as a mighty, noisy fighter jet roared overhead.......

Mom said to me once, after Dad had passed away, when she was later infirm and house-bound, how much she would have loved to come down to London again, travel on the noisy tube and stand in a pushy queue.

Stephen Stills was about to record his second solo album at Basing Street. The Americans arrived and set up their usual camp, this time in Studio One. Once again, the cases and cases of Coca-Cola and dozens of cartons of Marlborough cigarettes. I was booked in as assistant to Atlantic Records engineer, Bill Halverson. As I think I have already mentioned, I was by now engineering and producing my own sessions, so Sally wasn't sure if I would be happy going back to being an assistant, but Bill had requested me and I wasn't going to miss this for the world. Billy Preston on keyboards. The Memphis Horns. Bring it on.

After all, to be living a dream. This is what my Dad and Mom would have wanted for me.

Next to the Pontiac, the Maserati and the pink Jaguar----

Tea Towels at The Ready

The Island/Basing Street and Fallout Shelter studio worksheets would be the place to look for detailed records of all the sessions that ever took place between 1970 and 1990. Sadly, despite my best efforts, I cannot find a trace of them. More the pity, because they would go some considerable way in showing not only who was in the studios and when, how busy the studios were, but equally how busy we were as the in-house engineers. Every day working practices of the day did not apply. No forty-hour week here. No nine-to-five, Monday-to-Friday existence. We often worked nine to five, nine in the evening to five the next morning! I remember my first £100+ weekly pay-packet, in 1970, when the average weekly wage was about £40. Worth noting that I worked about seventy hours to achieve the earnings that week, the equivalent of what my father would have earned in two.

The worksheets would be filled out at the end of every session, usually by the assistant engineer. Details included would be the number of reels of tape used, two-inch as well as quarter-inch stereo and cassettes; artist name; record label/client; start and finish times; hire of equipment and instruments and number of taxis and mini-cabs used. Imperative to get the client's or producer's signature, as these worksheets would form the basis of all recording costs, to be either invoiced to the client or held as proof of artists' recording budgets, to be set off against artists' royalties at some later date.

The Stephen Stills sessions, for his second solo album titled, unimaginatively, Stephen Stills 2, were to take place upstairs in studio one at Basing Street. The worksheets, were they to exist today, would show start times as being eight in the evening, usually running through to the small hours of the morning, typically five or six am. As an assistant engineer, with responsibilities for setting up the studio microphones, headphones, screens, chairs and the like, editing out the previous night's master takes and carrying up the spiral staircase a half dozen or so new, blank two-inch tape reels, I would usually turn up for work at about six or six-thirty, to get a jump start on the forthcoming evening's musical journey. So again, no eight-hour work shift here. This was to be three weeks of twelve-hour days, seven days a week.

The musicians who were to turn up and feature on this album were world-renowned, and that I was to be in the presence of such talented and likeable people for the duration was to be my privilege.

On drums, Conrad Isadore. He had played with Eddie Grant and Joe Cocker as well as for Stephen Stills on his first solo album. I later recorded Conrad featuring on Paul Kossoff's solo album, Back Street Crawler, and again with John "Rabbit" Bundrick on John's first solo album, Broken Arrows. Also on drums, Dallas Taylor (Crosby, Stills, Nash and Young, Van Morrison) and, for good measure, Ringo Starr. Now here is a musician who needs little, if any, introduction. We all know his C.V. However, let me impart some first-hand inside information. The accepted, yet somehow unsubstantiated folklore of the day surrounding Ringo and his unique drum sound was the suggestion that he simply placed tea towels over the drum skins to deaden the sound. The result would be a short decay on the snare drum and tom-toms, as opposed to a more normal, open and natural sound. Listen to those Beatles records and it will become apparent. But did he use tea towels? Surely not something as mundanely domestic. You might expect to see a specifically designed piece of kit, for example, some kind of clip-on pad or damper, made especially for him by Ludwig Drums.

I was about to find out the veracity, or otherwise, of the folklore.

Ringo's, indeed, The Beatles' senior roadie/tour manager was Mal Evans. He was a tall, well-built, rather stocky man of immense strength, not only physically but also of character. Having been a bouncer at The Cavern Club in Liverpool, Beatles manager Brian Epstein had hired his services as a roadie for the Fab Four. Mal never left their side, continuing with the band until their demise in 1970. Here was a man I would get to meet again on sessions at Basing Street, where Ringo would come along to play drums for the, at the time, struggling Joe Cocker. Mal was someone I would get to know quite well a few years later out in Los Angeles, before his untimely death at the hands of the Los Angeles Police Department.

Mal arrived at the door of the studio for the Stephen Stills session early one evening with all of Ringo's drum cases quite literally under his arms. "Where do you want him?" he asked matter-of-factly. I led the way to the designated spot. "About here", I replied and asked if he needed a hand. He graciously declined, saying that he had done this so many times over the years that he could almost set up Ringo's drums blindfolded. I busied myself elsewhere in the studio, keeping one eye on Mal as he emptied the drum cases. Bass drum first. Then the snare, followed by tom-toms, high-hat and cymbals. Black, robust hard-shell cases, one for every drum and every cymbal, all the stands, drumsticks and required drum paraphernalia. After about half an hour, the drum kit was assembled and all the cases had been emptied- except for one, somewhat smaller, but nevertheless as durable, which remained teasingly unopened. Eventually, Mal put me out of my misery. He removed the lid of this final case, revealing an assortment of regular kitchen tea towels, some green and white, with stripes, and another one blue and white with a check pattern. You know the type I mean, the ones we all have in the kitchen at home or used to see in the school canteen. He placed them strategically over each of the drums, and there they remained for the duration of the session. Ringo arrived and was pleasantly unsurprised to see his studio drum kit covered in tea-towels, as usual, ready for him to play. He thanked Mal.

On bass, Calvin "Fuzzy" Samuel. His credits include Crosby, Stills, Nash and Young, Marianne Faithfull and Steve Winwood, as well as working on the first Stephen Stills solo album.

On guitar, Stephen himself, Nils Lofgren (Neil Young's *After the Gold Rush* album) and Eric Clapton.

Keyboards were shared between Stephen and the late, great Billy Preston. Preston had made his mark on the music scene in the 1960's playing with such formidable artists as Little Richard, Sam Cooke and Ray Charles. Preston enjoyed success with his own hits with songs such as *That's the Way God Planned It* and *Will It Go Round in Circles*. He co-wrote *You Are So Beautiful* for Joe Cocker. Probably his most notable and recognizable achievements came from his work with the Beatles, particularly with the Saville Row rooftop appearance on 30th January 1969, this being the Beatles last ever live performance.

A second grand piano was brought in for him to use on these Stephen Stills sessions. Billy had requested a Bosendorfer so that's what we hired in. Stephen played the in-house Steinway --- the one and only time I have ever miked up two grand pianos in the same room.

The crowning glory of musicians who were to play on this record would be a four-piece horn section. No ordinary players have these. The Memphis Horns at the time comprised of Andrew Love, tenor sax, Wayne Jackson, trumpet, Floyd Newman, baritone sax and Jack Helm on trombone. Look up The Memphis Horns and check out their discography. Here is a shortened list:

Neil Diamond, Al Green, Elvis Presley, Isaac Hayes, Otis Redding, Sam and Dave and everyone else on the Stax and Atlantic record labels. Truly legendary.

The Memphis Horns were part of the successful studio session world of Stax Records, which also featured the supreme musical prowess of Booker T. and the M. G's. I was to later record band members Steve Cropper, on guitar, Bassist "Duck" Dunn and keyboardist Booker T. out in Los Angeles in 1977.

But those tales must wait. Back to Stephen in London.

Henry Diltz, the photographer, came along for his second visit to the Island studios. He had made a name for himself amongst the musical elite of Hollywood's Laurel Canyon community as well as at the Woodstock festival. Also, his work with America's carbon copy of The Beatles, the world's first contrived boy-band, The Monkees.

Graham Nash, formerly with the successful British band The Hollies, but also now as part of the wistfully beautiful vocal harmonies that marked out Crosby, Stills, Nash and Young, came along to join Henry on backing vocal duties.

The man at the helm, behind the controls of the Helios console, the guy who would be an anchor of calm in the midst of the maelstrom of egotistical creativity that was to come, was Bill Halverson.

Throughout this book, I have referenced several sound engineers and producers from the period, many of whom it has been my pleasure to work with and a privilege to learn from. To most people, they will be faceless names, but to those in the know, all these people were a major part in the painting of the sonic wallpaper that covers the walls of the houses where our musical memories live. Bill Halverson was one such painter and decorator.

Bill had started his musical journey aged just thirteen as a budding trombone player, playing on the local band scene in California. He went on to work with studio owner Wally Heider as an assistant engineer on live, remote recordings, mostly around the Los Angeles club scene in Hollywood. At Heider's he handled engineering sessions with The Beach Boys and in 1967 recorded the Monterey Pop Festival. Then the iconic Johnny Cash album, *Live at Folson Prison*. Sessions for Chuck Berry, Jimi Hendrix and Joe Cocker soon followed. Bill is credited as engineer on Cream's groundbreaking 1968 album *Wheels of Fire*. There was the Eric Clapton solo album for ATCO records, a little of which was recorded at Basing Street when he was in town recording Stephen Stills' first solo album, the session on which I had assisted for the first time with Bill.

But undoubtedly, Bill's finest work was as an engineer on Crosby, Stills and Nash's first album for Atlantic Records in 1969. A work of art. The majestic, intricate vocal harmonies wrapping themselves around a romantic, country-rock style of musical sophistication that featured, amongst other gemstones, *Marrakesh Express* and *Suite: Judy Blue Eyes*. These were records I had listened to back home, before London, before Island, before the serendipitous magazine article stumbled upon one morning on my way to work behind the deli counter.

I was to be in the studio with this great man for three whole weeks and I couldn't wait to get started. By the end of the period, I was to have been shown multiple studio skills; microphone placement techniques, how to record a four-piece horn section, live in the studio at the same time as drums, guitar and pianos, with total separation between all the instruments. How best to record a Hammond organ, a Steinway and a Bosendorfer. Ways of simplifying the use of the myriad of equipment surrounding you, so as to be as quick and responsive as is required in this extremely demanding environment. Setting up individual headphone mixes for the different musicians that will require little or no further adjustments. Ergonomically de-stressed. Less use of the hands and fingers, more use of the ears. A golden chalice of pure experiential genius, generously passed on down to me by this kind, softly spoken giant of a man.

And then I put my foot in it.

One of the first questions I couldn't stop myself from asking Bill was regarding the beautiful acoustic guitar sounds on the Crosby, Stills and Nash recordings, especially on the classic track, *Suite: Judy Blue Eyes*. (This song was written for Judy Collins, the American singer/songwriter who had enjoyed success with, amongst other songs, her version of Stephen Sondheim's *Send in the Clowns*) The C, S and N song in question is a medley in four parts, joined together with an underlying, continuous accompaniment on acoustic guitar. It was the methodology of recording and capturing the sonic blissfulness of this guitar that begged my question. How do you get a guitar to sound like that? So clear, so crisp and yet so warm and full.

So, Bill, how did you do it? Can you let me in on the secret?

"Be more than happy to tell you" started Bill, in his warm, relaxed and soothing voice.

One second, I said, let me get paper and pen. O.k. I'm ready. Fire away.

"I used a Neuman U.87 microphone with the high pass filter on the capsule, no attenuation. About three or four inches from the sound-hole, parallel with the front body of the guitar."

I scribbled away.

"At the front end of the signal path I inserted a URIE 1176 compressor/limiter, set at a ratio of 4 to 1, with a fast attack and a slow release."

I noted the details. Priceless.

To the none initiated out there, this will all sound like technical hieroglyphics, but to a young, eager engineer such as myself, in the flush of his professional youth, this was the stuff of Holy Grails. The ancient sage, passing down the wisdom of ages to the young apprentice.

Is that it, I asked, perhaps expecting more?

"Oh yes," Bill continued. "Just two more things. You won't need to write these down."

"Firstly, you use a forty-seven-year-old vintage, Martin acoustic guitar, worth about four thousand dollars. Secondly, you get Stephen Stills to play it."

I ripped up my piece of paper. Bill smiled. Lesson learned.

I still to this day record acoustic guitars with a Neuman U.87, Bill Halverson style, so if the result is a far from perfect sound, then at least I know that the problem lies somewhere else.

On another occasion, early one evening as the musicians were beginning to assemble, I learnt another invaluable lesson from Mr. Halverson.

Stephen and Billy arrived first and asked if they could hear a playback of the song they had recorded the previous night. Bill wasn't around as yet, so I loaded up the tape with the correct take and pressed play.

The Helios desk had a separate monitor section where you would adjust the playback volumes of the individual tracks. For example, the bass drum would be on one track, the snare drum on another, overhead mics would be panned left and right, and separate faders for every instrument. Pianos would each be recorded in stereo over two tracks. Guitar on another, bass, guide vocal, horns, Hammond organ, etc. Quickly try and assemble a listenable balance, but with so many instruments, I was struggling. Looking from above, the faders on this monitor section of the desk looked like a map of the Manhattan skyline. Faders everywhere, at different heights and levels. A right old mess. Couldn't get the song to sound right. Impatient musicians. In walks Bill.

He slowly hangs his coat behind the door. Bill always did everything slowly. Wouldn't be rushed. Less haste, more speed would be his motto. I apologized for messing with the desk. Carry on, he encouraged. He gave me a few more minutes whilst he grabbed himself a can of coke.

Just a word on the coke.

Not sure about the Americans but I was addicted to the stuff. I was getting through about eight cans a night. The first thing I would do on arrival at the studio for the night shift would be to crack open a can. After the recording sessions were over and the Americans left town, I went cold turkey and came off the carbonized bubbles.

Other addictions, later in life, would prove considerably more resilient.

But back to my making a pig's ear of the playback. Bill moved in to the rescue as he took charge of the desk, pulled all the faders down and started again. Here came the lesson. He simply put all the faders at unity gain. In other words, he just placed all the faders in a straight line. Now press play, he said. So, there it was, the perfect balance. You could hear everything, loud and clear. Everyone was happy with the take and all went down into the studio to start rehearsing the next tune.

Bill explained.

Because of his background in live recording, he had learned, perhaps from his time spent with Wally Heider, that you keep things as simple as possible. Set all your monitors at unity gain and all your fader inputs at unity gain. Create your recording levels using the microphone and line amp gains at the top of the desk. Create the correct listening balance as you go. From scratch. Some instruments might be slightly over recorded, maybe the snare drum or the guitar, whereas others, such as the high-hat, you would slightly under record. Take an average and balance the instruments as you go along. Same with the overdubs. Just blend them into the music at the correct listening level.

Don't be hung up on what the recording meters are showing you. Use your ears!! The overriding benefit of this approach to recording is that when you switch from one song to another, you need to make few, if any changes to the monitoring section of the desk. Same with headphone mixes. Should be pretty much set from song to song. Eliminate as many tasks as possible and make life less tiring for yourself.

The weeks rolled by. Although I wouldn't become too involved on a personal level with most of the musicians, my duties as an assistant engineer required me to be seated at the far corner of the control room, on my own, next to the tape machines, I would occasionally join in the banter. In between, that is, my having to pay most attention to which take was to be the master, where to rewind back to for an overdub drop-in, responding to Bill's requests, such as moving microphones, replacing broken headphones, switching reels and running off cassette copies at the end of each session. The final duty of each evening would be to fill out the session sheet, get Bill to sign it, and have Tony the security guy, who sat on reception all night, order however many mini-cabs were needed to get everyone back to their hotels. Including one for me.

Sun-up, early morning. Sit in the back of the cab, too exhausted to speak to the driver, weary of any small talk. Gaze out the window, half asleep, winding through the streets of the morning rush-hour. The good people of London making their way to work, refreshed, a bright new day for them, the end of a very long, albeit extraordinary shift for me.

A moment of reflection, if I may. Over the decades I have witnessed and been a part of many technological changes in the industry. Fortunately, as with most of society's changes, they happen gradually, almost imperceptibly. As long as you pay attention, show an interest and recognize the potential benefits to your industry, you can keep abreast of change. Most importantly, the basic principles of the recording process remain the same; concentration, attention to detail, empathy with the musicians and above all else an almost hysterical passion for music. Having been exposed to the earlier technologies of recording has given me an advantage, in this digital age, over engineers and producers who have come to the business later than I.

In those days of analogue tape recording, signal-to-noise ratios, the tonality of the instruments at source and the capturing of real-time live performances were of far more importance than in today's digital world of cut and paste, infinite number of tracks and non-destructive editing. The skills that were needed had to be mastered with a great deal of expertise. The kind of expertise that would, during those early years, be generously shown to me by Brian Humphries, Frank Owen, Phil Brown, Andy and Glyn Johns, Kevin and the Grand Master of them all, Bill Halverson.

--half asleep, winding through the streets of the morning rush hour...

The Joyous Recklessness of Youth

I clearly remember studying the large map of The World that hung on the wall of the main office. The office with the round table, the modern, cream coloured, push button plastic telephones with the curly cables; the open boxes of black and white glossy publicity photos lying next to the white labelled test pressings of forthcoming releases; the walls adorned with pictures of all the Island artists of the day and worth mentioning again: Nick Drake, Traffic, Free, Fairport Convention, Mott the Hoople, Cat Stevens, Spooky Tooth, King Crimson, Quintessence, John and Beverley Martyn, Bronco and Jimmy Cliff. It was the summer of 1972 and I was still in awe of and mesmerised by the fact that I was living in London and working in the music business.

Time now to go off on my travels.

Two opportunities presented themselves to me. Both involved the need for a front of house mix engineer to go on tour with one of the label's bands. Free were about to embark on a tour of Japan and newly signed Head, Hands and Feet likewise to the U.S.A. I found myself engaged, not sure whether by choice or demand, providing my services to the latter. The first question asked of me: had I ever mixed live sound before? Well in actual fact I had. Even though my day-to-day duties were overwhelmingly inside the controlled conditions of the recording studio environment, I had on one occasion gone along to help out Johnny Nash and John "Rabbit" Bundrick at a gig they were performing one evening, probably to promote Johnny's next release, at The London Hilton on Park Lane. I sat behind the front of house mixing desk and balanced the sound coming over the p.a system. The desk was a very basic eight-channel affair, which was more than adequate for the event as we were only using two microphones and a couple of keyboard inputs. The room was small, as was the stage. There were about a hundred people present. In sharp contrast, my first gig with Head, Hands and Feet on their American tour was to be at the Los Angeles Forum in front of eighteen thousand!

Head, Hands and Feet were an English band, signed to Island in 1971 and about to be sent on a tour of America to promote their newly recorded album. In 1970 band members had performed at the Royal Albert Hall with the Johnny Harris Orchestra for his *Movements* concert, opening for Dionne Warwick. The main writers in the band, Ray Smith and Tony Colton, co-wrote and co-produced for Richard Harris and Shirley Bassey. They also co-wrote and performed the soundtrack for *The World of Georgie Best* BBC documentary from 1970 with orchestra leader Johnny Harris.

So there was some serious musical pedigree there, which was bolstered with the addition of Charlie Hodges on bass, guitar, fiddle and keyboards. He had played in English pioneer producer Joe Meek's band The Outlaws, along with Clem Cattini and Jimmy Page and was later one half of the "Rockney" duo Chas and Dave. Pete Gavin, formerly with blues legend Long John Baldry was on drums and Albert Lee on lead guitar. Albert had featured with Deep Purple and Chris Farlowe and the Thunderbirds, so the band was pretty hot!

A completed application form, a four hour wait at the passport office in Petty France, Victoria and within a few days I was on my way to Heathrow airport. I had studied the location of the first gig of the tour, Los Angeles, on the office map and spent days drooling over the prospect of actually being there. I had previously heard mentioned the gloriously exotic place names that were soon to become, once I had moved to Los Angeles permanently three years later, familiar neighbourhoods: Hollywood, Burbank, San Fernando, the Sunset Strip, Santa Monica ----.

We flew at night on a Boeing 707. My first ever time in the sky and I'm in economy class sitting next to and conversing with a very sophisticated, rather glamorous American woman who just happened to be the assistant editor of Time/Life magazine. How times have changed in the now, every day commonplace experience of flying. With no cheap package holidays to Florida, the only people who would fly in those days, especially to America, would be businessmen and woman. And of course, rock stars!

On reflection, it was the likes of us that probably marked the beginning of the end for those halcyon days of flying that previously had been the exclusive territory of the privileged few. We weren't particularly well behaved on that flight, or on others that were to follow. We drank excessively, made far too much noise and generally showed a poor example of ourselves. We collectively cheapened the experience for the other passengers and I regret it to this day.

Arriving at nighttime at New York's Kennedy Airport for a short stop-over, before our connecting flight onward to L.A., I found myself once again in a situation I could have only dreamt about some few years earlier. First impressions: cops and security guards with guns, openly on display in their hip holsters; larger than life Americans, talking out loud, sipping on cocktails as they awaited friends and families, or prepared themselves for flights. Massive baggage gondolas with a spectacular rotating array of people's luggage: suitcases, most non-descript but the occasional bespoke item such as a gentleman's Luis Vuitton or a lady's Pravda overnight bag. Large trunks, reminiscent of the 18th century Grand Tours. Musical instruments and sporting equipment, including several pairs of skis. Busy people in a busy airport. Numerous iconic yellow taxis jostling outside on the forecourts, horns honking. The brightly lit tails of the jetliners taxiing back and forth at the gates: American Airlines, T.W.A, United, Pan-Am, Alleghany ----. The energetic smell of the aviation fuel and the rush of excitement.

My first night in New York and my American Christening. It was simply awesome.

We arrived at Los Angeles International Airport in the wee hours, tired and jet-lagged. As we impatiently waited for our luggage to appear Charlie came over and said to me "this is going to be an amazing experience for you. (I think Charlie had been to the States, on tour before) You look a little dazed and confused", he sympathised. "Stick with me. I'll look after you." And look after me he did. I was a very young, inexperienced, somewhat naïve twenty-one-year-old and Charlie did his best to chaperone me around the United States, especially during the middle part of what was to be a gruelling tour. We grabbed our luggage and made our way to the arrivals lounge, looking around to see if any representative from Capitol Records (the band's U.S. label) might be there to meet and greet. And meet us and greet us they did, in typical flamboyant Hollywood style. Standing at the top of the escalator barring our further passage were six young Californian female beauties, in tank-tops and very short shorts, each with an individual word written in showy pink lipstick on their exposed, deeply tanned and very slim waistlines. They stood in a row in front of us, from left to right, spelling "WELCOME TO HEAD HANDS AND FEET".

It was love at first sight.

Not just with the array of physical beauty that stood before me, although one of the girls, I think she was the one on the far left, "WELCOME", was, unbeknownst to either of us that evening going to feature prominently in each other's lives for many years to come. It was the fact that, from that point on, the Californian experience had begun to drip into my veins. Now, at this moment in time more than ever before, I inexplicably felt a growing empathy with all the Beach Boys songs I had listened to in my youth; same too with Joni Mitchell's records, (I would soon be living near Laurel Canyon), the Eagles, (playing football every Wednesday night in Beverley Hills, near "Hotel California") and Linda Ronstadt, (across the road as my next door neighbour). I had been made "Welcome" and another of my Earth Spots had been created. I felt instantly at home.

But back to the top of the escalator. We were no longer tired or remotely exhausted. We were lifted, in more ways than one. Our spirits rose also as we, that is myself, the band members and their heavy-weight manager, Reg Lock, (who had previously been part of the management team for Irish actor Richard Harris) were ushered out into three awaiting limousines. Two girls in each.

The girls all worked for Capitol Records in the landmark circular tower building in Hollywood on the corner of Hollywood and Vine. The same building, I would have seen on the record sleeves of my Dad's old 78's back in Brum. The same image that was and still is the icon of the global brand that is Capitol Records.

For our first night in Hollywood, we stayed at the world-renowned showbiz hotel The Continental Hyatt House on Sunset Strip. Now known as the Andaz West Hollywood the hotel opened as The Gene Autry Hotel in 1963. In 1967 it was sold and renamed as The Continental Hyatt House and was used as a Hollywood base for many of the top rock bands of the seventies, including Led Zeppelin, The Who and The Rolling Stones. Its reputation for rock 'n' roll over indulgence was legendary and so it became THE hotel to stay at when your band was in L.A.

After checking in to my room, I took a quick shower. Strange how the smallest, seemingly insignificant experiences stay with you forever. I mean the shower. This was a shower unlike any I had been under before. Powerfully efficient and luxurious. Not the Luke-warm trickle of a shower back at number seven Cumberland Street. This was a big shower, American style.

We were to assemble in one of the downstairs bars. Reg wanted Hollywood to know we had arrived. I met Reg in the lift (oops, sorry, elevator) and as we descended the floors he, like a father to a son, took hold of the sleeves of my denim jacket and rolled them back, just a couple of turns over my wrists. He undid the top two buttons of my shirt. It was about looking cool. "This is Hollywood Digby, you gotta look the part" he said with a wry smile and a wink. "Let's go knock 'em dead".

Not sure, I thought there and then, that I'm going to be cut out for this sort of thing, but here goes; into the dimly lit, smoky crowded bar we went.

There were people from the record label, from the music press, paparazzi, band members from other groups that were in town and a scattering of what could only be politely, albeit accurately described as hangers on. No doubt a groupie or two. I couldn't be bothered to stick around too long. I've never been a big party animal. I get uncomfortable in the company of more than three. I slipped away back to the elevator, shirt buttoned up, jacket sleeves returned to a less hip but infinitely more comfortable position and retired to my room. My first night in Hollywood. My first rock 'n' roll party in the temple of rock hotels, on the famous Sunset Strip. Too much excitement.

An early night for me.

The next morning was momentous. I pulled back the curtains and looked out of the hotel window, above the legendary Sunset Strip. Out onto my first California morning. A new visual extravaganza of unfamiliarity: the curving, wide grey concrete road with the black tyre streaks and the bright red kerb markings; the unrecognizable style of blue street signs; the traffic lights suspended across the middle of the road; the tall green and brown palm trees; the giant colourful billboards; the curvaceously long, sleek motor cars, all driving on the wrong side of the road! The clear bright sunshine (no smog that day, Santa Anna wind conditions, which I was to learn later as being the meteorological explanation). But most vivid of all, the never before seen by me deep, rich blue azure of a southern Californian summer morning sky.

Breathtaking. I was smitten.

And so it began. Forty-eight gigs in fifty-two days. Seemingly endless daily internal flights between cities, zig-zagging our way across the country. Every central town and city in America, including some not-so-major ones. Collecting hire cars and trucks, checking into hotel after hotel. Hours spent on the highways, in all weathers. The cold of the East Coast, the wet, windy rains of the Midwest, the tropical tornadoes and floods of the Texas plains. The baking, scorching heat, west of the Rockies.

A typical day involved gathering all the crew and band members together in one place for breakfast. Not always so easy, depending on what had happened to whom, where they had either collectively or individually drifted off to after the last night's gig and the after-show revelry. Post breakfast in the hotel, drive to the airport and a short flight to the next city. The road crew would collect the hire cars and trucks, and we would all drive to the venue, usually the local basketball stadium or main theatre, where we would be introduced to other band members and crew who would be setting up the lights and the p.a., ready for the evening's entertainment. Tony, Reg, Albert and the band would most likely stop-off on the way at a local radio station to do some pre-gig album promotion. For most of the concerts Head, Hands and Feet were to be the main support band. Having not yet established themselves in the States as a mainstream act, this was hardly surprising. The downside to this would be that you had a smaller area of the stage, shared use of the front of house mixing desk and invariably less time to sound-check. But what did it matter? We were, over the coming months to be support act to some of the biggest bands of the era: The Doobie Brothers, Z.Z Top, Jethro Tull, Black Sabbath and The Allman Brothers are the ones I now recall. The established pattern was that you accompanied the headline act for maybe three or four gigs, as part of their own itinerary and then went on to support a different band for the next part of their tour. A logistical nightmare that would have been organized between the various band managers, in our case Reg and the relevant departments of the many record labels involved.

After a hurried sound check it would be back to the hotel, maybe a brief exploration of the local area, a bite to eat and then, early in the evening back to the venue. But to greet us there, a completely different scene from earlier in the day. Jam-packed car parks, queues of excited people in line outside, tickets in hand, paid for months earlier in anticipation of this night. Drive down the ramp to the backstage V.I.P. areas. Not now the hollow echoes of an almost empty stadium. No road crew to be seen. The stage is already set, lights dimmed, guitar amps and drum kits in position, microphones on their boom stands, sound levels set to deliver the familiar melodies, riffs and lyrics to the adoring waiting fans. Pre-recorded music blasting out of the p.a. Thousands of punters taking to their seats.

I stand out front, behind the mixing desk, right in the middle of the crowd, usually on the lower floor. Last-minute checks to fader positions, stage monitor levels, song running order taped to the desk, under the small lamp: sweaty palms and fast heart-beat. I feel sick to my stomach with nerves. Fade music. The master of ceremonies approaches the microphone (which microphone? Oh my God!! Please pick the right one). Spotlight. Crowd roars. "Please welcome, all the way from England, HEAD, HANDS AND FEET".

Bigger roar! Tony, Albert, Ray, Charlie and Pete appear on the stage. So tiny, so far away. "How ya doing tonight?!" shouts Tony. Crowd response, you know the drill, 'cause we've all been to a big gig. This is it. Showtime.

One or two encores and thirty-five minutes later it's all over. I'm exhausted. Can't imagine how the guys must feel. We meet up backstage and make a beer grab. Everyone gets a towel, even me! Tony says he needed more of his vocal in his monitors but less of Charlie's bass. Pete wanted more bass. Ray was happy with his mix but didn't think he sang particularly well. Albert didn't say a thing. He couldn't because he was already surrounded by local T.V and press. All this I thought and we are only the support act! Reg was buzzing and already talking about tomorrow night's gig and what we might all do to improve. More beer. Ray, Tony, Pete and Charlie get their turns to be interviewed and photographed with various local dignitaries. Climb into hire cars, back up the ramp and drive through the night sky back to the hotel. Find the bar.

Party time. Serious, full on, U.K band on tour of America type partying.

Two more months of this to come. I shuddered to think. I confess that in the beginning, I feared I might not survive. Maybe offering to come on this tour was a mistake on my part. Should have stayed in the U.K in the familiar surroundings of Basing Street, of Portobello and Fulham. Remained behind the comfortable desks of studios one and two with reels of tape and lots of tea. But survive I did. Thanks to Charlie in particular, but all of the guys, including Reg who enthusiastically emphasized the absolutely riotous fun of it all. So, if you can't beat them, I thought -------. I threw myself into the proceedings with an enthusism I had previously restrained.

I joined the party.

No further details can be revealed, not so much to protect the innocent as to protect the guilty.

By far and away the best part of all the tour travelling was, for me, the flying. We flew almost every day, from one city to the next. One day on a Boeing, the next day a McDonnell Douglas, then Lockheed. Loving the excitement of take-off and landing, the panoramic views from above and the exhilarating smell of aviation fuel. All the flag carriers of the day: T.W.A., Pacific Southwest Air, Delta, Braniff. Loving every minute.

Watching aeroplanes had always been a boyhood passion of mine. Growing up in Pype Hayes, Birmingham, the family was only a short distance from Castle Bromwich Aerodrome. Amongst many engineering accomplishments attributed to that part of the West Midlands during the war, newly assembled Spitfires were ferried across the road from one of the government's "shadow factories", built between the Fort Dunlop factory and the airfield, to be given their maiden test flights, often by female pilots. My Dad frequently described how he would, as a young man living in the house, witness the Spitfires performing a victory roll at the end of each test flight, to indicate the test pilot's satisfaction with the aircraft. Every year from this aerodrome, the R.A.F. would put on a Battle of Britain air display which could be watched and enjoyed from the comfort of our back garden. Overhead, Spitfires and Hurricanes, Lightning, Mosquito and Meteor jets. Lancasters and the Vulcan bomber. It was no wonder, therefore, that I found this aspect of the travelling, albeit repetitive and monotonous for some, to be overwhelmingly the best part of the experience. Looking effortlessly down from the skies onto glorious planet Earth, as opposed to the earlier limitations in our back garden, as a child staring longingly upward with a very stiff neck.

The first two weeks of touring were mostly along the west coast and on up to the Rockies. Places such as San Diego, San Francisco,

Denver and Albuquerque were most memorable to me, if only because of the mere sound of the names of these cities and the romance engendered in them. But this was no romance. It was bloody hard work!

Romance, however, was just around the corner.

We stopped off back at Los Angeles for a short two-day break. Reg had some record label business to attend to and we all benefitted from a couple of days pool-side, up on the roof of The Continental Hyatt House. By now I had taken many photographs, mostly from the air, but others of just about anything American that caught my eye. Photos of pick-up trucks, street signs, rental cars with the crew posing alongside, the guys in the band cavorting and up to no good in various airport lounges. Lots of pretty girls, especially flight attendants, mostly the ones who cavorted and were up to no good. On return to the U.K. the band recorded an album, *Old Soldiers Never Die* which I engineered and my photographs were, used as a montage on the double-fold inside of the album sleeve. Check out the record and see for yourself the photographic history of our tour of America.

I shared a room at the Hyatt House Hotel with Pete, the drummer. One late morning, a telephone call came through to the room. It was for Pete, but he wasn't around. "Can I tell him who called?" I asked the rather sexy sounding female on the other end. Tell him Janet from Capitol Records. I said I would, thinking to myself that this must surely be "Welcome" on the line. "Welcome" had made a beeline for Pete when we all were greeted at the top of the escalator some two weeks earlier, and I guessed right. In a moment of uncharacteristic bravery, curious perhaps as to how welcoming she might be, I asked Janet if she knew of any place where I could get a couple of hundred photographs developed (no digital cameras as yet, so no downloading). Sure, she replied helpfully, just across the street from the Capitol, there is a 'photo booth and they can do it for you in one hour. Only in America, I thought. Nothing like that in the U.K in 1972. Maybe if I meet you there perhaps you might care to have lunch with me, while the photos are being developed?

Essentially, that lunch went on to last fourteen years, because we became close, fell in love and a few years later were married. A young, optimistic and precarious love it must be said. But if that kind of love can't be found in the joyous recklessness of youth, then there is no prospect for those of us who find and commit to a longer lasting, deeper, more solid and realistic love later in life.

I never went back to The Continental Hyatt House. I nearly missed the flight to Chicago, which was where we were heading next. Janet and I had spent a couple of fun days together in her apartment up on Beachwood Drive in the Hollywood Hills, just below the Hollywood sign, smoking weed, drinking wine, listening to music and making love. I didn't want to leave. Just finish the tour without me. Oh, and by the way, I'm not coming back to England. Just leave me here in Paradise.

But a slightly annoyed Reg had other plans for me, so I got a lift to the hotel, said "see you soon" to Janet and jetted off. The rest of the tour was a haze. I had lost interest. We stopped off in L.A. one more time and the guys all stayed at The Hyatt. I checked in to Beachwood.

The last gig of the tour was in a place called Ipswich, Massachusetts. A far cry from the giant basketball stadiums and arenas of the previous forty-plus shows, this was in front of a small crowd in a local "saw-dust on the floor" bar, a hundred people at the most. It was good to be able to see the guys in the band on stage, close up. You could even hear clearly what they were playing! It was a little sad to know that this was the end of a memorable couple of months of us all being together, close bonds and all that. The conclusion for me of a one-off experience. I have never toured with a band since. Would never do it again. Just not suited.

Flew out of Boston, headed east, and six hours later descended through the gloomy grey skies of England. Walked through the inevitable rain and got the crowded tube train to Victoria, resentfully noticing how grim and pale-faced everyone looked; their dirty shoes and slovenly drab clothing; the noise and the smell. No sunshine. No orange blossom. But wait a minute, this is London, the exciting place you live and work—the place you love.

Yet somehow things had changed and would never be the same again. I had found another beautiful, dream-like Earth Spot almost halfway around the world, and I was confused.

I got back to my flat on Cumberland Street and immediately picked up the phone and rang my girlfriend in California.

---you might care to have Lunch with me, while the 'photos are being developed.

154

Back To The Day Job

I was by now one of the Island's full-time senior engineers and working flat out. Non-stop, one album after another, sometimes working on two or three albums at a time. Session after session, the months just rolled by. Hereby follows a brief synopsis, again in no particular chronological order, of some of the sessions worthiest of note.

Joe Cocker, with Denny Cordell producing, in Studio Two. Denny had enjoyed success producing The Moody Blues, The Move and Georgie Fame. Big hits came for him with Procol Harem's *A Whiter Shade of Pale* and Cocker's seminal cover of The Beatles classic *with a Little Help from My Friends*. Joe had, by all accounts, been unwell, unwilling and physically unable to record. The sight of him quietly sitting in a darkened corner of the control room, rolling spliff after spliff, hardly conversing with anyone for the majority of the time over those next two or three days would serve to confirm that. Denny had assembled an experienced collection of musicians to inspire Joe creatively: Chris Stainton on keyboards and Alan Spenner on bass. Both had been with Joe in his backing band, The Greaseband and along with guitarists Henry McCullough and Neil Hubbard and drummer Bruce Rowland, they had all played together with Joe at the legendary 1969 Woodstock festival. On drums for the first two days was B.J. Wilson from Procol Harum. Day three, and Ringo turned up. He lasted about three or four hours and despite Joe coming to the microphone on two or three occasions, in vain attempts to perform, Ringo was professional enough to realise there was to be nothing productive coming from his time spent with Joe and duly summoned Mal Evans, his roadie, to pack up the drums (and the tea-towels) and head for home.

So that was that. Even with a bit of help from his friends, we had spent three days in the studio and had nothing to show for it. Sad really. The musicians wanted it to work for Joe, as they all had an appreciation of the state of mind and health that he was in at that time.

I was to work with Denny again a few years down the line, for artists on his Shelter Records label in Los Angeles.

Greats from the world of jazz, Cleo Laine and Johnny Dankworth, booked into Studio One for the day, to cut an E.P. of covers of tunes by the American soft-rock band, Bread. With David Gates as the primary writer and vocalist in the band, Bread enjoyed numerous top ten hits in the seventies, most notably *Baby I 'm-a Want You* and *Make it With You*. Cleo and Johnny were consummate professionals and extremely likeable, relaxed and easy to get along with. There were pages and pages of manuscript everywhere, both for the musicians and me. Fast-paced and mildly chaotic, the session was also being filmed by BBC Two for a documentary to be shown later in the year. There were cameras, lights, cables and a film crew, assorted technicians, producers, directors, make-up artists, personal secretaries for all and sundry, all adding to the excitement. What's more, I was going to be on the telly!

Or so I thought.

A few months later, back home in Birmingham, I was in the front room with Mom and Dad, sisters Pat and Jayne, sitting expectantly in front of the television, Radio Times at hand to confirm the start time of the Cleo Laine and Johnny Dankworth documentary, which was going to feature me as the chief sound engineer. Fame and glory awaited—lights, camera, action.

The first scenes were of Cleo and Johnny arriving at Basing Street, meeting the musicians and their producer. They ascended the steps to Studio One and posed for questions beside the recording console. This will be me next, I thought. But no. Not just yet. A few shots of the studio, microphones, music stands, conductor, that sort of thing. Then Cleo was at the microphone, singing away in her beautifully dulcet tones, Johnny responding with lyrical dexterity on his gleaming tenor sax. Then back into the control room for a playback. Here it comes. Me next. We were all struggling to contain our excitement, especially Dad, who was so proud of his son, the soon-to-be television celebrity.

Then the moment came. And it was only a moment. One shot of the back of my head and another featuring my right hand moving some faders. And that was it—credits roll, no mention, program over, news headlines next.

Mom and Dad didn't know whether to laugh or cry. I wanted to cry. Jayne said something gracious like "---- oh, that was good, wasn't it?" Pat was speechless, somewhat disappointingly bemused. My big break in showbiz had come and gone. Blink and you would have missed it. I'm on the cutting room floor somewhere.

John Martyn had teamed up with bassist Danny Thompson for the 1971 recording of his fifth Island album, *Bless the Weather*, a partnership that was to last until John died in 2009. Danny has been, and still is, a top double bass session player, having played with the likes of Roy Orbison, John McLaughlin, Nick Drake, Ronnie Scott, Kate Bush, Donovan and many more. He was a founder member of the legendary British folk-jazz band, Pentangle. Danny worked with John on the iconic *Solid Air* album, the title track being a torturous tribute to John's close friend and Island stablemate, Nick Drake. The album was released in February 1973, just eighteen months before the untimely demise of Drake.

Chris Blackwell chose me to engineer on the following two John Martyn albums, *Inside Out* (1973) and *Sunday's Child* (1974).

Danny played bass on both the albums, and the three of us developed the kind of close relationship that can only come from spending many hundreds of hours in each other's company. Such that, for example, on one of the tracks (I forget which, of course) on the *Inside Out* album, the three of us, over a very long weekend at The Fallout Shelter studio in British Grove, Hammersmith, managed sixty-three uninterrupted sleepless hours in the studio. On one song! Chemically assisted, as I recall. Starting on Friday at 6 pm and on to mine and Danny's departure at 9 am on the following Monday, John grabbed a passing engineer and carried on for a further eight hours! I reminded John some months later of this epic feat of studio endurance. He laughed and was quick to point out that, by his reckoning, we had spent approximately twenty-seven of those hours drinking in the Cross Keys public house across the road from the studio, so not all work and no play.

As work on the *Inside Out* album progressed, I was both surprised and astonished when walking around the popular market in Camden, north London, one Sunday morning on a rare day off. On display amongst other "bootleg" cassette tapes that were commonly for sale at one of the many stalls was an amateurish-looking tape of a John Martyn album. It was the *Inside Out* album! "How much?" I enquired. "Five quid to you, mate", came the terse reply. "Funny that", I continued. "The album isn't finished yet!" "How do you know that?" he snapped. "Because I just know, mate, and I will bring you a licensed copy when it is finished. It will have the Island Records logo on it, and you will be able to sell it for more than a fiver."

I walked away, leaving one bemused stallholder to contemplate the authenticity of at least one of his grubby tapes.

Many years later, working at Gateway Studios in Battersea, south London, I joined in a conversation with a group of engineers having their lunch break. The subject matter was the merits or otherwise of various techniques you could employ to record a double bass. One chap insisted quite vociferously that you simply had to use a contact microphone, attached to the side of the instrument, as well as two mics in front of the "F" holes. Never works, said the other guy. You get all sorts of "phase cancellation" issues that way. What you have to do is use a dynamic microphone about four inches from the fingerboard. Rubbish, came the response. This was all getting a little heated. I was listening intently and awaited my chance. "Well, Digby, how do YOU record a double bass?" I paused for a moment as I recalled the first time I had met Danny and his beloved bass, how I had asked him what microphone(s) and where he would place them to get the sound that, in his years of studio experience, had proved most pleasing to him. Danny explained that the best results come from a simple approach: one microphone, a Neumann U.87, placed a couple of inches from the bridge, cardioid pattern, with the high-pass filter (to remove the "boom" from the low-end), and just a little compression. I addressed the committee, repeating the above procedure, only to be admonished by the more senior of the two engineers. He was a little irate that his methodology had not been seen as gospel, and then went on to hoist himself by his own petard. "The best double bass sound I have EVER heard on a record", he proclaimed, "is on John Martyn's *Inside Out* album".

I finished my cup of tea and, walking away, softly suggested he should check out the engineering credits on the back of that album.

I related this conversation to Danny when we were back in the studio recording John's next album, *Sunday's Child*. Danny shook his head and smiled. I have a similar tale, he said, that goes even one better. Pray to tell, Danny:

I was booked for an overdub session at E.M.I. studios in north London, he began. I was introduced to the engineer and the producer, set myself up in the live room, donned a pair of headphones, and was good to go. The engineer came in and set up several microphones. The scene resembled one of those essential press conferences, you know the type, with all the microphones surrounding the podium. The engineer retired to the control room and pressed the talk-back button. "Play, please, Mr. Thompson". He started doing what engineers do: lifting faders, switching channels on and off, coming back into the live room, moving microphones an inch here and there, back into the control room. A lot of frowning and scratching of the chin, the producer towering behind him, looking earnestly at his watch. Engineer in complete dismay presses talk-back. "Can you please come into the control room, Mr. Thompson?". What seems to be the problem, I ask politely. "Can't seem to get a decent sound out of that old double bass. Just sounds rubbish. Have you got another one we could try?" I most certainly do not. Do you have any idea how many records this bass has appeared on? I was making records with this bass before you were born.

The producer steps in to keep the peace and wishes to know where we are going with all this. He glances once more at his watch. Time is money. The engineer took his last gallant stand, which proved fatal. He reached up and grabbed a record from the shelf, a twelve-inch vinyl recording titled "Sounds of the Orchestra". Track four. Double bass. The beautiful depth and resonance. The harmonic integrity. The presence and clarity. Sheer musical joy to the ears as the sound of this classic double bass, beautifully played, came out of the speakers.

Can you guess as to what is coming next?

Danny told me how the engineer's face had dropped to the floor once he read the sleeve notes. Not only did the recording he had played feature Danny and his "rubbish" double bass but to pour salt into the hapless engineer's egotistical wound, it had actually been recorded in that very same room, using the same desk and equipment, some four or five years earlier.

Danny put his vintage bass back in its faded cloth bag and left the building. Will never know who got to play bass on that track or who, for that matter, engineered the session.

A last reflection on being in the studio with John Martyn. One early morning, at the end of a long night of recording, we had all ordered taxis and were passing the time chatting in the reception area. John enquired as to whether or not there was any blank space on the end of the last reel of tape we had been working with earlier. Yeah, sure I said, there are about ten minutes worth left. The vocal and guitar mics were still in place because we were coming back later in the day so no need to strip down the studio. John said he had a song he wanted to record, that a certain mood had come over him, and that he just wanted to capture something.

We slid back into the studio and John put on the headphones, gathered up his guitar and I put the tape machine into the record. What happened next can only be described as magical. I love that guy's voice and his guitar playing, but this time he excelled even my expectations. The song is *Ellie Rhee* and it appears on the digital re-issue of *Sunday's Child*. Written by Septimus Winner (1827-1902) this is a poignant tale about the loneliness of separation during the slavery days of the American Civil War. If you have never listened to John Martyn, then I humbly suggest you start with *Ellie Rhee*.

Whenever I hear the track today, I find myself expecting a taxi to arrive.

Muff Winwood, Island head of A+R, always had an ear for a hit, so when he brought the American duo of brothers Ron and Russell Mael to the label, there was little doubting their potential.

"*Sparks is an American band formed in Los Angeles in 1971 by brothers Ron (keyboards) and Russell Mael (vocals), renamed from Halfnelson, formed in 1968. Known for their quirky approach to songwriting, Sparks' music is often accompanied by intelligent, sophisticated, and acerbic lyrics, and an idiosyncratic, theatrical stage presence, typified in the contrast between Russell's wide-eyed, hyperactive frontman antics and Ron's sedentary, scowling demeanour. They are also noted for Russell Mael's falsetto voice and Ron Mael's keyboard style*". (Sparks: Elegantly Whimsical. David Dye. Npr.org 2006. Shooting Off Sparks. Skylaire Alfvegren. L.A. Weekly 1998. Sparks Profile. Jesse Ashlock Epitonic.com 2007)

Muff took me along with him as his engineer to The Who's Ramport Studios in south London to lay down backing tracks for their Island debut album, *Kimono My House*. I'm not sure why we didn't record at Basing Street, but at least it was a change of scenery for me. The Mael brothers had advertised in The Melody Maker for band members and the following personnel were selected: Martin Gordon on bass, who later went on to enjoy success with the band Jet, who were produced by Queen's producer Roy Thomas Baker. Adrian Fisher was recruited for guitar duties. He had previously played with ex-Free bass player Andy Fraser in the band Toby and later with Mike Patto in Boxer. Adrian moved to Thailand in the late eighties and sadly died so young, in 2000 from a heart attack. Norman "Dinky" Diamond was hired on drums and, unlike Martin and Adrian, went on to record several albums with Sparks. He was voted Drummer of the Year in a Premier Drums poll in 1975, but was ultimately replaced later that year as the band sought out more electronic sounding productions. "Dinky" married Muff's secretary, Lee Packham in 1976, but they were later divorced. He was never to fully get over his disappointment at being dropped by the band and in September 2004 he committed suicide in his Berkshire home.

Such a warm, kind-hearted, gentle soul and a superb drummer, whose musical contribution to Sparks' early albums for Island cannot be overstated.

Overdubs were carried out at Basing Street, despite problems with the unstable electricity supply. Under Edward Heath's 1970-1974 Conservative government, policies were introduced to help manage an ailing economy with the introduction of power cuts and the three-day working week, which didn't apply to the label or the studio engineers working there. Bill and Joe, the studio technical engineers simply hired in a couple of petrol-powered generators and life went on almost as normal.

We enjoyed a number 2 in the charts with the classic *This Town Ain't Big Enough* and, as always, working with Muff was a joy. His attention to detail, combined with a methodical yet relaxed and often humorous approach to studio life, made for a very fulfilling session time. Somewhat less fulfilling would be the visit to the studio by the B.B.C. "Top of the Pops" representative. This would occur once it was established, usually by Thursday afternoons in the publicity and marketing departments of the label, that one of the Island artists, in this case Sparks, was expecting to make an appearance on this all-important television music program. You had a record heading for the charts. A hit. The B.B.C., in conjunction with the Musicians Union, would expect to witness the re-recording of the chart-bound track, live in the studio, before their very eyes and ears, for purposes of authenticity. The lead vocal, however, had to be performed "live" in the television studio. Almost impossible to recreate a backing track in a few hours of studio time that may have taken days or even weeks to produce, so a pre-prepared instrumental version of the original master recording on an alternative reel of tape was mixed down ahead of time. A surreptitious sleight of hand and all was well. The B.B.C. knew the deal, as did the M.U., so in time this archaic practice was discontinued.

A second album followed, *Propaganda* which I co-engineered with Island engineer Tony Platt, Muff Winwood once again producing. Tony went on to become a successful engineer/producer in his own right, working with bands such as Thin Lizzy, AC/DC, Iron Maiden, Cheap Trick and Gary Moore.

Some years later, on my return from living in the States, a little battered and bruised shall we say, Muff was one of the first who offered me work back in the U.K., helping me to get my feet firmly on the ground again. I shall always be indebted for the repeated vote of confidence shown to me by this industry giant.

Top American producer Richard Perry booked into studio two to record and overdub on tracks with Harry Nilsson for his R.C.A. album *Nilsson Schmilsson*. Perry had produced for Barbara Streisand, Carly Simon, Diana Ross, Andy Williams and Manhattan Transfer. In 1978 he created Planet Records and I was to engineer for him a few years later at his studio out in Los Angeles.

He was a quite serious, somewhat illusive man whose luminous ego was matched only by his overwhelming stature in the business. He knew his music and how he wanted it to sound, was meticulous to the point of tedium and worked Harry and me extremely hard. On one occasion, before Richard had arrived at the studio, there was just Harry, myself and a blank piece of tape. Harry had an idea. He went out to the vocal mic and I pressed record. He made some strange drum sounding percussive noises with his mouth. An early example of "Beat-Boxing" I guess. Then he overdubbed a bass line, again with his mouth, followed by many orchestral sounds: oboes, French horns, harmonies, counter melodies -----, all executed with perfect aural mimicry. Took him and me about twenty minutes to create an amazingly unique, slightly odd sounding piece of music. We played it back and fell about laughing.

Then the door opened and in walked Richard. Laughter stops. Straight faces. Back to work.

Should have made a copy for myself. Don't know what became of my track with Harry. Still, it was fun to do and I will always remember him as a kind, fun-loving, creative genius, who was a joy to be with.

Mott the Hoople, despite the eccentric name, were a very down-to-earth bunch of regular guys from Hereford. They had been signed to Island by label producer Guy Stevens, who himself came up with the name for the band, after reading the Willard Manus novel of the same name, about life in a circus freak show. A brief word about Guy Stevens:

"Stevens was involved in the early history of Island Records and also ran the UK division of the Sue record label for Chris Blackwell. Stevens used the Sue label to put out obscure American singles not only from the U.S. Sue group of labels, but from any number of tiny independent record companies, and some of the bigger ones. He became widely influential. Stevens was also president of the Chuck Berry Appreciation Society, and had a say in the UK releases that Pye International put out by Chuck Berry, Bo Diddley and others on the Chess and Checker labels. It was Guy Stevens who brought Berry to the UK for his first tour after paying his bail to get him out of jail for offences under the Mann Act." (The Generalist. 26/02/2012).

Mott's first two albums for Island were produced by Guy, with Andy Johns as engineer. I assisted on some sessions for album number two but for the third album, *Wildlife*, having received little success on the previous two, the band decided to produce themselves. Along with Tony Platt and Brian Humphries, I engineered on those sessions. Most notable was one Saturday morning when only myself and Mick Ralphs (lead guitarist) turned up for the session. Some confusion amongst the other band members' diaries resulted in Mick and I having the whole studio to ourselves. The instruments were all set up, microphones in place, just nobody there to play them. Except, that is, Mick. I was about to discover what a talented multi-instrumentalist of a musician Mick is, because he suggested that he had a song of his own that he had wanted to record for some time, so now was the perfect opportunity.

He laid down a couple of guitar parts, overdubbed some drums and bass, lead vocal, guitar solos, we did a quick mix and were home by late afternoon. Genius, I thought. Oh, and what was the name of the song? It was *Can't Get Enough of Your Love* which Mick later recorded with his next band, Bad Company, for their debut album *Bad Company*. That album topped the Billboard charts and has been certified as a five times platinum album by the RIAA.

Nice to know I recorded one of the demos.

Mott the Hoople's fourth and final album for Island was *Brain Capers* and for this, they brought back the old team of Guy Stevens and Andy Johns. I remember Andy and Guy bursting into the Basing Street reception area on the first day of recording, dressed as Batman and Robin, in complete costume, including capes and face masks. Armed with fully loaded water pistols they ran up and down the stairs, in and out of all the offices, firing at and soaking everybody. Utter hysterical lunacy. But what else might you expect from those two crazy guys!

Another word about approaches to music production. One early evening in studio one, Andy Johns and I are engineering, Guy Stevens is producing, and Mott the Hoople are going for take seven. It sounds lacklustre, dull and uninspired despite Guy's encouragement down the talkback microphone. Take eight. It's going from bad to worse. So what does Guy do to inspire the band?

He climbs onto the desk, feet astride Andy's puzzled brow and starts jumping up and down like a madman, in time with the music! The band looks up from the studio floor and, bearing witness to Guy's bizarre antics in the control room, are suitably galvanised and respond accordingly. Volume and intensity increase, enhanced passion and excitement in the performance evident for all to see and hear. Take nine and it is nailed. I'm looking at Guy Stevens and thinking to myself what a crazy, outrageous and clever man he is. He also happened to have an infectious laugh and a warm sense of humour and I admire him for illustrating how it is sometimes necessary to employ a production technique that isn't in any of the textbooks. Young students of the profession take note.

Despite this reunion of superheroes, the album still failed to create any momentum for the band, so they parted company from Island. They were on the verge of breaking up when, fortuitously for them David Bowie, a big fan of the band appeared with a song for Mott to record. *All the Young Dudes* was a turning point in their careers, especially for lead vocalist Ian Hunter. Bowie produced the album of the same name and this was released on Columbia in the States and on C.B.S. Bowie took Mott from a potential non-entity to being champions of the glam-rock movement, but much credit must go to Chris Blackwell and the Island team for supporting the band during the making of the four albums that preceded any success.

I doubt that would happen today.

The Manor in Oxfordshire was the second residential studio built in the U.K., the first being Rockfield in Monmouthshire. Along with members of the Island band Fairport Convention, Australian record producer Trevor Lucas invited me to engineer one of the earliest commercial recordings to take place at Virgin magnate Richard Branson's luxurious studio retreat. The album was to be called *Rock On. The Bunch*, the bunch being members of Fairport plus others, including Sandy Denny, Richard and Linda Thompson, Pat Donaldson, Ashley Hutchings, Gerry Conway and Dave Mattocks. Simply Google this impressive list and get a sense of the quality of musicianship. The album was to consist of covers of the band's favourite songs by, amongst others, Elvis Presley, Buddy Holly and The Everly Brothers. We spent two wonderful weeks out in the Oxfordshire countryside, being wined and dined, banquet style, every evening. Croquet on the lawn just after breakfast and a dip in the pool before lunch. Lavishly très chic.

Shortly after the completion of the record, Trevor handed me a copy of the production vinyl in its glossy cover and thanked me on behalf of all the band members for the hard work I had put in. I turned to the back of the album sleeve, as you do when looking to see if they have spelt your name correctly under the "engineered by" credit. But oh dear. No mention. Not anywhere. I pointed this out to Trevor. He scoured the sleeve notes for my name as his face turned an apologetic red. No matter, I said. I've had a great time and I'm glad everyone is pleased.

Rock On.

Studio one. Phil Spector as producer. George Harrison and Harry Nilsson on acoustic guitars. A song for Phil's wife, Ronnie, written by George, *Try Some, Buy Some* was later re-recorded at Abbey Road for George's own album. Lasting memory? Phil Spector's dogmatic, humourless autocratic style of production and his appallingly cheap looking hair-piece!

Jesus Christ Superstar album, studio two. Alan O'Duffy chief engineer, me assisting. Mostly vocal/chorale overdubs. Hectic paced couple of days in the company of a very youthful Andrew Lloyd Webber and the delightful gentleman that is Tim Rice.

Brian Eno. Recording his single *Seven Deadly Fins* in one day, mastering the following morning at Apple studios in Saville Row and released the same day. A record for a record. I've listened to it recently and it doesn't sound too good! I think we might have rushed this one.

The beautifully played and gorgeously rich sounding mandolins of Bryn Haworth's Island albums. I recorded and produced two albums with Bryn: *Let The Days Go by* in 1974 and *Sunny Side of the Street* in 1975. Happy and relaxed times spent with this talented musician and his kind, good-natured wife Sally.

The Dundee Horns, later to become The Average White Band and the recording of audition tracks in studio two for the label. Island, in a rare case of ill-judgement, passed on the band.

John "Speedy" Keen. Formerly with Thunderclap Newman, a one-hit band with the classic *Something in the Air*, they were formed by Pete Townsend in 1968 to showcase the talents of the Who's former chauffeur, John Keen, pianist Andy Newman and guitarist Jimmy McCulloch, later of Paul McCartney's Wings fame. John's album was aptly named *Y'Know Wot I Mean* as this was one of John's most frequently used expressions.

Jim Capaldi's *Short Cut Draw Blood* solo album for Island, featuring the hit single *Love Hurts*. Produced by Muscle Shoals legend Steve Smith, that particular track was entirely my mix and whenever I hear it on the radio I still think the crash cymbals are far too loud! Still, didn't prevent it from getting to number four in the U'K charts.

Gordon Haskell's 1971 album *It Is and It Isn't*. Overdubs in studio one with senior Atlantic Records' producer Arif Mardin.

Such a well-turned-out gentleman of immense charm and character. Sheet music everywhere.

I remember walking into the studio two one morning for a session to overdub piano on a track (not sure who the artist was --- I know, should have kept a diary). The session musician, who had been recruited by the engineer for the day Clive Franks, was a shortish, balding chap called Reg Dwight. He was sitting on the sofa awaiting the arrival of Clive. Reg struck a rather solitary, sad figure as he sat there, white plastic melting beaker of hot tea in hand. He didn't say much at all, seemed quite nervous and a little introverted. He listened to the song we had recorded earlier, made some musical notes and went out into the main studio and sat at the Steinway. Microphones in place, recording levels and headphone balance satisfactory, two takes, job done. He chats briefly with Clive, who he was obviously close friends with and leaves the building. Later that same week Clive invited me to go along with him to Trident Studios in Saint Anne's Court, Soho. Reg, he informed me, was actually recording his own album there, his third to be precise. I sat in the control room at Trident and listened to the most wonderful music coming out of the studio monitors. Robin Cable was the in-house engineer and Gus Dudgeon the producer.

I will always remember him as Reg Dwight, but Elton John is a much more attractive professional name.

Mike McGear had been a member of the Liverpool comedy, poetry and music group The Scaffold. Their most considerable success had been with the 1968 Christmas number one, "Lily the Pink", and Mike was signed to Island to record his 1972 solo album, "Woman". Mike's real surname is McCartney, but because another member of the family had already achieved a considerable amount of success as a bass player, vocalist and composer in a popular beat-combo of the day, Mike chose not to coast-tail on that success, subsequently changing his name to McGear.

It was a Saturday morning when we met up at Basing Street for the day's work in studio one. I had been scheduled by Sally to engineer and was standing in the kitchen making the obligatory morning tea when Mike announced what the day would involve. He produced out of his rucksack a seven-and-a-half-inch plastic spool of tape. He described how he and his younger brother, "our kid", had recorded this at home the night before and his idea was to transfer the recording over to the multi-track tape machine and that his brother and his brother's wife were coming down to the studio to overdub some guitars and vocals. Sounds good to me, I said, enquiring of him as to whether or not he took sugar in his tea?

Mike wandered off into the studio. As I stood there in the tiny downstairs kitchen, waiting for the kettle to boil, a thought occurred to me. His younger brother, the one he referred to as "our kid", wasn't he ---- could it be ---- is it?

It was!

I stood in the reception area looking out through the circular window of the main door as the bright yellow Rolls Royce pulled up on Basing Street. Out stepped Paul McCartney, in an even brighter yellow suit, his wife Linda alongside, guitars in hand. As they approached the door I had a brief flashback. I was outside my sister Pat's bedroom door. It was 1963 again and I'm listening to the "Regentone" record player and this man that was coming towards me was the same person who had shouted out the count-in to that first Beatle track. This was Mister "One, Two, Three, Four---".

Some days in the recording studio, as with any occupation, are better than others. There are those you may choose to forget; unproductive, dull and tedious. Not many, but enough for you to wish away. In contrast, the studio experiences that stay fresh in your mind are usually a combination of all the essential elements arriving in one place, at the same time: great music, solid players, quality sounding instruments and above all else, really genuinely lovely people.

This was to be one such day.

Paul was keen to get cracking, so I showed off my best. I knew this desk and equipment as if it were all a physical part of my body and soul, so as quickly as he played one part, I switched tracks, adjusted headphones and pressed record, always ready for the next overdub. And they came thick and fast. Linda joined in with backing vocals and percussion. She was good! Rumours had abounded as to the musical skills, or lack of them, from this lady who, like Yoko Ono, had been, unjustly, I always think, responsible for breaking up the Beatles. No evidence of that here. Linda had good pitch and timing, took instructions well in terms of picking out and executing harmonies. Together, they sounded very tight and proficient. What is more, they were so obviously very deeply in love. In between takes, during playbacks, they sat on the sofa kissing and cuddling like a couple of teenagers, playing guitar and practising harmonies. We all took turns putting the kettle on! (Sorry to any of my readers if, once again, I shatter any illusions regarding the exciting, glamorous world of Rock'n'Roll, but that's the way it is, folks.)

Wrapped around in such a convivial and creative atmosphere I was made to feel like one of the family and just wish now that I could have taken a snapshot with them, but as a professional studio engineer, you just didn't do that. Maybe today with a selfie, but not then. More the pity. By early evening we were done. Paul and Linda graciously thanked me, jumped into the yellow roller and sped off. Wow! What a day I thought. I'm still glowing all these years after!

A few days later, there was a production meeting with Mike and the label bosses, including Chris Blackwell. I was invited to attend. By all accounts, Mike, Paul, and Linda thought the session I had engineered had gone well. There was talk of finding the right producer for the record. I was encouraged to join in the debate and yet somehow felt strangely disengaged with the whole process. Sure, it had gone well. I knew that. Were they offering me the gig as a producer?

My mind was elsewhere.

In California, to be precise.

"Play please, Mr. Thompson".

Two Tickets, Please

Every time I earned five hundred pounds I jumped on a 'plane to Los Angeles. I flew so many times back and forth that one airline, TWA, gave me a frequent flyer "getaway" credit card, which meant I could go pretty much whenever I felt like it. After all, I had been freelance since the summer of 1972, in order to be able to tour the States with Head, Hands and Feet, so I wasn't tied down any more by regular employment. In fact, I see myself as having been not so much self-employed, as unemployed since 1972. I have thereby always had the freedom of being able to look for work of any description. For the past 49 years, I have been an active member of what is now commonly referred to as the "gig economy" and believe me, it makes for a varied and often challenging existence. Over the decades I have worked on building sites, driven forklift trucks, courier driving, landscape gardening, a German cake factory and of course, whenever possible, in recording studios.

The predominantly creative side of me always wanted to be a musician/songwriter. I realised a long time ago that song writing was not to be my strong point, but as a musician? Maybe one day. Out in California?

Janet, my "Welcome" girl, flew out to England one time and hated the place. One afternoon, we were standing in Saint James' Park, me pointing out to her the glorious splendour of Buckingham Palace. She just looked, squirmed and said, "Call that a palace?!" I think she had conjured up thoughts of a more Disneyesque place of residence fit for Kings, Queens, Princes and Princesses, so I wasn't surprised by her disappointment. She struggled with the climate, understandable if you were born in Southern California, went to Hollywood High School and lived all your life in paradise, so I could forgive her that.

A few months later I am missing Janet and California, so once more to the TWA ticket office on Piccadilly. As I am ascending the escalator to the first-floor ticket office I notice one of the booking agents, who must have just seen the top of my head first, rising up before her, begin reaching into her drawer of blank tickets and start to write out the travel details before I had even arrived at her desk. "Hello again, Mr. Smith. The usual?" Yes please, next Thursday, for a couple of weeks. I would always travel light, with no check in luggage, just an overnight bag. I had plenty of clothes, shoes, toiletries etc. in Hollywood on Beachwood Drive because I was essentially living there half the time. On one occasion I flew to Los Angeles on a near empty Boeing 747. Reason being, in those days during the winter months TWA reduced the number of flights per week due to the seasonal drop in demand. Usually in late March or early April, they would re-instate their full flight schedule. This was the first flight within the full timetable and I don't think TWA had advertised the date correctly because myself and nineteen other people, including the flight crew had the jet all to ourselves. Sit anywhere you like. A flight attendant each. Pure luxury.

Another method of travel to the States in those days would be as a courier. You could travel for free. Businesses that required documents to be delivered the following day between the U.K and America would book a seat on a commercial airline and you would simply be required to occupy the seat and retrieve a sack of mail from the baggage area on arrival, bring it through customs and hand it over to an awaiting company representative. All above board and strictly regulated, and in a pre-internet environment, this was common practice in the world of multi-nationals. For individuals like me, it was as cheap a method of travel as possible. I went to New York a couple of times as a courier, on one occasion being provided with a top floor, Manhattan penthouse apartment for the night, as I was expected to accompany the documents forward to Los Angeles the following day. I made direct trips to Los Angeles about three other times this way.

Perhaps Chris Blackwell was becoming a little uneasy with my regular absences from the studios because he created a job opportunity for Janet in the U.K., having her head up the coordination of cross-pond business for the company. After all, he had already flown me out to L.A. for the day, with Jim Capaldi's latest single, so he knew of our relationship. Besides, it was typical of the thoughtful kindness of the man that he would create a position within the company for Janet, thereby also keeping me closer to the studios, where I was needed and at the same time saving me a small fortune in airfares.

Janet and I took on the rental of a two-bedroom basement flat in St. John's Wood, northwest London, just a short distance from the Abbey Road studios. We travelled to work at different times, but would hang out with Island people together, both at work and socially outside of office hours. No such thing as out of studio hours --- they just operated around the clock. Janet made many friends at Island, not least of all with Suzette Newman, studio manager at Island's Hammersmith studios, The Fallout Shelter. (Suzette would later go on to become Chris' P.A.) Janet and I had lived in St. John's Wood for about a year, it was the summer of 1975 and I was off on my travels again. I was heading to The Manor for a second time.

Nigel Thomas had managed Alexis Korner, Joe Cocker and Ray Davis of The Kinks, so he fulfilled the title of "heavyweight" in no short measure. Later in his life, a year before his death, he had handled the affairs of Morrissey from The Smiths. In an interview with music journalist Tony Parsons for Vox magazine in

1993, Morrissey paid tribute to Nigel Thomas at the manager's funeral in Gloucestershire.

"It has been the most exciting year of my life and the most fruitful," he said. *"I would not have had that year if it had not been for Nigel. It is not a very dignified business, but Nigel managed to make it so. All the things I remember about him are good and happy. I am a reasonably pessimistic person, and he was very optimistic. Everything he said could happen happened, most notably selling out the Hollywood Bowl.*

It was an achievement in which he was entirely instrumental. I was enormously proud of that."

How strange then, that when I mentioned to some industry people that I was off to The Manor to record one of Nigel's bands, Boxer, some strongly recommended I get paid first, don't sign anything, be careful, he is a bit of a villain. I never found him to be so. Quite the opposite, as this tale will tell.

Boxer were formed in 1975 by vocalist Mike Patto and guitarist Ollie Halsall. I had engineered recordings with Mike's previous band, Patto, along with Tony Platt at Basing Street, with Muff Winwood once again producing. Mike's soulful, Cocker-esque style of vocals, along with Ollie's uniquely gifted guitar playing and Muff's relaxed approach to production, had made for happy times in the studio, so I was looking forward to the sessions at The Manor.

On drums, Tony Newman. He had played with Sounds Incorporated, T. Rex, Jeff Beck and David Bowie, so he was no slouch on the skins. On bass, Keith Ellis, who had previously played with Van der Graaf Generator and Juicy Lucy. My fondest memory of Keith from those Manor sessions was him sitting on a stool in the live room next to Mike, sipping on a bottle of Doctor Collis Browne's cough mixture. Potent stuff, due to high levels of opium, but it was Keith's little treat and it cheered him up no end. Until the cry came out from Mike --- "We have a green bass player.

Somebody call a doctor". I peered through the glass from the control room and, yes, Keith had definitely turned a shade of soft lime. A couple of sips of water and a quick walk around the croquet lawn and he was fine.

The recording progressed as all tapes do. A week passes by, and half the album is done. Then comes one of those phone calls that changes everything in your life.

It was Janet calling from London. There had been a slight disaster. A freak cloud burst had resulted in our St. John's Wood flat being flooded and all of the contents being swept into the garden. Seriously. The flash flood of August 14th 1975, centred over Hampstead in north London had taken out the bay window at the front and the French windows at the back. Chairs, tables, books, everything gone. Washed away. Everything, that is, except my beloved TEAC reel to reel four track tape machine and all my tapes which Janet had thoughtfully managed to save. She was phoning from the bedroom, floating on a mattress, holding onto our cat, smoking a cigarette with Suzette, who'd popped over for a visit after work. They were both laughing hysterically. Why not, if it helps?

When Nigel heard of our dilemma, he did what those good men do. He arranged for a car to bring Janet and the cat across the country to join us at The Manor. He moved us into a double room and added Janet (and the cat) to the dining list. Another week and the album was complete. What are you and Janet going to do next? asked Nigel, genuinely concerned. Not sure, got nowhere to live. So Nigel pulled out all the stops and checked us into the luxurious Portobello Hotel in Holland Park. Stay there as long as you need, 'till you figure out what to do next. Oh, and here is another £400 to tide you over. (£400 in 1975 in today's money is about £3k) The band and myself are really pleased with the record, so consider this, a performance related bonus.

So much for the villain. Another kind and thoughtful man. But what *were* we going to do?

We stayed at The Portobello for two weeks, courtesy of Nigel's generosity, by which time we had made a decision. A telephone call was made to our friend in Los Angeles, Bernadette Gorman, who worked for Denny Cordell at the newly established Shelter Records in Hollywood. She said we could come and stay with her in Santa Monica while we look for our own place.

Janet had spent about eighteen months in England, working for Island, catching the bus to work every day, sometimes in the pouring rain and the cold. She never much liked living in England, but made a good show of herself and rarely complained. It was time for me to go back with Janet to her neck of the woods and give life a new start. We would find work. Janet still had contacts in Hollywood, and I would take my guitar, buy a new tape machine and write songs. Become a musician.

I was suffering from recording studio burnout, having recorded over twenty albums in the previous five and a half years and simply needed a break. If I can be forgiven for stealing and modifying part of a Steve Redgrave, Olympic oarsman quote: If you ever see me anywhere near a recording studio again -----. So in the summer of 1975, we left London. No fanfare, just casually slipped away, almost unnoticed. Told a few close friends, but no one seemed to notice. Who was it that said: "We probably wouldn't worry so much about what people thought of us, if we knew how seldom they did"? That was never, it has to be said the case with my close family, as I knew how much they all loved and cared for me, as they had always done, but Mom and Dad must have thought, just as they had when I first went to London with The Great List of Thirty-Eight, that I was crazy! As it happens, I got to visit family in Birmingham more often when I lived six thousand miles away than I ever did living one hundred and twenty miles down the motorway.

The next nine years would be an exciting, eventful roller coaster period in my life and that I was to survive and live to tell the tale is in itself a miracle, thanks again in no small part to my thoughts never being too far away at any one time from my wonderful family in Birmingham. Piccadilly. TWA. Two tickets please, Los Angeles.

--the glorious splendour of Buckingham Palace---

A Christmas Card View of London

In the summer of 1975, the President of the United States of America was Gerald Ford. He had assumed the office of the Presidency as a consequence of Richard Nixon's resignation following the Watergate "dirty tricks" scandal of the early 1970s. Under Ford's presidency, America's involvement in Vietnam was to end and despite the nation's optimism and relief, the country was at the same time suffering its worst economic conditions since The Great Depression, which didn't bode particularly well for a young couple arriving from the U.K about to start a new life together in the U.S.A.

On the positive side, America in the mid-seventies was a relatively easy place to travel to and from. This was a pre-9/11 and Lockerbie world, so security and immigration issues at airports were considerably less restrictive than they are today. Most aircraft hijackings and terrorist activities were taking place in Europe and the Middle East, so the U.S was not only relatively disconnected but also, particularly it has to be said out on the west coast, naively unaware. Santa Monica, California, situated at the far west of the country, with its miles of golden sandy beaches and warm, refreshing on-shore sea breezes, was as beautiful and unsuspectingly safe, pleasant a place to be at this time as anywhere else on earth.

Located approximately eleven miles from downtown L.A., just south of Malibu, Santa Monica has long been a popular coastal resort for British ex-pats. In the mid-seventies, there was a British population of about 30,000, mostly elderly and retired, so it would not be uncommon to see them out bowling, knotted handkerchiefs on head, eating ice-cream and enjoying the quality fish and chips provided by "Ye Olde King's Head" at the end of Santa Monica Boulevard. Founded in 1974, (I believe by a chap called Phil, who came from Birmingham?) this is now a world-renowned restaurant and bar. Yet at the time of my living in L.A. it was simply a place to go after a Sunday morning game of football up at Pepperdine University in the Santa Monica mountains, where you could drink English ale (albeit served too cold), read day old English newspapers, (quite pointless really) eat the best fish and chips (definitely worth it) and listen to English builders, painters and decorators, plumbers and brick-layers, who were working out in California, constantly complain that "it's too hot" or that Americans are "too loud". Another common complaint amongst this disgruntled group of ungrateful individuals would be that there wasn't any English footie on the telly. I was very nearly involved in an altercation with a couple of the lads, when I was about to walk up to them and suggest they "piss-off back to England" only to be wisely advised by a slightly soberer friend of mine that it wasn't worth getting your teeth kicked in for the likes of them.

Our arrival at LAX (Los Angeles International Airport) was as routine as it had always been. Janet took her place in the queue with American nationals and I waited in line with all the foreigners. "Purpose of visit to the United States, Mr. Smith?" queried the customs officer. "Business and pleasure" was my reply, as it had always been. He stamps my passport for a six-week visitor's visa. "Enjoy your stay in the United States and have a nice day Mr. Smith". By now I had collected so many LAX entry stamps on my passport that, unbeknownst to me at the time, I was sowing several seeds of potential discontent with American customs officials, seeds that would, in the very near future, flower into the ugliest and troublesome of weeds.

Janet and I meet up in the arrivals hall, to be greeted by Bernadette and driven the short distance to her Santa Monica apartment. All so matter of fact, as if we were never meant to be anywhere else. Within a couple of weeks, Janet had found herself a job and somewhere for us to live. So simple. So quick and easy. So American. We thanked Bernadette for her generous hospitality and moved into a small but quaint two-bedroom first floor apartment in the Hollywood Hills, just off Franklin Avenue, in between the Hughes supermarket and the Holiday Inn. 2007B, Pinehurst Avenue was to be our home for about eighteen months and the place where the first building blocks of our life together in California were to be laid. We grabbed odds and sods of furniture from Janet's family and friends, car boot and garage sales. We found an old upright piano from somewhere/someone and miraculously managed to drag it up the one flight of stairs and through the narrow front door. Janet bought me a Yamaha acoustic guitar for my 25th birthday in November, so by the end of that year I was playing piano and guitar, writing songs and living the new dream.

What could possibly go wrong?

Janet had easily found employment back at Capitol Records, doing the same thing she had been doing in England for Chris, only this time in reverse, liaising between the Hollywood office and their numerous overseas licensing partners. I had been a frequent visitor to the Capitol Tower building during my visits to Janet on Beachwood Drive. You could walk there from her apartment, which I did on many a sunny morning, that being most mornings because this is Southern California. Walk down the gentle, spotlessly clean hill towards Vine Street, grab an orange for breakfast from an overhanging branch, watch and listen to the water sprinklers and admire the lavish attention paid to the neatly kept lawns by the predominately Hispanic gardeners. Spot Hummingbirds darting between shrubberies. The intoxicating fragrance of the warm morning air --- a perfect mix of orange blossom and catalytic converters. Delicious. And I could make a similar journey from Pinehurst Avenue to The Tower, because it was about equal distance, just a little more to the west. A narrow, steep, tree-lined road leading up to one of the many winding canyons that abound in this part of Hollywood, Pinehurst was as picturesque and secluded a spot as you could hope to find so near to the busyness of Hollywood Boulevard. Lined with assorted small ranch homes, Mediterranean and Spanish Mission style inspired bungalows with their terra cotta roofs, cactus plants, avocado trees, laurel, fragrant lilac and sage (and of course, the orange blossom) the location of our new home together was nothing short of perfect. From the bottom of the avenue, at the corner of Franklin, you could see the top floors of the famous Capitol Tower and each time I would approach the building it was still with the same sense of awe as the first time back in 1972 when I was touring with Head, Hands and Feet. Looking upward at the sunshade awnings that cover every floor, I was always picturing Dad's 78 p.m. records back in Birmingham. Designed by Welton Becket and built in 1955 the thirteen storey, earthquake resistant building was the world's first circular office block. Nicknamed "The House That Nat Built", because of Nat King Cole's immense financial contribution to the success of Capitol Records, the building coincidently resembles a stack of records. This was not, however, the intention of the architects, but has become somewhat of a Hollywood urban myth. (www.emporis.com)

Once inside this landmark building you are at first simply stunned by the array of silver, gold and platinum discs. Hundreds of them, floor to ceiling, on every single floor. And as you walk around, literally around the offices you are reminded that the building is as circular on the inside as it appears on the outside. Janet used to roller-skate around and between the different departments, as if each floor were a roller-rink. This was representative of her somewhat unorthodox, outgoing style, which was a part of her nature that drew me to her in the first place. She tied feathers in her blue and green streaked long, shiny auburn hair, wore torn Levi jeans and sandals most of the time and drove a small yellow two door Toyota. She swore a lot, smoked a little pot now and then, especially when listening to music and could only be described as a real Lady of The Canyon. What we in the U.K might refer to simply as "a bit of a hippie". I was a shy, reservedly quiet Englishman so we were a perfect match and the people where Janet worked loved seeing us together. We became, in their eyes, somewhat of a Hollywood item.

I was introduced to many of the key players at Capitol Records, the guys and girls who ran the various departments. With no diaries to fall back on, I can only remember their first names: Denis (head of the press department), John (art) Carter (A+R) Stu (studio manager). There was an older, well-dressed lady who handled studio bookings and I wish I could remember her name because she listened to one of my songs (co-written with Richard Reeve back in London) and gave me a day's free studio time. In Capitol Records' studio in Hollywood! The Sutherland Brothers and Quiver were in town and I got them to come along and play on the track. Capitol passed on the demo.

One evening out in the car park Janet introduced me to music producer David Foster, who had just parked his car as he was working that evening at Capitol's studio. Most importantly, he was a rising star on the Hollywood music scene and was to go on to have 16 Grammy Award winning hits with the likes of Natalie Cole, Whitney Houston, Rod Stewart, Madonna and Celine Dion. Janet knew this man was going places and her logic was that it would be good for my career to make friends and mix. After all, this is Hollywood and it's what we do here. She would bring celebrities over for dinner, unannounced, people like singer Dobie Gray, who'd had a big hit in 1973 with *Drift Away* and in 1975 he helped decorate our Xmas tree. Bob Harris, the English presenter of the highly rated, late night television series, The Old Grey Whistle

Test, enjoyed a plate of Janet's Grandmother's Sicilian recipe spaghetti Bolognese. I was frequently invited out to dinner with Capitol executives, most memorably one evening to the famous Musso and Frank bar and restaurant on Hollywood Boulevard. Founded in 1919 as "Francois", the restaurant changed its name in 1923 and it was and still is frequented by all the Hollywood stars. I sat next to Janet across the table from Bhaskar Menon, the CEO of Capitol Records. Indian born, Menon was a world renown music industry executive who, as chairman of E.M.I. Group's worldwide operations, had moved to Los Angeles to rescue a struggling Capitol Industries Inc., in which E.M.I. held a majority interest. His motto for his employees was simple: "*Uncompromising excellence in what you do goes without saying. We expect more than that.*" (New Musical Express, 1978).

I was touching hands with some of Hollywood's elite inner circle. Such a promising start.

Despite the rejection from Capitol of my demonstration tape, (no taste in music these record company people) I continued to write songs in my Hollywood apartment. Only they were never really proper songs, just meandering, predictable chord progressions with the occasional suspect melodic accompaniment and even less lyrical content. Here's an example: *"I put my key in the door, walk in the room and find myself saying, "Is anybody home?"* Complete clichéd rubbish! The more I persisted with this futile pursuit the more frustrated I became. Surely, with all my years of recording some great songwriters, spending hours and hours in the studio being a party to many master classes in this process of song writing, I should see that I wasn't cut out for it. Didn't have the necessary talent. Stick to being a recording engineer. Stay with what you are good at. The signposts were clear. There was plenty of writing on the wall --- I just didn't want to read it.

So I just got pissed instead. Pissed as in drunk, not the American "pissed" as in annoyed, although I was becoming somewhat annoyed with the world as well. Should have been more annoyed with myself. I had mastered the craft of drinking and smoking heavily and to excess back in London and here in Los Angeles, with the addition of cocaine to my list of dependencies, I was to excel. I would stay up all night, blindly determined to come up with a song idea, mumbling incoherently into the microphone, drinking, snorting and puffing 'till dawn. Janet would arise early morning, off to work. Me, crashed out until the middle of the afternoon, whereby I would start the whole silly nonsense again. This went on for a few months until a very loud penny dropped. I was broke and I would need to find a job.

On reflection, I can now see how disappointed Janet must have been with me. After all, she had introduced me to so many important people and I hadn't responded in a way she might have approved of. And I didn't even need to take the short trip down the hill into Hollywood to seek a career opportunity. Across the road from our apartment lived a successful L.A session keyboard player, Brock Walsh. He'd worked with The Pointer Sisters, Karla Bonoff, and Jennifer Warnes and had a beautiful baby-grand piano in his front room. I would longingly watch from my window and enviously listen to him play. Most days he would be visited by other musicians, not least of all songwriter and Asylum records' artist Andrew Gold, who regularly showed up with country-rock singer, Linda Ronstadt. Gold was born in Burbank, California and followed his parents into show business. His mother was singer Marni Nixon who famously provided voice-overs for the likes of Natalie Wood in *West-Side Story*, Deborah Kerr in *The King and I* and Audrey Hepburn in *My Fair Lady*. His father was Ernest Gold, the Austrian born, Academy Award-winning composer for the movie *Exodus*. (Daily Telegraph Obituary, 2011).

Gold played many of the instruments on Linda Ronstadt's 1974 breakthrough album *Heart Like a Wheel* and on her following four albums. He went on to record his own albums, most notably his 1976 offering *What's Wrong with this Picture* on Asylum records, which featured his massive hit *Lonely Boy*. He was most probably sitting around the piano working on that album with my neighbour, Brock, and with Linda, who was always there with them. But I just couldn't summon up the courage to go across the street, knock on his door and introduce myself. Didn't have the confidence. Perhaps I was reluctant to present myself to them as an engineer, despite, or even because of my fairly impressive C.V. from my Island experiences in London. Studio burnout had taken its toll on me. I longed to be part of their world as a musician and that was never going to happen. The standard was set far too high for me to be involved on that level and I must have known that, so I stayed away, drank more beer, puffed and mumbled some more.

Island Records had very plush offices up near the strip at the smart end of Sunset Boulevard. Chris Blackwell was in town and invited me to meet the Los Angeles team. He introduced me to Lionel Conway, head of publishing, the man who had played The Sutherland Brothers original recording of *Sailing* to his football playing buddy, Rod Stewart. Lionel and I talked football and he invited me to come along to the running track in Beverley Hills where the predominately ex-pats regularly played on Wednesday evenings. Also, I met Spencer Davis, who was doing some A+R for the label. Spencer had achieved considerable success playing alongside Steve and Muff Winwood, and with drummer Pete York back in the day with the band he had formed in Birmingham, The Spencer Davis Group. *Keep on Running*, *I'm a Man*, *Gimme Some Lovin'* and *Somebody Help Me* had all been massive hits and here I was in Los Angeles finally getting to meet one of my musical heroes. I told him about the leather brief case from my old school days, which had his named blazoned across it and he was flattered and a little embarrassed. I liked him all the more for that. We became good friends and I would soon be engineering for Spencer on a number of albums.

Chris Blackwell also introduced me to Kent Duncan, who ran his own studios, Kendun Recorders, in Burbank. He was a very likeable man and I spent a couple of weeks at his studio, recording, if I remember correctly, a band called Stray Dog, featuring on guitar my old buddy from Island/Heartbreaker days, "Snuffy" Walden. But my reluctance to set foot in a recording studio again persisted and I probably turned my back on what might have been a very lucrative association with that particular studio. However, an opportunity came my way that I simply couldn't decline.

Muscle Shoals, Alabama producer Steve Smith, who I had worked with back in London on the Jim Capaldi album *Short Cut Draw Blood* approached me to engineer for him on the next Robert Palmer album. Robert had already recorded two albums for Island and expectations in 1976 for this, his third, were high. We were booked into Clover studios on the corner of Santa Monica and Vine for three weeks. Steve assembled a collection of some of L. A's musical elite to play on this record: Richie Hayward, drums (Littlefeat), Chuck Rainey, bass (Steely Dan, Quincy Jones, Aretha Franklin), Paul Barrere, guitar (Littlefeat), Bill Payne, keyboards (J.J. Cale, Bryan Adams, Doobie Brothers, James Taylor, Littlefeat) and Jodie Linscott, percussion (Elton John, The Who, Eric Clapton, Tom Jones). Also on drums, Jeff Porcaro (Steely Dan, Joe Cocker, Hall and Oates, Pink Floyd, Paul McCartney, Lionel Ritchie). And of course, the charming, sophisticated gentleman himself, Robert Palmer on vocals. In the coming weeks, I was to experience the absolute electrifying, exciting and terrifying madness of studio life in Los Angeles, typical of the mid-seventies music scene in Hollywood. The vast amounts of alcohol and marijuana that were to be consumed would only be supplanted by the excessive use of an extraordinarily enormous quantity of that cruellest of drug mistresses, cocaine. Not by all, it must be said. Some were more sensible than others, particularly Robert, who was by far and away much more in control than many. Let's just say that Steve, myself and Ritchie stood shoulders, or should I say noses above everyone else as we attempted our level best over the next couple of weeks at single-handedly propping up the economy of South America.

I had first come across this devilish substance back at Basing Street on the Stephen Stills sessions when I was assisting Bill Halverson. Not Bill, it must be said, but some of the participants in the recording of that album were enthusiastic users. Then later, on the John Martyn sessions, especially during that epic 60+ hours studio adventure, when John, Danny and I were to be a testimony to the edict that "cocaine is God's way of saying you have more money than sense". So by the time I got to Clover studios in Hollywood, I was already a pathetic wretch of an addict. And if anyone ever tells you that cocaine is not addictive, then they haven't tried nearly hard enough to enjoy themselves. If you were ever fortunate (or rather, unfortunate) enough to acquire the finest slivers of Peruvian flake cocaine or the crystallised iridescent beauty of the Bolivian variety, as opposed to some cheap, off the street imposter of contraband, half cut with Mannitol or some other such laxative, then you will have experienced the most powerfully mind altering, confidence building, high energy induced feeling of utter joy.

The body and mind can never forget that.

Nor should it be forgotten that the destructive effects of an addiction, be it alcohol, cocaine or beyond can only serve, in the long run, to destroy its beholder. The constant, endlessly pathetic pursuit of the next high, the next fix. Perish the thought of ever being without your "go to" substance. The lengths to which irrational behaviour will be stretched. One example (of many) of my own reckless conduct, whilst under the influence of drugs, was on one of the Robert Palmer sessions. It must have been about four in the morning. We had run out of coke. Aagh! Desperate men in desperate times require desperate actions. Somebody needs to drive over to Lenny's place and get some stuff. There was a whip round and between us, we scraped together about a hundred bucks. All we needed now was some drunken, stoned, foolhardy mug to get behind the wheel of a car and drive the twenty-mile round trip to North Hollywood.

Steve threw me the keys to his Cordoba and I was gone.

An hour later I was, miraculously, back at the studio with "the stuff" and normal service was resumed. However, it wasn't possible to conceal from Steve that I had managed to make a meter long scratch down the left-hand side of his beloved Chrysler. This I had done when squeezing out of the studio car park in a rush to get to Lenny. A few weeks later, Steve presented me with a copy of the four-hundred-and-fifty-dollar repair bill, this amount being deducted from my engineering fee. That proved to make it one of my most expensive cocaine deals. However, if the Los Angeles Police Department (L.A.P.D.) had caught me behind the wheel of a car that morning, drunk and high on cocaine, the price would have been immeasurably higher.

Steve and I shared other, more pleasurable and considerably less catastrophic experiences. Like the time he took me along to a training session with the Los Angeles Rams football team. Steve knew of my love of sport, and I had decided that, when in Rome, support your local football team, so I had become a fan of The Rams. After all, this team had won four straight NFC West championships between 1973 and 1976 and was to go on to win three more consecutively. For those not conversant with this beautiful game, you have to imagine a cross between rugby and chess. It epitomises the perfect blend of brute force and mathematical savvy. A precision sport that combines physical fluidity with intellectual prowess. What's more, it's fun to watch.

I was introduced by Steve to their head coach, Chuck Knox, star quarterback Jack Youngblood and several other players. This team were the U.S. equivalent of British football's Manchester United and I was very privileged to be amongst them. I was most impressed by the depth and technical teachings of the coaching staff. A team of three were working with the kickers, lining up different conversion scenarios within varying field positions. The quarter back coaching staff were placing fifty cent coins on the field, at ten yard intervals and I watched in amazement how accurate the throwing arm can be as the coins bounced up in the air when the ball hit them, twenty, thirty, forty or fifty yards away.

Steve also hired me to engineer a 1977 soft-rock album for Elektra Records with American duo Paklameredith (Jimmy Packla and Larry Meredith), again at Clover Studios. This time, Steve pulled out all the stops in terms of his musical connections by employing Steve Cropper, Booker "T" and "Duck" Dunn to play on the record. These three were essentially the backbone of the successful Stax Records house band Booker "T" and the MGs, the guys who had put Southern and Memphis soul music on the industry map. They had played on records for Wilson Pickett, Otis Redding and Sam and Dave and enjoyed their own individual glory with the number one Billboard instrumental hit *Green Onions*. My most lasting memories are of the extremely laid-back, un-hurried approach these musicians employed, and who at all times were polite and respectful of the studio environment. How quickly and effortlessly they learnt the chord progressions and the song arrangements. Consummate professionals at the top of their game. Time spent in the recording studio with musicians of this calibre would be a welcome addition to any recording engineer's C.V. and, despite the album dipping into relative obscurity, I was once again privileged to have worked alongside such giants of the music industry.

On another occasion, Janet and I spent an evening with Steve and his close friend Isaac Tigrett, the American businessman, up at Isaac's sumptuous Malibu home. (Lots of cocaine that night, Peruvian flake, I recall). Tigrett will be best known for starting up, along with British restaurateur Peter Morton, the Hard Rock Café chain of American diners, the first one being in London's fashionable Mayfair, in 1971. Steve and I used to regularly frequent the Hard Rock Cafe in London, especially after a long day in the studio together. Waltzing passed the long queues, we enjoyed V.I.P. status and instant access. We would take along cassette tapes of the day's studio mixes and get one of the staff members to play them out over the speakers in the café. This was as good a way as any to check out the quality of the sound and the integrity of the mix, not to mention looking around to see if any of the customers were tapping their feet.

Steve and I were to work together again at the end of 1976, back in the U.K. The album was *Rough Diamond* and featured David Byron, ex-Uriah Heep vocalist, Clem Clempson, guitarist from Humble Pie, bassist Willie Bath (the Wild Angels, Champion) and former Wings drummer Geoff Britton. Co-engineered by myself, Phil Brown (ex-Olympic but by now a senior Island engineer) with Dave Hutchins assisting, these were the sessions I referred to earlier when we were under a deadline to deliver the album to Island, so we're utilising all three Island studios of the day: The Fallout Shelter Hammersmith, Basing Street and the mobile recording truck parked in the icy car park on British Grove. It was the winter of 1976.

I was flown to London and booked in to The Royal Garden Hotel in Kensington. Steve never did things in half measure and I was pleased to be staying in such luxurious five-star surroundings. It was just a few days before Christmas and I remember looking from my hotel room window one morning, out across a snow-covered Kensington Gardens, thinking how beautiful London looked. The wide walkway leading down to Kensington High Street. People wrapped up in winter clothing, walking with their dogs (also wrapped up in winter clothing) couples holding mitten-covered hands, kids on skateboards and bicycles taking advantage of the slippery paths to put on even more heroic displays of skill and courage. The snow-covered tops of the trees and the iced over ponds. A Christmas card view of London.

   Yet despite this idyllic scene, I was thousands of miles from home, missing the Capitol tower and couldn't wait to get back to my Christmas tree in California.

---a snow covered Kensington Gardens, ---

-Many Millennia Before-

The Magic Castle, located at 7001, Franklin Avenue is an exclusive nightclub for magicians and magic enthusiasts. Built in 1909 as a Chateau style mansion by philanthropist Rollin B. Lane, the mansion remained in the Lane family until 1955, when it was sold to its current owners, the Glover family. In 1961 the building was leased to Milt and Bill Larsen who converted it to its present state and they opened for business as The Magic Castle in 1963. (Los Angeles Office of Historic Resources)

Living on Pinehurst we were only a stone's throw away and often thought of going there for a meal and to see a magic show, but because of the selective nature of the clientele, limited for the most part to members of "The Magic Circle", we could only dream of ever entering this legendary palace of the supernatural. Unless, of course, there was to be some external assistance from one of the less mysterious forces of nature.

The force in question was to be a traffic accident.

I was partaking of my customary morning walk (usually to clear my head after another night of heavy drinking, puffing, snorting and mumbling) along Franklin Avenue to buy a newspaper from the Holiday Inn when I heard the almighty thump as the sporty white convertible Mercedes crashed into the back of the sedate black Lincoln Continental. The Merc' reversed, pulling pieces of the rear bumper and tail lights with it, drove around the damaged Linc' and sped off. I took a mental snapshot of the licence plate number and approached the shaken occupants. The two elderly gentlemen who were sitting at the front wrote down the number and thanked me. We exchanged phone numbers and addresses, for purposes of insurance claims and just before they drove off, one of them handed me his business card. As I waved goodbye, I was reading the card and observed the somewhat disabled Lincoln turning right into the driveway of the Magic Castle. The card had a picture of the chateau, and his occupation was stated as "magician".

About two weeks later, a letter dropped through our door, with a Magic Castle logo in the top left-hand corner. Inside were two tickets for a meal and a show.

Another road accident, this one less beneficial, happened one afternoon when I was sitting at the piano, mumbling away as usual. I had become the proud owner of a high-mileage, 1963 Dodge Polaro. A beautiful gas-guzzling beast of V8 proportions, white bodywork with the red and silver plastic moulded interior, this classic of American automobiles was described in the sales literature of its day as "the luxury land yacht", and it certainly did seem to sail down the freeways. Janet had borrowed the car to do some shopping, and I heard the distinctive sound of the returning Dodge as she approached the apartment up the hill from Franklin. As was customary, due to the narrowness of the road, it was necessary to drive to the top of Pinehurst, where there was enough room to turn around and come back down the hill and park. Only this time, Janet didn't park the car. I heard it as it came back down the mountain, expecting to listen to her slow down and pull over. But she didn't stop. Out of the front room window, I saw the car speed past, back down the hill, out of control. Next came the sound of a parking bollard being ripped out of the ground as the Dodge shuddered to a halt some hundred yards down the hill, near the bottom, at the junction of the main road.

Diabetics take note. If, after you have taken your prescribed morning dose of insulin, you don't eat anything, then you are likely to drop into a coma by lunchtime. If you are behind the wheel of a car when this happens, the results could be fatal. Thank goodness for the bollard at the bottom of the hill, or else Janet (and my Dodge) would have careered across the main road into traffic. I had always known about Janet's type one diabetes, and she had told me what to expect in the event of an insulin reaction. Carbohydrates are required quickly. Sugar is best, sweets or spoonfuls of honey. From that day onward, I would religiously and repeatedly ask her, usually to her annoyance, but if only for my peace of mind, in the morning, and again at night, "Have you taken your insulin?" and "Don't forget to eat something".

The Dodge proved impractical, due in part to its size and weight, making it difficult to drive, especially for a lady, so we traded up to a more contemporary Ford Granada; power steering, fuel efficient, etc. I looked online the other day at 1963 Dodge Polara. One was on sale for $65,000.

Ford Granadas are ten a penny, and diabetes is on the increase.

In the summer of '76, I made a short trip to England to visit family and friends—any excuse to fly. We are inbound to Heathrow and approaching Shannon on the west coast of Ireland. As the westernmost airport between Europe and the Americas, Shannon had been used as a refuelling stop during the early days of trans-Atlantic flying. Today, its primary role is as the first and last point of radio communication between ground control and pilots travelling across the Atlantic to and from Europe. The usual flight path from the U.K. outbound to the west coast of America is via the "polar route", which will take you on a northerly path up the spine of Britain, over Scotland and across Iceland and the southern tip of Greenland, rarely over Shannon. However, inbound to the U.K. from the west will often find you approaching over Shannon. I know all this because I flew so many times to and from America, and I am an air travel geek.

After a long-haul flight from Los Angeles of about ten or eleven hours, it is a welcoming sight to see the verdant grass of Ireland

34,000 feet below, knowing that you will now be making your final descent into the south-east of England.

Only in 1976 was this not the case. I looked out of the left-hand side of the Boeing only to be startled by the sight of the brown, parched earth below. We must be being diverted to southern Spain, I thought. Terrorist alert at Heathrow? Bad weather? Nobody had informed us over the p.a., unless, of course, I had been asleep. In any event, it certainly wasn't the familiar plush, green landscape I had seen from the air so many times before. Not to worry, we will soon be on the ground and all will become clear. As we got nearer to Heathrow, I began to recognise familiar landmarks: The Severn Estuary, Salisbury Plain, the Thames Valley, and Windsor Castle; the holding stack at Ockham, circling awaiting a slot. Peel off to the north-east, turn left over the City of London and follow the river and the A4. Final approach, lock on to I.L.S. (instrument landing system). Runway 27 left, seven miles out, one hundred and fifty knots, fifteen hundred feet, gear down, land, taxi.

Heathrow.

But once outside, driving into town along the M4, I was to witness the damage caused by the most prolonged period of intense heat (by British standards) as a consequence of the hottest summer average temperature since records began.

This was the summer of 1976.

The verges along the motorway were strewn with dry tumbleweed. The fields were barren and straw-like, and the reservoirs and lakes that surround Heathrow were almost empty. The drought was at its most severe in August of 1976, when parts of the southwest went 45 days without any rain in July and August. As the hot and dry weather continued, devastating heath and forest fires broke out in parts of Southern England. Fifty thousand trees were destroyed at Hurn Forest in Dorset. Crops were badly hit, with £500 million worth of crops failing. Food prices subsequently increased by 12%. (thisiswiltshire.co.uk)

But these unusual events were not to be alone in making my visit to England that summer a remarkable one. The heat was on the rise in Notting Hill and not for meteorological reasons.

After visiting my family in Birmingham, where all the talk was about the weather, I returned to London. I dropped in first of all to Island Records in St. Peter's Square to say hello to Trevor Wyatt, studio manager and Suzette Newman, who was now working for Chris as his full time P.A. Chris once again showed immense generosity and gave me the keys to his luxury penthouse apartment high above the Basing Street studios, where I stayed for a week or so. It was from this vantage point that I was to witness, first hand, scenes of riotous violence never before, or at least not in my time, seen on the streets of West London. It was August and the traditional annual bank holiday festivities of the Notting Hill Carnival were to end in tears.

The history of the Notting Hill Carnival can be traced back to 1959, where a "Caribbean Carnival" was first held at St. Pancras Town Hall. Even before that, the idea of carnival in the U.K. goes way back. As David Dabydeen, Guyanese writer and academic, states:

"Carnival is not alien to British culture. Bartholomew Fair and Southwark Fair in the 18th century were moments of great festivity and release. There was juggling, pickpocketing, whoring, drinking, masquerade — people dressed up as the Archbishop of Canterbury and indulged in vulgar acts."

It is undoubtedly the case that the Notting Hill Carnival, since it first flowed through the streets of the Royal Borough of Kensington and Chelsea in 1966, revitalised our spirit of carnival.

Unfortunately, however, in that summer of '76, tensions between black youths and the police were at a turning point, due in no small part to the correctly perceived view of the Caribbean community youth that they were the victims of undue police harassment. In any event, on the evening of Monday, 30th August 1976, it all kicked off.

Looking out of the penthouse window from my privileged view above Basing Street, I first remember seeing three policemen crouching down, holding galvanised metal dustbin lids above their heads as bricks and stones rained down on them. Not something you see every day on the streets of London. The BBC reported:

1976: Notting Hill Carnival ends in riot:

More than 100 police officers had to be taken to hospital after clashes at the Notting Hill Carnival in west London. Most were released after treatment but at least 26 have been detained overnight for observation or further treatment. Around 60 carnival-goers also needed hospital treatment after the clashes which led to the arrest of at least 66 people. The trouble is believed to have started after police tried to arrest a pickpocket near Portobello Road on the main carnival route. Several black youths went to the pickpocket's aid and within minutes the disturbance escalated. The police were attacked with stones and other missiles. They armed themselves with dustbin lids, milk crates and wire fencing and charged the rioters.

At one stage a group of black youths were seen moving up Westbourne Park road smashing windows. Gangs of white youths were also said to have been involved in the violence. One witness, Raymond Hunter, who lives in Westbourne Park Road said he saw a police van set alight. "The two policemen managed to get out of the van and fled. The gang then turned the van over and set fire to it," Mr. Hunter said. Police sealed off roads and closed pubs in the area as well as shutting down Ladbroke Grove underground station in an attempt to contain the violence. In the past, the carnival - now in its 10th year - has been largely peaceful in spite of tensions with police. A member of the Notting Hill Carnival Development Committee, Selwyn Baptiste said they had been optimistic after the first day of the festival passed off peacefully.

"We had no reason to suppose it would be any different today. This was supposed to be about fun and love - not violence," Mr. Baptiste said.

I switched on the television and saw wider reports of the same images I had seen first-hand as I looked out of the window. There was a commotion taking place outside the main entrance of the studio so I went downstairs to investigate. People on the street were banging on the door, pleading to be allowed in, for their own safety. A number of Island staff, including some of the artists (John Martyn and Chris Wood I recall, amongst others) were assembled in the reception area. We were allowing people to come inside to shelter from the street violence, as if we were some sort of U.N. peace-keeping base camp! I went back upstairs and telephoned the family in Birmingham. I spoke to my Dad who was watching the events on the family television. I described to him the scenes I was witnessing, live, as if I were a war correspondent on some foreign frontline. It was all both alarming and surreal. Most definitely time to return to the relative peace and quiet of Los Angeles.

Our Santa Monica friend Bernadette was working at Shelter Records in Hollywood,, and she suggested Janet come and work with her at the label. Janet was looking for a new challenge away from Capitol, so this was ideal. Founded by Tulsa, Oklahoma keyboard player Leon Russell (the guy on the mellotron in Studio One) and Buenos Aires born record producer Denny Cordell, the label was situated along the less fashionable end of Sunset Boulevard, nearer to downtown. Not the velvety manicured lawns of Sunset on the palm tree lined approaches to Beverley Hills, where Island had offices, this end of Sunset is a tangled mass of liquor stores, tattoo parlours, beat-up old Chevys parked outside pool halls and Budweiser bars. Infinitely more interesting by virtue of its authenticity, I took an instant liking to this part of Los Angeles.

Located in a funky, single-storey wooden building, with its recording studios in the basement, there was plenty of character not only in the ramshackle premises but also in the whole set-up of the Shelter business. Denny had a very relaxed, informal approach to his artists and his staff, not immeasurably different to the vibe at Island. The label was to enjoy early success with J.J. Cale, Freddie King, Phoebe Snow, Willis Alan Ramsey and, most importantly, Tom Petty and the Heartbreakers. By the time Janet arrived on the scene, this band was well down the road with the recording of their debut album. I would hang out at the label, get to meet the guys, and listen to early versions of the tracks as they were coming down the pipeline. I must admit I was hoping to get a chance to work in the studio with them, but they already had their production team in place, so that was never going to happen. I did, however, work with the guitarist, Mike Campbell and the keyboard player, Benmont Tench, on sessions at later dates.

The album was being recorded in Shelter's own basement studios. One morning, after dropping Janet off at work, I was pouring myself a cup of coffee in reception. Janet, who had been down to the studio to collect some paperwork, came over to me with an excited grin all over her face. "You gotta come and see this," she said, leading me by the hand downstairs to the studio. Outside, looking into the rubbish tip of a garden was a dead tree, its bare branches completely covered with crushed empty beer cans; there must have been a hundred. It was a beer-can tree.

But that was only the beginning of this early morning visual feast of the extraordinary. We walked into the studio kitchen area only to find the walls, floor, ceiling, sink and taps, fridge, all the doors and handles completely covered in aluminium foil. Same in the studio control room. The desk, the speakers, floor to ceiling. And the live room. Microphones and stands, headphones, absolutely EVERYTHING.

We were enclosed inside an aluminium world.

An example of studio boredom taken to a hitherto unknown zenith. The complete collapse of rational judgement and common sense, almost certainly created with chemical assistance, but despite, or even because of that, the album went gold and launched the band's career. My favourite track off the album is a song aptly called, *Breakdown*.

After only a couple of months back in Los Angeles I received a call from London requesting the services of my engineering skills, for a once in a lifetime trip to North Africa. Island had been approached by former theatrical agent and film production impresario Emilio "Mim" Scala with an idea to record an album of North African Dervish music, as performed by the ancient Saharan tribe of the Ganoua. These musicians can trace their music back across the Muslim world to its roots in Sudan and as an expression of religious celebration is believed to have magical and healing powers. To add to the cultural music mix, Mim enrolled Ghanaian conga player Reebop Kwakuh Bah to come along. I had recorded Reebop on many occasions in London; he was the "go to" conga player on any and all sessions, thanks in no small part to his wonderful work with Steve Winwood and the band Traffic. I have a sneaking suspicion that it was Reebop who had recommended me to engineer on this project. On a number of occasions in the studio he had complimented me on my studio style; "You have good rhythm and always hear the detail" he used to say. Most kind, Reebop and thank you.

After telephone conversations with London regarding dates, my fee, location and the approach we were going to take to recording on location in Tangier, Morocco, it was decided that I should bring along my trusty TEAC four track reel to reel tape machine. We were going to keep the recording simple, just four microphones plugged directly into the inputs on the back of the machine, so no mixing desk and no outboard equipment. Any equalisation, compression or reverb would be done post-production back in London.

Island put me up at the familiar surroundings of The Portobello Hotel, until such time as we were ready to depart. I was accompanied on the British Airways flight to Tangier by Island maintenance engineer, Chow. An Anglo Chinese technical wizard, Chow was to come along to supervise the set-up of the recording environment in what would prove to be challenging conditions. We flew at night and on arrival I could just make out in the dark my TEAC being gently handled onto a luggage trolley and was much relieved at its safe transit. As Chow and I descended the wheeled-up steps onto the tarmac of the African Continent we each responded, unrehearsed, by kissing the ground! This was after all, we agreed, where many millennia before, we had both come from.

We travelled by chauffeur-driven car from the airport, through the dimly lit city of Tangier and north towards the Mediterranean. Mim greeted us at the palace gates. A short journey along the driveway and there it stood in all its magnificent splendour. The palace where we would be staying for the next ten days was somewhat of a crumbling ruin, a shadow of its no doubt glorious past. Still, nonetheless it appeared majestic, towering above us in the North African evening sky. It was huge! As are, I suppose, most palaces and this one would have impressed even a sceptical Californian lady who most definitely would have made derogatory comparisons with a certain palace in London. But how on earth Mim had managed to find this unique location, only he would know. He had, I later learned, spent some considerable time in the '60's living in this part of the world, so he would have real estate connections. He brought along, as co-producer, Island film director Richard "Dickie" Jobson, whom I knew from Basing Street days with Bob Marley. Dickie had managed Bob from 1973 to 1975, as well as Jimmy Cliff and Toots Hibbert (Toots and the Maytals). He would later be most remembered as the writer/director for the 1982 masterpiece of Jamaican film, *Countryman*. Shown at the Cannes Film Festival the movie has gone on to become a cult classic.

Back in the palace for our first night, suitably wined and dined, I retired to one of the many bedrooms. As I drifted away I couldn't help but notice a strange wave like movement on the wall opposite. It appeared as a dark wide shadow, twisting and curling its way from the floor to the ceiling. I got out of bed to investigate and upon closer inspection, I could make out a sea of red ants, winding their way up from the wooden floorboards and out through the crumbling, ornate plasterwork of the ceiling. Tens of thousands of them, in constant motion. I climbed back into bed and watched them, hypnotised, dreaming of what might come tomorrow.

The first thing Chow and I did was to check that the tape machine was operating correctly. With suitable transformers and electrical cabling in place, we switched her on, loaded a reel of blank, quarter inch tape onto the spools and pressed play. Oh dear. It very soon became apparent that the voltage coming from the mains supply of the palace was unstable. You could see the spools slowing down, then speeding up, sometimes even grinding to an almost complete stop. The fact that the house lights were also going up and down in brightness might have been a clue. What to do? Chow did some rough calculations on a scrap of paper and concluded that battery power was the only way to go. So off we went to the marketplace. A six-foot Chinaman and a five foot eight blonde-haired Brummie, walking around the Kasbah searching for batteries. Not in the slightest bit conspicuous! We were immediately seized upon by a couple of young Arab boys who never left our side. Every day that we went there for more batteries they appeared, as if by magic, which it probably was. But bless them, because they found us all the batteries we needed. Most likely, in the next eight or nine days we bought every battery available in Tangier, because the two boys made sure we never ran out. Chow gave them some money and I bought a camel leather bag from one of them and they were happy with the deal. Chow taped together a long cardboard tube and stacked the batteries one on top of the other, to create the correct electrical conditions so that recording could proceed. Chow returned to London after the first week and left me with a pile of batteries, a basic circuit diagram and two slightly confused young Arab boys who said they missed the Chinese man and hoped he would return soon.

The large, marble-floored dining room, with the enormous "sit-in" fireplace, was chosen as the recording space. It was early evening and there was a chill in the air. Fires were lit and carpets were spread across the floors to help warm the room and dampen the acoustics. Reebop set up his congas and as we awaited the arrival of the Ganoua musicians, he started to play. Right on cue, the Arabs arrived, complete with their traditional instruments, the likes of which I had never seen, let alone recorded before. Gimbris, three stringed plucked lutes covered in animal skin; Kocobars, or Karkabas, castanet like bells; reed flutes known as Nais and finally handheld drums of varying sizes. The drummers and the Gimbri players sat themselves immediately in front of the fireplaces, warming and tuning their instruments. There was a lot of laughter and derisory pointing of fingers at Reebop's conga drums, which they all seemed to agree were far too loud, so Reebop obliged and played with a lighter touch. I couldn't understand a word that was being said and I doubt Reebop could either, but a mixed soup of West-African and Arabic words were swirling around the room amidst many smiles and much merriment. I imagined the Arabs were winding up the Ghanaian; "Call those drums?! This is a real drum!" as one of the Ganouas struck his drum at the same time as dancing and spinning it wildly in the air. The Gimbri players were already swapping "guitar riffs" and soon the drummers were all joining in. The sound was so excitingly hypnotic that I immediately put the TEAC into record, feeling pleased with myself that I had set up the microphones earlier in the day.

The musicians played for a couple of hours and it was time to eat. Huge cauldrons of piping hot food were brought into the room, prepared by an army of Moroccan chefs hired by Mim for the duration. Handfuls of lemony couscous, mixed with chopped Medjool dates, dipped into the spicy goat, mutton and chicken casseroles, washed down with gallons of sweet, minty green tea. I had set up a basic playback system so that whilst we ate we could listen back to what had been recorded earlier in the evening. Judging by the looks of astonishment on their weathered Arab faces, I was convinced they had never heard themselves being reproduced from a tape machine before. Pipes were lit and a smoke of marijuana flower top seeds was enjoyed by all. From what I could glean from the conversation, with the help of Mim's street Arabic, the pipes used by these men were special family heirlooms, passed down from father to son and were as important a part of the smoking ritual as the herb itself. I thought of my Rasta friends back in London. A kindred calm wisdom of brotherhood, accompanied in no short measure by almost continuous laughter and a sense of utter joy.

Each sunny morning, we would sit on the sloping lawn outside on the front terrace, overlooking the sparkling blue Mediterranean, speakers facing out into the garden, playing back the music from the night before. We would enjoy a breakfast of toasted Moroccan crusty cumin bread with jam, pan-fried semolina flatbreads and more mint tea, served to us by young, smartly dressed Arab boys. I can see Mim now, lying back on his recliner, sun on his face, glowing with pride at what was being achieved. That evening, we would do it all again. The Ghanaian and the Arabs improvising and jamming on rhythms, riffs and trance-like melodies. The album was to be titled *Trance*, and no wonder.

One morning after an early breakfast on the lawn I explored the surrounding rocky hillside, watching the wandering goat herdsmen in their white robes, Fathers' pipes stuck neatly in their belts, next to their leather pouches of marijuana. This timeless motion of man and beast was abruptly interrupted, when I was suddenly chased from the field by a large adult bull who possessed no pipe and was quite unconcerned about timeless motion, etc.

Today, I look back on that time spent with those tribesmen who came down from the Atlas Mountains to perform their magical music in front of me as being a gift from them. To have shared with me their music and cuisine, along with no small measure of their wisdom and humour helps in my understanding of their culture and outlook on life. As to why, perhaps, the proud and ancient Arab can be forgiven for feeling somewhat superior to, despite being, over the centuries, repeatedly put upon by their western counterparts.

Granadas are ten a penny-

A Quarter of an Inch Thick

I first kicked a football when I was three and a half years of age. Walking back from nursery school with my Mom and my best friend Colin Farmer, we marched into Smith's the newsagents on the Chester Road. A red, plastic "Frido" football was purchased and once on the green outside our house, Colin and I enjoyed our first of many games of football.

That small patch of grass in front of the terrace of four council houses that stood at the bottom of Hale Grove was to become, in our imaginations, Wembley Stadium (if we were playing in The F.A. Cup Final) or the Santiago Bernabéu Stadium (I was Alfredo Di Stefano playing for Real Madrid) or simply Villa Park or Saint Andrews if it was just a Saturday English league match. Whenever there had been any footie on the telly that day, then all the local lads would assemble afterwards on the green, with the red ball, pick sides (sometimes there might only be three of us, so one in goal and one a side) and play. As we grew in size and numbers, Pype Hayes Park became the place to play and over a period of the next fifteen years, I must have kicked a football on every single square inch of grass in that vast park, in all weathers, sometimes in a foot of snow, often late into the evening when it was too dark to see. Playing football was my earliest love and I can comfortably say, in all modesty, that I was bloody good at it! I played for all my school teams, and won many cups and medals, the most accomplished coming from being victorious in the Birmingham Schools F.A. Championship Finals for Paget Road Junior School, scoring the winning goal and receiving a winner's medal. It sits proudly to this day on the shelf behind me.

Fast forward thirteen years and I am standing alongside Lionel Conway, head of Island Music Publishing, west coast, on another patch of grass, this one in the middle of a running track in

Beverley Hills, California. Next to the fire station and within kicking distance of the Beverley Hills Hotel (Hotel California from the Eagles song writing perspective), surrounded by fragrant conifer and avocado trees, this oval track was used as a keep fit location for many of the movie stars of the day. Robert Vaughn, star of the '60's T.V. hit series *The Man from U.N.C.L.E.* was regularly there on Wednesday evenings, which was when all we ex-pats met up to play. On odd occasions I saw Burt Reynolds running around the track, Telly Savalas, Karen Black, Julie Christie, Jacqueline Bisset and many other celebs of the day, all in their track suits and trainers, working on their "body beautiful", seemingly pleased to be away from the glare of the cameras. There were a few famous people on the pitch as well as off. Ray Davis from The Kinks turned up to play a couple of times, Robert Plant likewise, usually wearing the shortest of shorts exposing his long, somewhat lanky but perfectly functional legs. Joe Bugner, the Hungarian born British heavyweight boxer honoured us with his presence for several games, his most notable footballing asset being that he could kick a ball further and harder than any man who has ever graced a football pitch. Comedian and writer Marty Feldman joined forces with us a couple of times when he was in town. He had made appearances on the Dean Martin television show, having risen to fame in the U.K. with *At Last the 1948 Show* after previously being a successful comic script writer for political satirist David Frost. Marty's famously bulging and misaligned eyes made for interestingly sarcastic comments on the field regarding the importance of making eye contact with your fellow players, especially when passing the ball and he took all of the jibes in the best of humour. A kind, softly spoken man who was very popular with all his teammates.

Another successful British comedy writer popped along a few times. Ian La Frenais had enjoyed a fruitful relationship with fellow writer Dick Clement, penning together such television comedy classics as *The Likely Lads*, *Porridge* and *Auf Wiedersehen, Pet*, but fortunately for the world at large Ian chose, wisely I think, not to pursue a career as a sportsman.

But undoubtedly the most prestigious, gifted and regular player on the park was Rod Stewart. Lionel introduced me to Rod who immediately asked where did I want to play? "We are a bit short up front" he said, pointing out that the team, who had been playing together out in L.A. for about two years by now, were in need of a couple of new strikers. "Up front for me please, Rod. I usually play inside right". Jumpers for goal posts, the Wednesday evening kick around would be an informal affair, with the rest of the team being made up of people such as myself; back-room staff who worked in various technical aspects of the entertainment industry, along with a handful of aspiring musicians and songwriters. But don't ever make the mistake of trying to take advantage of being in close proximity to Mr Stewart by going up to him at half-time with a cassette tape of one of your new songs that you think would be perfect for him to record, as one hopeful youngster found out at his peril. As the kid handed Rod the tape, Rod exploded. "Don't ever do that to me when I am playing football" he screamed at the, by now reduced figure. "This is the one time a week when I am not a pop star, I'm just me, relaxing with my mates doing what I love best. You go through my management company like everyone else". To his credit, Rod very kindly wrote down the number of his management company and handed it to the lad. The rest of us budding songwriters took note.

The west coast representative of Adidas sports equipment, Andre I think, became close friends with Rod and provided us all with an assortment of boots, socks and jerseys, which appeared regularly from the boot of his car, courtesy of the company. On subsequent concert tours, Rod would be surrounded on stage by footballs, which he would liberally kick out into the audience at the end of every show. These footballs were usually provided by Adidas, thanks in no small part to Andre's impressive footballing skills, his professional sales pitch and his persistent Italian charm.

It was a Wednesday night at the running track, in Beverley Hills, playing up front in my first game with Rod, Lionel and the ex-pats. I needed to impress. I scored three goals.

Sundays were an altogether different affair. The same Wednesday evening attendant ex-pats would meet up at the San Fernando Valley end of Coldwater Canyon at a variety of different football pitches. Proper pitches these; goalposts, pitch markings, sometimes even corner flags and nets. There was nearly always an assortment of Hispanic teams assembled, some looking for willing opponents and we were always happy to oblige. After all, "soccer" was mostly enjoyed in those days in America by only the Hispanic communities and the standard was high. We were by this time being managed (if that's not too an inflated appraisal) by one of our more senior players, John, who worked at The Los Angeles Times newspaper. Mancunian by birth, John had already been living in Los Angeles for about fifteen years when I arrived, so it was all the more remarkable that he exhibited not the slightest reduction to his deep, rich Manchester accent! He arranged matches for us, discussed tactics and generally kept us organised. More especially, his gentle, softly spoken Mexican wife, Lupie, laid on platefuls of delicious home-made Mexican food for the whole team to enjoy after a game back at their place in Hollywood, near Universal Studios.

As an aside, I might just mention the time we were driving to John and Lupie's house for one such feast, on New Year's Day. As we approached the house, driving along the Hollywood freeway, I felt the car swerve involuntarily to the left and then to the right. Must have been a defect in the road surface, I thought, or maybe I need to check tyre pressures. We arrived at the house and everyone was noisily assembled in the back garden, pointing at the cracks in the paving, staring in astonishment at the roof tiles that were lying broken on the ground. This was to be the first of three earthquakes that I would experience during my time in California.

John arranged a game for us against a young side from U.C.L.A. (University of California, Los Angeles). Most of us weren't aware that soccer was on the curriculum at such a prestigious all-American facility. Their sporting prowess would surely be aimed towards American football and baseball, so we were quietly confident of showing them the finer points of the "beautiful game" whilst at the same time giving them a good thrashing. As we assembled pitch side in our assorted patchwork quilt of jerseys, socks and shorts, their luxury air-conditioned team coach arrived and our hearts sank. When they stepped off the bus, there was an audible gasp amongst us. The U.C.L.A. squad was about fifteen in total, all six-footers, mostly blonde and with physiques that would put David Beckham to shame. They wore all white, including their boots and were accompanied by three or four senior looking coaches, each one carrying a bag of footballs, a medical kit and a clipboard. We all turned and stared at John.

The entire game was played in our half of the pitch. It soon became apparent that this was to be a damage limitation exercise, because I don't remember even touching the ball. Don't think I passed the ball once, let alone a shot on goal. Lionel ran around a lot. Joe Bugner would have helped if he could have landed a couple of right hooks out of sight of the referee, but he couldn't catch up with any of them to even try. Rod probably fared the best out of all of us, being quite tall and certainly very fit. He played, as he always did, in a "mid-field general" type role, similar in many ways to the style of England World Cup winning captain Bobby Moore and the Netherlands international Johan Cruyff. But we may just as well have been playing the Dutch Champions because no matter how you look at sport, as in it's the playing, not the winning that is important, an eleven nil whitewash is humiliating at best.

This was to be the one and only time that we never went for a beer after a game.

Off the pitch, I was experiencing what we self-employed refer to as a rest period. In other words, I had no work. My good friend, English guitarist Steve Webb, was in a similar position of unemployment. He and I had worked together in London with Island Artist Jess Roden and Steve was also living here in Los Angeles, putting a band together and looking for a label deal. His band, Lion, (later to be renamed The Difference) also featured Rod Stewart's guitarist Robin LeMesurier (son of actor John LeMesurier and comedienne Hattie Jacques) and they achieved much success in California. In and around band rehearsals, gigs and recording sessions Steve had found temporary employment at a German cake factory out near Van Nuys airport, in the San Fernando Valley. His role was as warehouse and freezer manager and there was a vacancy for someone to stick English labels over German labelled sauce bottles. Six thousand of them. Kept me busy for about two months and brought in some much needed dollars. Whilst the cake ingredients were authentic and imported from the Motherland, the bakers were both Mexicans and when Steve introduced me to José and Pedro, I took an instant liking to them both. Steve and I tried explaining to them that we were professionals in the music industry, simply needing a short spell of "normal" employment but they would have none of it. To them we were just a couple of "limey gringos" and they made as much fun of us as they dared. Steve and I gave as good as we got, chasing them around the factory with real knives and toy guns pretending to be Clint Eastwood or John Wayne, always resulting in the four of us collapsed in a heap on the warehouse floor in floods of laughter tears.

Mexicans can fly. I don't mean aero planes, which no doubt they do, but as in Superman fly. This can't be true I hear you say, But I witnessed this aerial phenomenon for myself in the car park of the cake factory. This is how it came about.

Every Thursday a container truck would arrive from Germany via the port of Los Angeles, with about twenty-five tons of flour, cake mixes, sauces and bottles of schnapps. I don't suppose many people, even those who live in Los Angeles, realise that this great city even has a seaport. Located in San Pedro Bay, south of the city near Long Beach, the Port of Los Angeles has existed since the early twentieth century. Employing nearly 900,000 people with around $1 billion worth of cargo coming in and out every day, this part of town was always a favourite haunt of mine. Unfashionably on the wrong side of the tracks for the majority of Hollywood folk, I always found this industrial landscape, reminiscent of both the manufacturing environment of the West Midlands and the busy docklands of the Thames estuary, to be an essential reality check for one so far from home. I would drive there and park for hours, watching the ships roll in and out of the bay. Combine this activity with my having worked with Steve Cropper, means I have two things in common with Otis Redding.

The truck that delivered the ill-fated container to the warehouse door in Van Nuys had long since departed, leaving the four of us, with the aid of two pallet jacks, to transfer the contents inside. Whilst inside, re-arranging the warehouse to accommodate the newly arrived cargo, we all felt the ground shake. Another earthquake? That was the consensus, so we prepared to take cover. But the shake was too short lived to be of the seismic variety, so we went outside to investigate. Only the top half of the container could be seen above ground level. She was lying at an angle, rear end lowest with the doors pointing upwards at an angle of about thirty degrees. The weight of the container had exposed some weakness in the surface of the car park and she appeared to be sinking, stern first. José went in first. Brave man. We peered inside and could see the chaos of broken pallets, ripped apart drums of flour, broken bottles of sauces everywhere. No use now for the pallet jacks. This was going to be a salvage operation performed manually, so we formed a human chain, with José inside, deep down in the lowest part at the back, Steve next, about mid-way, myself near the doors and Pedro outside. Slowly but surely we began to empty the contents, the scene reminiscent of an emergency relief effort as parcels and packages were handed on down the line. Then it happened. The noise was sudden and loud. The container was evidently on the move again, this time in an attempt to seek a resting place in even further depths beneath the car park. José was not prepared to go down with the ship and within a fraction of a moment had flown through the air, past Steve, past me and out into the fresh air. I jumped off and Steve clambered out. There could be no other explanation as to how José had exited the doomed container so quickly other than his ability to fly. This act of super-hero proportions only added to my admiration, respect and love for Mexicans as a whole. That and Lupie's cooking.

A considerably more sedate responsibility given to me at the cake factory was frequent trips to Palm Springs in the company's refrigerated van. This would be to deliver to the upmarket restaurants and hotels of this prestigious desert community the finest hand-made German Black Forest, Apple Strudel and Cheesecake Kuchen and Torte. Could never bring myself to let on that these were all mass made in automated machines, dozens at a time, by two Mexicans.

But no matter. Judging from the few left-over samples enjoyed by Steve and myself, they were delicious. What was even more enjoyable would be the two-hour drive, alone with my thoughts, staring and marvelling at the beauty of the desert landscape. Palm Springs sits at the foothills of the imposingly stark San Jacinto Mountains, within the Coachella Valley of Riverside County. On approach you drive past industrial size wind farms and huge, solar powered roadside advertising hoardings, the wide-open arid space dotted with resilient Joshua trees, brush-shrub and Mojave Yucca. Once in Palm Springs, the grandeur of desert-chic is all around. Irrigated golf courses abound, along with hundreds of tennis courts and swimming pools. Spotlessly clean sidewalks with street signs such as *Bing Crosby Drive*, *Jack Benny Road* and *Frank Sinatra Drive* give many clues as to the opulence that surrounds you. I've heard Palm Springs described as "The Gay Nineties", suggesting that most residents are either gay or ninety! Not sure about that, but as I am infinitely nearer ninety than gay and with my love of golf and tennis, warm sunshine and lengthy day light hours, I could think of worse places to live.

Lunch times back at the cake factory would be spent in the warm sunshine sitting across the road, outside the Taco Bell Mexican fast-food restaurant, situated perilously and delightfully near to the end of the runway at Van Nuys Airport. Steve and I would watch with horrified laughter as the trainee private pilots attempted their first solo landings under the watchful eye of their instructors, who were no doubt glad to be out of the cockpit and safely on the ground. Many happy hours spent talking music and watching 'planes crash-landing. Finish off my Burrito Supreme and return to more sauce bottle labels, creep up on the Mexicans and scare them! Complete the afternoon shift then jump on the back of Steve's Kawasaki motorbike, stop off for a couple of pints of Guinness at the Robin Hood pub on Burbank Boulevard, then whizz home down the Hollywood freeway, sun in our faces, wind in our hair, holding on for dear life.

There were other, similarly less well-known parts of Los Angeles that I grew drawn to. Another long-time English friend and co-soccer player, Harvey Shield, lived in Angelino Heights in the Echo Park district, just a few miles west of downtown. In terms of its history, Angelino Heights is one of the oldest parts of the city. Built around 1886 to coincide with the gold and banking boom of California, the area boasts many uniquely Victorian houses, most noticeably on Carroll Avenue, which is where Harvey lived. Back in England, in the mid-sixties, Harvey had been in a band called Episode Six with Ian Gillan, who was later to become lead singer with Deep Purple. They toured with Alan Price of the Animals and Dusty Springfield. In 1975 Harvey had moved to Los Angeles and wrote the Bay City Roller's hit song *The Way I Feel Tonight*.

After a particularly heavy drinking session one night at The Cat and Fiddle on Laurel Canyon, I staggered back with Harvey to his Angelino Heights' home to continue into the small hours, drinking and listening to music. We were both awoken at about nine thirty in the morning to the ferocious sound of wind and rain. It was also pitch black. We switched on the television at the same time as looking out of the window. The damage was to be seen all around, with palm trees bent over and snapped in two, roof tiles missing from the houses across the road and trash bins scattered everywhere. According to television reports, a tornado had swept through nearby downtown and ripped the roof off the Convention Centre. How Harvey's wooden built, two-hundred-year-old house had survived such a violent weather phenomenon can only be a credit to the design and build skills of the Victorians.

Harvey and I shared a fondness for Mexican food and one evening we jumped in his old convertible Chevy, sun-bleached and torn top rolled down and drove the short distance to a favourite haunt of his in East Los Angeles. This area was a predominately

Hispanic part of town (probably still is) and renown for the violence amongst a number of local Mexican gangs.

A short history lesson, courtesy of streetgangs.com:

"Encompassing the land east of the Los Angeles River, East Los Angeles is a central historical area of the City that has for many years been anchored by communities such as Boyle Heights and Lincoln Heights. This area was home to the Gabrielino Indians since the 1st Century, but the area fell to the hands of the Spanish in the late eighteenth century, with Mexican and American ranchers taking control of the land for much of the nineteenth century. East Los Angeles became a popular immigrant destination during the early 1900s for Russians, Jews, Japanese, and Mexicans. Living east of the river and working in nearby factories, or travelling by electric rail into downtown Los Angeles, immigrants and their children helped fuel the prosperity of the growing City. By the onset of World War II, East Los Angeles was a nearly exclusively Latino community, soon reinforced by Mexican workers who arrived to man the machines in the area's burgeoning war industries. Remnants of Jewish influence still remain in the form of street names and an old synagogue, but this primary Latino community is one of the most popular in the Country. This area also includes the northern section of City Terrace. It is the largest Mexican-American community in the United States and home to over 1 million people in an area bigger than Manhattan or Washington D.C. Barrios west of Indiana are in Boyle Heights, which is actually part of the City of Los Angeles policed by the Hollenbeck division of the LAPD. The East Los Angeles area is policed by the LA County Sheriff's Department."

So when we pulled up outside what appeared to me to be almost literally a hole in the wall, down an unlit side street, Harvey led the way and knocked firmly on the non-descript door. We entered and were greeted by a large, jovial Mexican lady, who squeezed

Harvey tightly, kissed him on the cheek and laughingly asked if he wanted his usual seat by the window. Was this wise, I asked Harvey, what with being in the gangland centre of Los Angeles, drive-by shootings and all that. Not to worry Harvey bellowed. Safe as houses, he reassured me. We are white Anglo-Saxons and have nothing to fear from this community. They love me here and as my friend you will be equally welcome, as indeed I was. A lot of beer was drunk as we watched Mexican football on the television and shared in the noisy ambivalent atmosphere of the Cantina. Must have been a relatively quiet night for the regulars because, somewhat disappointingly, there were no shootings that evening, drive-by or otherwise.

The food was deliciously fresh, homemade and as authentic a Mexican meal as is possible to enjoy anywhere north of the Tijuana River. Even more remarkable, Harvey had confidently left the top down of his parked Chevy and when we returned to it, his Sony Walkman was still there on the front seat.

Far less explosive pleasures could be found just a short distance from Harvey's house. If you continue east and drive two and a half miles along Sunset from Angelino Heights you eventually find yourself passing underneath the intersection of the Interstate 110 Harbour Freeway and the U.S. Route 101 Hollywood Freeway. You are now in downtown Los Angeles.

Founded in 1781 by settlers who had moved north from Mexico, this historic part of the original city is the least well known by residents and visitors alike. The full name for Los Angeles is: "El Pueblo de Nuestra Señora la Reina de los Ángeles de Porciúncula" (in English: "town of our lady the Queen of Angels of the little Portion"). You can understand why we simply call it L.A.

As far back as 1920 "--- *the city's private and municipal rail lines were the most far-flung and comprehensive in the world in mileage, even besting New York City. By this time, a steady influx* of residents and aggressive land developers had transformed the city into a large metropolitan area, with Downtown L.A. at its centre. Rail lines connected four counties with over 1,100 miles of track". (Westworld 2000)

As numerous banking institutions set up their headquarters along South Spring Street, the district became known as the "Wall Street of the West". To accommodate this commercial growth, numerous grand hotels were built, the most impressive of which must be The Biltmore. Opened in 1923 as the largest hotel west of Chicago, the Spanish/Italian renaissance exterior, designed by architects Schultze and Weaver is only exceeded in its external beauty by the breathtaking interiors, decorated with *"frescos and murals, carved marble fountains, wood beamed ceilings and panelled walls. Lead crystal chandeliers, bronze stairwells and doorways"*. (Los Angeles Office of Historic Resources).

I would frequently take the bus (unheard of if you lived in Hollywood and weren't black or Hispanic) and travel into the downtown area. I wasn't working very much and couldn't afford to run the car, so the bus was ideal. You see so much more of a city when someone else is driving. Walk down Seventh Street and explore the largest jewellery quarter in the United States, or visit the Mexican market on historic Olvera Street, with its craft shops, restaurants and dancing troubadours. Enjoy an unaffordable cappuccino in the glorious "Art-Deco" Biltmore.

So much to see and do.

Who said Los Angeles has no history or culture? Someone once described California as being a thousand miles long, four hundred miles wide and a quarter of an inch thick! Most unkind and wildly inaccurate.

If, on the other hand, you simply wish to get up to no good and do something childishly reckless, then get on the back of Steve's motorbike, after a stint at the cake factory, and ride to the very top of Beachwood Drive, park up and scramble your way up the steep and dusty side of Mount Lee. Then stand tall, 1,708 feet above sea level, alongside and behind the famous Hollywood sign. See the enormous individual letters up close, hold on to the flimsy steel framework, look down and across the whole of the Los Angeles basin, catch the sun glistening on the distant Pacific, and then wonder how the hell you are ever going to get down again.

With both feet firmly back on the ground, I walked into Island's offices and re-introduced myself to Spencer Davis.

   Perfect timing.

See the enormous individual letters up close-----.

Happy Days

The London production of the hit musical *Hair* opened at The Shaftsbury Theatre in September 1968 and had a performance run of 1,997 shows.

Hair: The American Tribal Love-Rock Musical is a rock musical with a book and lyrics by James Rado and Gerome Ragni and music by Galt MacDermot A product of the hippie counter-culture and sexual revolution of the 1960s, several of its songs became anthems of the anti-Vietnam War peace movement The musical's profanity, its depiction of the use of illegal drugs, its treatment of sexuality, its irreverence for the American flag and its nude scene caused much comment and controversy. The musical broke new ground in musical theatre by defining the genre of "rock musical", using a racially integrated cast, and inviting the audience onstage for a "Be-In" finale. ("The Age of Hair" Barbara L. Horn. Published by Praeger.)

The London cast included such stage luminaries as Paul Nicholas (BBC 1983 sitcom *Just Good Friends*), Elaine Page (*Evita* 1978), Richard O'Brien (*Rocky Horror Show*), and the little-known singer/composer Paul Korda. Along with Marsha Hunt, actress and singer, his was one of the silhouetted outlines of "Big Hair" featured in the heavily publicised promotional posters. When I met him for the first time in California, Paul was still in possession of his generous locks. Mine, on the other hand, were quickly diminishing.

Paul had moved to Los Angeles in 1977 to progress his career as a songwriter and recording artist, having already written songs for Roger Daltrey, Dave Edmunds and Franki Valli. Both his mother and father had impressive musical backgrounds, so it was inherent in the genes for Paul to succeed. Independent label Janus Records, part of the Pye Records group of companies, with

Paul's approval, hired Spencer Davis as producer and Spencer hired me to engineer. In the early summer of 1978, we moved into studio A at Village Recorders on Butler Avenue in Santa Monica to record Paul's *Dancing in the Aisles* album. Mark Sanders played drums, and Chris Pinnick handled guitar duties. Despite much research, I can find little information on the musical heritage of these two musicians, so apologies. On bass was Charlie Harrison, who had found fame and success working with American country rock band Poco and with Byrds lead guitarist and vocalist Roger McGuinn. On saxophone, we brought in Liverpudlian Phil Kenzie, who, along with his work with Rod Stewart and Roger Daltrey, will be best remembered for his beautiful thematic saxophone on Al Stewart's *Year of the Cat*. We were pleasantly surprised to have the band Supertramp as neighbours next door in studio B. They had already been deeply entrenched in the studio since May, working on their *Breakfast in America* album and would remain there long after our departure. Released on A&M Records in March 1979, this was to be the band's most successful album, reaching quadruple platinum in terms of sales. As for Village Recorders, we were entering into a recording environment with a hugely prestigious musical history and would be adding our modest accomplishments to an industry hall of fame. Here is an abbreviated list of clients that would have recorded there in previous years: The Beach Boys, The Eagles, Johnny Cash, Ray Charles, Eric Clapton, Elton John, Fleetwood Mac, Tom Jones.

At the time we were there, the studios were being managed by music publicist and promoter Dick LaPalm, who had risen to fame working with such jazz greats as Count Basie, Mel Torme, Sarah Vaughan and Nat King Cole. The desk and walls in Dick's office were completely covered by pictures of his family and business associates and most mornings before the start of our days recording, we would be invited upstairs to enjoy a morning coffee (or occasionally other more adult refreshment) and listen to wonderful stories of life on the road with the likes of Nat King Cole and his band. I remember Dick telling us that most times, Nat and his closest entourage would stay in the finest hotels. In contrast, he, as the only white person, would invariably have to settle for considerably more austere accommodation. An early and little-known case of reverse discrimination, shrugged off by Dick with a hearty laugh and a tear in his eye.

He had obviously been very fond of Nat.

Dick LaPalm passed away in 2013. He was an immensely likeable man and took especial care to look after us whilst we were working at his wonderful studio. I hope his son Todd will be pleased for me to include his quote:

"He was a kind and gentle soul and touched the lives of many, many people throughout his lifetime. The people he worked with in the business were not only his clients, but more than anything else, they were his friends and for some, it was many years. He wouldn't have wanted it any other way".

Back in the studio, the recording of Paul's album progressed well. In between takes I would wander into studio B and catch up with the Supertramp boys, frequently conversing with Pete Henderson, their English engineer and co-producer. We would share in the frustrations that all engineers endure; the seemingly endless hours spent capturing the demanding artists' performances, the meticulous attention to microscopic musical detail and the detrimental health consequences of experiencing no natural daylight for weeks, indeed months at a time.

There are in fact, serious negative life outcomes that result from too much time spent in recording studios. Apart from my own relatively mild state of studio burn-out, of which I dip in and out of even now, I know of at least two studio engineers for whom the whole process of making an album came at a huge personnel cost. The names of the engineers and the artists for whom they toiled shall remain unspecified, but suffice to say they are mentioned earlier in these writings. One previously normal, sane and mild-mannered soul of many years of experience became a crazed, alcoholic divorcee after a three-month stint, locked in the same studio night after endless night with the same demanding musicians. Another professional colleague of mine would never set foot in a recording studio ever again, as a direct consequence of been driven completely bonkers by the band's unrelenting demands during the recording of an extremely well-known album, to the point of his suffering from a peculiar form of Post Traumatic Stress Disorder.

Choosing a career path as a recording studio engineer should come with a government health warning.

There were lighter, more relaxed and amusing moments to be enjoyed at Village Recorders. One such example was to come from my ownership of an early hand-held computer game. I had become a massive fan of American football and this compact electronic toy was an assimilation of that great game. The small screen mimicked the one-hundred-yard-long football pitch, and the idea was to "catch" the ball thrown by your quarterback and race down the field, avoiding tackles and score a "touchdown". Upon which, if successful, a robotic beeping sound would follow, accompanied by yelps of joy and fist-pumping in the control room. I lent the game to the Super tramp guys next door and it disappeared for a week.

Next time you hear the track *Logical Song* from Supertramp's *Breakfast in America* album, listen carefully at about 3mins 22secs, hear the sound of a "touch-down" and think of my computer game, of Village Recorders and most respectfully of Dick LaPalm.

The 1979 gasoline shortages in the United States were the inspiration behind another venture into the recording studio with Paul Korda. In California, at that time you could only buy fuel for your car every other day, based on a system of odd and even numbers on your licence plates. Paul wrote a song called *Out of Gas* and after a rushed recording session, the track was released by R.C.A. records. It was broadcast on the main C.B.S. television news and was later featured in a documentary series *The History of America* presented by veteran American television news reporter Ted Koppel. The success enjoyed by Paul was perhaps enviously overshadowed by his keyboard player Dave Kaffinetti and drummer Rick Parnell, both being chosen as band members in Rob Reiner's cult classic spoof *This is Spinal Tap*. Paul makes a brief appearance in this mockumentary as a party-going rock-star and I watch this hysterically funny and sadly accurate depiction of music business life at every opportunity and never tire of it.

I almost made a guest appearance myself in a popular television series of the day. I was driving east along Sunset one early evening to collect Janet from Shelter. The traffic was bumper to bumper and I was stopped outside a pool hall when suddenly, all hell broke loose! Bursting out of the swing doors came two guys, one with blonde hair the other brown. Both men showed considerable athletic prowess as they rolled over the bonnet of a parked Ford Gran Torino and onto the road. They ducked down low, took cover and drew their weapons. They looked kind of familiar, but when the gun shots started ringing out I hadn't a care for who they were and I dropped below my steering wheel in fear of my life. The next thing I heard was the reassuring voice of a film director shouting "CUT! Let's run it again. Take nine". An unconcerned policeman appeared and moved us all along. The blonde was David Soul and his partner was Paul Michael Glaser. Pity they didn't use take eight because I would have made a brief appearance in an episode of *Starsky and Hutch*.

It was not uncommon to see film crews on location around Los Angeles, particularly in Hollywood. After all, this was and arguably still is the capital of the movie industry. Another striking example for me of the sometimes alarming wonders of living amongst the movie-making community was when we had moved to a new, larger apartment in the soon to be very fashionable part of West Hollywood, just off Melrose Avenue. One afternoon, standing on the balcony gazing up into the Hollywood Hills, the quiet stillness of a perfect blue sky was violently interrupted by the sound of attack helicopters. There were four of them and they were military in appearance. One was particularly large, blue, sleek and very heavily armed. The other three were in hot pursuit and smoke appeared from the sides of the fuselages. The aerial combat was an exhibition of aerobatics of the highest level and I would have been terrified if it wasn't for the fact that it was so captivating. Besides which, I had lived in Los Angeles long enough by now to hazard at a guess that this was a movie in the making. Indeed, it was. Directed by John Badham and starring Roy Scheider, *Blue Thunder* is an action thriller that features a high-tech helicopter of the same name and was released in 1983. Some of the scenes were filmed above my head.

Bordered by Santa Monica Boulevard to the north, Beverley Boulevard to the south, La Brea Avenue to the east and Fairfax Avenue to the west, West Hollywood was at one time an assorted mix of old Jewish tailor shops, second-hand record and bookstores, run down furniture outlets, a couple of strip clubs and dodgy burger bars. The smart money had always gone to Beverley Hills, Brentwood, Hancock Park near the Wiltshire Country Club and high in the Hollywood Hills, but West Hollywood was on the up. The houses that are situated in the latticework of the many narrow streets in between the outer boundaries are well built, mostly detached and of Spanish/Mediterranean style. There is also some spacious purpose built quadro-plex apartments lying on beautiful tree-lined streets, just a stone's throw from the Farmers Market, Cedars-Sinai Medical Centre, C.B.S. television studios and the Pacific Design Centre. We rented one such apartment just in time to watch the beginnings of an area rocket to the upmarket, fashionable district it is today. Fabulous boutiques and restaurants, trendy coffee shops and vegan cafes. Organic burger bars and no strip clubs.

    Our move to this up-and-coming part of West Hollywood coincided with Janet's appointment as P.A. to George Harrison, working for his label, Darkhorse Records. Situated on the old Charlie Chaplin film lot on La Brea Avenue, Darkhorse rented space from the main owners, A+M Records. Janet had always been well connected in the industry and no doubt had used her vast knowledge and experience to influence the right people in securing this prestigious position with the former Beatle.

    A+M Records was formed in 1962 by trumpeter and bandleader Herb Alpert and industry executive Jerry Moss. The label took its name from their initials. The company had headquarters in La Brea from 1966 to 1999 and enjoyed success with artists such as Liza Minnelli, Captain and Tenille, Herb Alpert and the Tijuana Brass, Quincy Jones, Supertramp and probably most importantly, with The Carpenters. As well as having their own recording studios A+M had world famous vinyl mastering facilities and I had already used the services of Bernie Grundman, the senior engineer, from as far away as London for the mastering of many Island records. A+M also distributed many of the Island artists for American release, including Cat Stevens, Free, Spooky Tooth and Fairport Convention so I felt an affinity to the label even before Janet and Darkhorse. I became a frequent visitor to the parking lot and got to know the security men who held court at the guarded gates. Mike always had a gun at his waist and there was a rifle hanging in the hut, where he must also have kept a bottle of something soothing because you could always smell the booze on him. But he did his job and always smiled at me as he waved me through. Pity the outcome, I thought, if you were to upset him.

One evening I turned up as usual to collect Janet. Parked outside the recording studio was a brand new, bright red, convertible top of the range Jaguar XJ6. I enquired of Mike as to who the owner was. Maybe some bigwig, high flying executive was visiting Herb and Jerry? But no. It belonged, he informed me, to the Carpenters' recording engineer. Richard and Karen Carpenter had bought the luxury car for him as their way of saying thank you for creating the exquisite vocal sounds that typify all those wonderful Carpenters records. Whenever I hear a Carpenters song I picture that Jaguar parked there and wonder whether I should have worked for A+M instead of Island.

The single-storey offices of Darkhorse records were small and basic. Pieces of Beatle memorabilia on the walls, some pictures of Ravi Shankar, the great sitar player and a few rather drab artificial plants in one corner gathering dust. Maybe it was an unjustified impression but it didn't seem to be too bubbly a place. Not compared to Shelter, or Island. I sensed a certain sadness in the air. A discontent. Just a feeling I had. Most evenings I would arrive to collect Janet and George would be sitting alone in the reception area, maybe taking a telephone call or just walking aimlessly around. He would always smile politely and I would do the same back. Never quite knew what to say to the man. Could have, maybe should have said "Don't you remember me? I was on recording sessions with you in London. I've got all your records and I am a huge fan. Grew up learning to play guitar listening to you, so I just want to say thanks for the inspiration". But I never said anything to him. Not once. I have never been the most overly confident person and I suspect my nerves just got the better of me again. Which is odd when you consider that on two or three occasions he gave Janet the keys to his magnificent palatial Bel Air mansion so that she and I could go and play tennis there, which we did, only because I knew that we would be there alone. Janet had dinner with George and his wife Olivia numerous times and I was invited but couldn't bring myself to go. What a silly, insecure little fool I was. Must have embarrassed Janet as well, though she would never have shown it. On reflection, I suspect that my, by now heavier drinking and puffing were getting the better of me. These substances have a dreadful, lasting after effect, creating deep feelings of depression and anxiety. I know that now, just didn't realise it then. Add to that my becoming wedded to the villainous seductress that is cocaine and you have the correct recipe for a complete lack of confidence and the resultant manifestation of under achievement.

A band called Attitudes had signed to Darkhorse and were in the studio putting the final touches to their album, so there were pictures of them on the wall too. This was a formidable musical ensemble with David Foster on keyboards (the producer whom Janet had introduced me to earlier) Jim Keltner on drums (George Harrison and John Lennon solo albums) and Danny Kortchmar (James Taylor and Linda Ronstadt) on guitar. If I had kept myself more together I might possibly have engineered on that record. I know that Janet put a word in for me and I would have cultivated a close relationship with the label and with George Harrison. Maybe the sadness and discontent I sensed were not emanating out of Darkhorse but from within myself. Janet and I were frequently arguing, usually over money and lifestyle choices. My lack of ambition and her desire to spend increasing amounts of time shopping in Beverley Hills created conflict between us. It was not so much the cost of all the shoes, leather coats, perfumes, jewellery and more shoes that she came home with on an almost daily basis; after all, she was spending her own hard-earned money. It was more the fact that my jean wearing, pink streaky haired Canyon Lady was moving up-market to Rodeo Drive and I couldn't keep pace.

Which was a real shame because we had not long been married.

The previous Easter had been spent with my family back in the U.K. Two weeks of complete and utter misery. If Janet hadn't been particularly fond of London, then Birmingham was to prove too great a challenge. It was winter-like conditions in England, cold and wet. Janet did not want to be there and sulked the whole time. My efforts to impress upon her the importance of spending some of our time, especially this festive period with my family were futile. On the flight back to L.A. the mood lightened, that is until we were separated at immigration control and I was arrested. "Purpose of visit to the United States, Mr. Smith?" "Business and pleasure" I replied, as usual. The immigration officer spent longer than normal examining my passport, which of course was peppered with page after page of LAX entry stamps. Those weeds that I had planted. "You seem to spend a lot of time in Los Angeles, Mr. Smith." "Yes, I love it here." (First incorrect answer). "Do you have somewhere to live?" "Yes, we have a beautiful apartment in West Hollywood." (Second incorrect answer). As he wrote it down, I heard him mumble under his breath ---"maintaining a residence." "Do you work when you are here?" "I am a freelance recording engineer and I work all over the world." I boastfully replied. (Third and fatal.) More mumbling. ---"seeking employment." That was it. I was a condemned man. I was escorted into a back room, given a bible to hold and with my right hand raised I had to promise to tell the truth, the whole truth, etc. I was kept waiting in that room for two hours before a representative from Trans World Airlines arrived. Some documents were signed and I was told by the uniformed immigration officer that I had two choices. I could simply get on the next flight back to London and nothing further would happen. Alternatively, I would be placed under custody of TWA, appear before an immigration judge in the morning and risk deportation, the consequences of which would mean I could never again enter the United States. At this point, I was exhausted and somewhat annoyed at the inconvenience of the whole affair and felt unjustly treated. In a rare moment of bravado, I chose to take my chances with the judge.

As soon as we arrived back at our apartment, I telephoned Steve Smith, the producer I had worked with on the Robert Palmer album. He kindly arranged for a lawyer to meet with us at the courthouse the following morning and it was there that I met Randy Blotky. A tall, dark haired, elegantly dressed man who reminded me of a young Raymond Burr, the Canadian-American actor who played the lead in Perry Mason and Ironside. I hoped Randy would be as successful representing me in the Los Angeles County Superior Court as in his T.V. shows. We were taken into a small side room that looked more like an office than a courtroom. There was a grey haired, bespectacled elderly gentleman sitting at a table, surrounded by books and paperwork. Randy approached him. I was both astonished and relieved as I overheard their conversation. It went something like this;

Judge: Hi Randy, nice to see you. How are Tina and the boys?

Randy: They're fine thank you Ken. And Sheila?

Judge: Still waiting on the results, but she'll pull through. Now, who have we got here?

Randy: An Englishman with a loose tongue. He's no trouble. Usual nine holes on Thursday?

Judge: You bet. Send him over.

The kindly judge suggested that next time I pass through immigration I should keep my big mouth shut. He had my passport, which he stamped and wished me well. Randy followed me and Janet into the car park. "How long have you guys known each other? Why don't you just get married, get yourself a Green Card and you won't have a problem anymore going back and forth." It seemed to make sense. So Janet and I went to a coffee shop in Beverley Hills, I got down on one knee, Janet laughed and said don't be silly.

We got married in a small chapel in the picturesque city of Ojai, Ventura County, but only after I had asked her dad's permission.

Janet's dad, Ron, was an ex-navy man who had served during the Second World War in the South Pacific. He was a short man but well-built, always immaculately dressed and with his thick mane of wavy grey hair and rich moustache, he cut a very sharp figure. He drove a large Cadillac and was a deeply proud and patriotic all-American guy. He had many illustrious tales to tell of life on the ocean waves and had a wonderful sense of humour to match. No doubt one of his proudest days was when we all travelled down to San Diego to attend his grandson Mark's graduation parade at the U.S. Naval Academy. We all sat there in the stands overlooking the parade ground and I remember it being an extremely hot day, even by Californian standards. To add to the excitement and the heat of the day, sat immediately behind me was the beautiful English actress, Audrey Hepburn. I was repeatedly chastised for continually glancing over my shoulder. Janet's mom Katherine was, like Audrey, very slim and petite, with twinkly eyes and an extremely pleasant, easy-going disposition. She worked in a health food store on Hollywood Boulevard and would bring me all manner of remedies designed to prevent hair loss; brewer's yeast tablets, folic acid, wheat germ, scalp creams, you name it, I tried them all! Bless her. Janet had a sister, Pat, who married a member of the Cannon family, who were and still are leaders in the manufacturing of fine quality towels. His family were immensely wealthy and when Pat's husband Dave went to jail for tax evasion it was all the more bemusing. Ron and Katherine also had two sons, Ronnie Jr. and Richard, who like me was music mad. He played a mean guitar, so we wrote some songs together. A very kind, thoughtful and softly spoken young man who loved his sport, he patiently talked me through all the complex rules of American football, usually on a Monday night in front of the television, both of us drinking can after can of limp American beer and smoking an awful lot of weed.

Happy days.

The head of the family was unmistakably represented by Janet's grandmother, also Katherine. She had immigrated to America as a young girl from Sicily and now lived in Orange County. As the name of the area suggests, her garden was unsurprisingly full of orange trees, remnants of earlier orchards that once covered the county. These mature, lush citrus trees seemed to bear fruit all year round. Every time we would visit her she would be in the kitchen cooking: meat loaf, Bolognese, stuffed peppers, platefuls of hand-made pasta, mountains of food, yet she would always apologise that she "donta cook like I used to!" Out into the garden and fill ten carrier bags full of the sweetest, juiciest oranges imaginable, load them into the car, take them home and enjoy fresh squeezed Californian orange juice for days and for free.

Janet's mom and dad could never stay put. When I first met the family they lived in a modest suburban tract home in Universal City, Los Angeles. They moved to just outside Denver, Colorado for a few years, where it was always good to visit them up in the fresh mountain air, in their rented trailer home. Pat and Dave usually followed Ron and Katherine, as did Richard, wherever they moved to, so the family were always together. Then there were a couple of years of them all living in Garland, Texas, where we visited twice. Next stop, Las Vegas and another trailer home. Pat, Dave and Richard all followed. Always great fun to visit the family when they live less than two miles from the strip. Pat and Dave used to go gambling almost every night, like you and I might go to a restaurant or the pub and they learnt how to play the tables, the cards and the bandits well, so as to increase their chances of winning, which they did more than often. We accompanied them many times and I remember one night witnessing a punter collect the $100,000 jackpot playing a card game called Keno at the Circus Circus casino. We had enjoyed a burlesque show and a meal that night, but entertaining though it was, it wasn't as life changing an evening for us as it must have been for that lucky card player.

   I became very close with Janet's family and loved them all dearly, as any decent son-in-law should. Ronnie Jr. and Richard were like the brothers I never had, which made it all the sadder when Janet and I eventually separated. Ronnie Jr. was very academically gifted, clever at math's like my Dad and very intelligent in debates about politics and society in general. Richard was more of a dreamer, a bit like me, in a world of his own. His only downside, other than his consumption of large amounts of alcohol, was his penchant for certain mind-altering chemicals, such as P.C.P. (Phencyclidine or Angel Dust), an extremely powerful hallucinogenic anesthetic, to which he pitifully became extremely addicted. He had started up his own small business manufacturing bees-wax candles and was doing rather well in Vegas but sadly his time spent at the roulette wheel of drug and alcohol excess proved too costly and directly resulted in his early death. For Ron and his wife, again the saddest of all losses ... that of your own child.

   At this point, I am once again sunken and confused. Time to stand on my balcony, in the perfect surrounds of a comfortable West Hollywood apartment, look out across the evening sky at the flickering lights of Tinsel Town, take another drag of a spliff, a gulp of Jack Daniels, a desperate snort of coke. Begin to wonder what the hell am I doing here. Missing my family in England. Longing for the familiar surroundings of Portobello Road. For some grey skies. Some rain. Some normality.

the flickering lights of Tinsel Town.

Loud And Clear

A constant challenge for any Englishman living abroad is to find a place that sells Typhoo tea. Marmite can be elusive, unlike Australian Vegemite which is globally omnipresent. Cadbury's milk chocolate, McVitie's Digestive biscuits and Colman's mustard might be a quest too far, but seek and thou shalt find.

Chalet Gourmet on Sunset, near Beverley Hills was the closest continental grocery store to where we lived and they sold a wide variety of English and European food, as well as exhibiting in the doorway as you came in an impressive, well-stocked super-sized fish tank full of live lobsters; pick one, they'll stick it in a vat of boiling water and kill it for you. Ready to eat. You could also get English butter and cheeses, Cornish ice-cream and Jammy Dodgers. Heavenly! The other go-to rescue centre was a small shop in the foyer of the Ambassador Hotel on Wiltshire Boulevard. Opened since 1921 and home to the famous Cocoanut Grove nightclub, I always felt a sense of guilt entering this distinguished place for such a relatively trivial, self-indulgent matter as English grocery shopping. This was after all the location of the 1968 assassination of presidential candidate and former U.S. Attorney General Robert F. Kennedy. I could always sense the ghostly reverberation of that awful event whenever I was there and I wasn't too displeased when I heard of the buildings demolishment in 2005.

Another commodity in short supply in Southern California is rain. As I sit here in England writing this during the wettest December in seventy years, I struggle to remember how dreary and dull it was to see clear blue sky and feel warm sunshine day after day after day. Three hundred days a year where the only variation in the climate was that some days would be hotter than others. Living in Hollywood I would eagerly await a telephone call from Bernadette, out in Santa Monica, near the beach. "It's cloudy here today, Digby" she would announce, knowing how uplifting those words would sound to me. "On my way, Bernie".

February and March, being part of the rainy season in Southern California might bring some respite and in 1978 this was most certainly the case.

After a relatively busy work period, I was in a position to treat my Mom and Dad to the trip of a lifetime and sent them two tickets to come out to California and visit. It was to be in February for two weeks, several days of which coincided with the worst flash floods in Californian history. After a couple of days of adjusting to the time zone, Mom and Dad were raring to go. We visited all the usual tourist spots: Universal Studios, Disneyland, La Brea Tar Pits, Venice Beach and Malibu, where they came and watched me play football. Mom held Rod Stewart's coat and got her picture taken with him. She dined out back in Birmingham on that picture for years and became his biggest fan! I took my Dad for breakfast to a diner named after him, *Bert's Mad House* on La Brea, the inside of which features as the location for the back sleeve photograph by Mark Hanauer for Supertramp's *Breakfast in America* album. Took them for lunch to The Original Pantry Cafe in downtown, one of the oldest, 24-hour restaurants in Los Angeles, whose proud boast is that it has never, ever closed:

"The Original Pantry Cafe is an iconic coffee shop and restaurant in Los Angeles, California. Located at the corner of 9th and Figueroa in Downtown L.A.'s South Park district, The Pantry (as locals know it) claims never to have closed or been without a customer since it opened in 1924, including when it changed locations in 1950 to make room for a freeway off-ramp; it served lunch in the original location and served dinner at the new location the same day". (pantrycafe.com).

We flew up to San Francisco for a couple of days, and Dad particularly liked the place, especially the helicopter ride we took out over the bay, around the famous Alcatraz prison. "$20 per person --- 20 min flight around Alcatraz", said the handwritten sign at the harbour side heli-pad. We approached the relatively young-looking, all-too-casually dressed pilot and $40 changed hands. Mom was having none of it. As we lifted off at speed, vertically into the clear sky, waving at the tiny disappearing figure on the ground, I remember thinking how small and alone she looked and sensed she was regretting her decision to remain earthbound. The flight didn't last anywhere near 20 minutes. Within 10 minutes, we were back on the ground, and enjoyable though it was, Dad and I were a little peeved at the brevity of the flight.

One afternoon, we took the folks up to Laurel Canyon to visit our friends John and Joanne. John was the art director for Capitol Records, and Joanne was writing a book about the Beatles with their tour manager, Mal Evans, whom I had met and worked with alongside Ringo on sessions back in London. We enjoyed a pleasant lunch, and I was pleased that John was tactful enough not to dish up the cocaine for dessert, as would most certainly have been the case if it had just been me and Janet there. Many Very Happy Xmases had been spent with John and Joanne in their log-cabin canyon retreat. Mal was often there, relating amusing and sometimes shocking tales of his Beatles days, all of us listening to music, sitting around the piano, laughing and smoking, boozing and snorting into the wee hours, but not this time, thank you, John.

Very sadly, the book that Joanne was working on with Mal was never completed. (Not to my knowledge, unless Joanne, you managed to complete the work, in which case, my apologies and I will search for it later.) In January 1976, Mal was cruelly the victim of an overzealous Los Angeles police department. Upon being sent to Mal's home in response to a telephone call from his girlfriend, who told them that he was confused and had a gun, and mistaking the air rifle Mal was holding for a proper rifle, the police shot him dead.

Such a shockingly sad and unnecessary early death for this warm-hearted, larger-than-life character, who had so much more to say and to give.

It was whilst we were at John and Joanne's with my parents that the aforementioned rain came down. The sky turned a bluish shade of brown, the wind picked up, and within minutes, the canyon was a river. The sound of the rain against the wooden cabin roof was deafening. We all gazed out of the window in amazement at the tree branches, pieces of shrubbery, furniture and most alarmingly, cars that were floating down the hill in the torrent. Fortunately, our car was secure in a parking bay above the cabin, but Joanne wasn't so lucky. "Look, there's a pink VW just like mine," she exclaimed as we watched the bobbing car float past the front door. John caught a glimpse of the licence plate number. Oh dear.

The next day, we drove through the deserted streets of Hollywood, cars and trees piled high at the bottom of Laurel, Coldwater and Topanga Canyons, at the intersections of Franklin Avenue and Hollywood Boulevard. Like a war zone, a scene out of one of Hollywood's finest disaster movies. Only this time it was for real. C.G.I. is not required.

A few weeks later, after Mom and Dad had returned to the U.K., I was sitting in a dry Farmers Market enjoying a morning coffee, reading the Los Angeles Times. Hidden away on page eleven, bottom right-hand corner, about two column inches, the headline read: "Helicopter crashes into San Francisco Bay, killing all four occupants. $20 tours around Alcatraz suspended indefinitely."

Gulp.

I know from later conversations with Mom and Dad that they had a wonderful time in California, although it came to pass that for the whole of their time spent there, Mom had been unwell, just hadn't let on. It was the beginning of problems with her thyroid gland, issues which were to trouble her for many years to come. She hadn't wanted to spoil the trip for any of us. But knowing how intuitive she always was, there is no doubt that she would have sensed the underlying tension between me and Janet. The unhappy stirrings of discontent that were about to come to a head.

I continued to be in demand as an engineer and producer on many more albums during my time out in L.A. I worked at all the major studios and some smaller independent ones as well: Wally Heiders, Crystal Sound, the Record Plant, United Western, Eldorado, Sunswept Sound, Mama Joe's. I recorded tracks for guitarist Albert Lee's first solo album, *Hiding*, up at Indigo Ranch.

Set in 60 acres of the beautiful Santa Monica Mountains, the studios were built in 1974 by engineer Richard Kaplan and Moody Blues keyboard player and vocalist Mike Pinder. Famous for its rare Aengus recording console, artists such as Neil Young, Olivia Newton-John, Limp Bizkit, and Neil Diamond all recorded there, until its closure in 2006. We recorded there in 1979 with an illustrious team of musicians, including Buddy Emmons (steel guitar), Bill Payne and Charlie Hodges (keyboards), Pete Gavin and Gerry Conway (drums).

We would drive back to L.A. each night and visit with Albert's friends Sonny Curtis and Jerry Allison, two former members of Buddy Holly's backing band, The Crickets. They would listen to our mixes of the day's work in the studio and give us their critique. Also with Albert, I attended a party celebrating the wedding of country singer Emmylou Harris to the record's producer Brian

Ahern and Albert got up on stage to play alongside Elvis Presley's guitarist James Burton. I was mingling with the stars.

I had two hit singles, Now and Zero Hour, produced by Island's Danny Holloway, with local band The Plimsouls on Planet Records, the label owned by Pointer Sisters and Harry Nilsson producer Richard Perry, (who I had worked with in London). Both tracks received heavy radio air-pay but rival band The Knack had a massive hit with My Sharona and simply blew us out of the water in terms of being the most successful L.A. band of the time.

Working at The Record Plant, Clover and United Western studios I recorded Swansong records' band (Led Zeppelin's label) Detective, who featured on guitar Michael Monarch (ex-Steppenwolf) Tony Kaye on keyboards (ex-Yes) Michael Des Barres lead vocals (Silverhead) Bobby Pickett (Sugarloaf/vocals) on bass and John Hyde (vocals for Hokus Pokus) on drums. A star-studded line up with, once again, Steve Smith producing. I most remember spending about a week trawling around EVERY recording studio in Los Angeles, searching for the perfect sounding room with the right acoustics for John's drums. Also, Steve jetting off to New York for the day to watch a baseball game, when he should have been on session. We found the right room for John but never saw Steve in the studio with this particular band again!

Dirk Hamilton was a little-known singer/songwriter from Hobart, Indiana. He was signed to Elektra Records and I recorded two albums with this intelligent and witty man. Meet Me at the Crux and Thug of Love will always be two of my favourite albums. Both were recorded at United Western Recorders (later renamed Ocean Way Recording) on Sunset.

With so many top-notch, high-end recording facilities in the Los Angeles area available to choose from, it wasn't always easy to pick which one to use for any given project. All would have quality acoustics, drum and vocal booths, Neve or Harrison, A.P.I or Trident consoles, usually sixty-plus channels. Wide selection of microphones, every make and model, usually at least four of each. Classic outboard gear, including vintage compressors and signal processors to die for; racks and racks of them. And always first-class engineers to assist you, often females. Rarely saw that in the U.K. in those days, but in the States, quite common. (I have always wondered as to the reasons for the lack of female recording engineers and producers in this, admittedly, male dominated sector. Women have the right temperament and required sensitivities for such demanding roles and I would encourage any young aspiring females to get more involved in this side of the music industry.)

So what was it that United Western offered us that determined our using that particular facility to make Dirk's albums? Quite simply, they offered free beer! Done deal.

Guest appearance on the *Thug of Love* album playing accordion was Garth Hudson from The Band, whose album *Stagefright* I had mixed with Glyn Johns back in London, all those years ago. As a reference to interesting/unusual recording methodology, I must relate the experience we had with Garth. A tall, bearded, quiet and reflective man, he introduced himself to us and sat in front of the speakers as we played him the track that required the accordion overdub. He rolled himself a small marijuana cigarette, lent back in the sumptuous leather chair and requested we play the track again. As he was listening, he told us a tale of time spent on the road with Bob Dylan and the rest of the band, something about getting thrown out of a hotel or some such event. We listened intently, the anticipation of him about to play creating a wonderful atmosphere. He slowly walked into the studio, strapped on his accordion, signalled to me to play the track in his headphones and I hit record.

On this first pass through the track he hardly played a thing, just two or three notes here and there, seemingly at random. Very odd, we all thought. He must just be practicing. At the end of the song he put the accordion down and walked back into the control room, sat in the leather chair and rolled himself another spliff. Shall I play it back? I asked. No need, he replied and began to tell us another "on the road" story. It began something like this:

"We were driving east on route 66, out of San Bernadino, -----

Ten minutes later he got up and walked towards the studio and picked up the accordion again. "Record this on another track" he requested, "oh, and don't play back what I did on the take before. Just hold onto it for later". So I pressed play and record and once again the selective sparseness of what he played was underwhelming. Is this for real? The keyboard player with The Band doesn't seem to have much of a clue. He came back into the control room, rolled a smoke and related another anecdote. "We were five miles out of Louisville, Kentucky, pushing for Columbus, Ohio -----". All very interesting but what about our song? Back on the accordion, another take, another puff, another tale. Where was this all heading? We recorded about five takes in this fashion and didn't have the heart to tell him, as he was putting on his coat and getting ready to leave, that we weren't too pleased. "Been mighty fine meeting you folks, good luck with the record." We were speechless. His last remark as he left was almost as an afterthought. "Just play back all five takes at the same time. Good day to you". And off he went. So we did as he said and played them all back together. Guess what? Bloody genius! All the right chords and phrases, tasty little overlapping licks, sounded like one take.

Another short anecdote regarding United Western studios is worth a mention here. On arrival one morning at the studio, I couldn't help but notice how clean the exterior of the building looked. The alleyway down the side had been swept and washed down and all the dustbins that were usually present there had been removed. There were a couple of men wearing shades patrolling the entrance area. A feeling of something special, if not even sinister hung in the air.

Once inside I asked the lady on reception what was going on. She said she wasn't supposed to say anything to anyone, but seeing as I was a regular visitor she let on. Frank Sinatra had booked the main studio for the day, so that particular part of the building would be out of bounds to all but essential crew. I knew a couple of the resident engineers so was given an escorted visit to where the great man was going to sing. The studio was set up for a big band, about twenty musicians. Headphones, microphones, music stands, the band leader's lectern with its own microphone. I immediately had a flashback and thought of Kevin back at the Island. He would have approved. Then we had to leave and I walked into the smaller studio to greet Dirk.

Now I can't exactly recall how it came about that I was crawling on my hands and knees through a galvanised steel air-conditioning duct, but that's what I was doing. I followed my leader who was one of the studio maintenance engineers and as we approached the grill cover that vented air into the main studio, he signaled to me to be absolutely silent. You could hear the wonderful music loud and clear. What you couldn't hear too well was the vocal, drowned out by the power of the big band. But I saw his trousered legs. Both of them. And his black, highly polished shoes. Not sure where the guys with the shades were, so we quickly shuffled around and returned from whence we had come.

Never did get to see Frank Sinatra in concert, but I got closer than most.

I travelled to Edmonton, Alberta with Spencer Davis to engineer another album with him as a producer at Darryl Goede Studios, for a band called U.S.K. I fell in love with Canada and the Canadians. All the conveniences of an American lifestyle but without the bullish hype. It was October and incredibly warm for the time of year in that part of the world. I asked one of the locals when did they expect the inevitable snow? A week after next he confidently replied. Sure enough, about two weeks later when I was back in L.A. I made a telephone call to the studio manageress regarding some tape copies of the final mixes. How much snow was there I enquired? "Oh, the usual" she said. "About two feet. Might get heavy next week."

Another memorable studio experience for me was working on the Sammy Hagar live album *All Night Long* which I mixed at The Record Plant in Sausalito, just north of San Francisco, with Capitol Records' producer John Carter. John had fostered Bob Seger's career at Capitol, culminating in his 1976 platinum album *Night Moves*. John Carter was also credited with relaunching Tina Turner's career, producing her first album for Capitol in 1984, *Private Dancer*. John was good friends with Janet, from her days at Capitol and we enjoyed lunch with him and his charming wife Jenny on several occasions in their beautiful and very exclusive Frank Lloyd Wright house up in the Hollywood Hills. He kindly flew Janet up to the Bay to join me on a weekend off. He was returning to L.A. for a couple of days so he threw me the keys to his hired Ford Camaro, the use of which was heavily utilised. We drove miles exploring this picturesque part of Northern California, especially around the sweeping vineyards of the Napa and Sonoma valleys, a most beautiful part of our planet where I vowed to return one day. Maybe next year. Anyway, I was suitably refreshed when Janet flew back to L.A. and went back into the studio with John to put the final touches to the record. Released in the U.K. in 1980, the album was renamed *Loud and Clear*.

What was becoming increasingly loud and clear to me was that, despite our exciting and eventful life together, Janet and I were growing in different directions. As we sat down to dinner one night in our West Hollywood apartment, I ventured to suggest that perhaps I should move out, get my own place and have some time apart. I was quite taken aback when, without hesitation, she over enthusiastically agreed, to the extent that the following day she had picked up a copy of one of the local papers and had found me a couple of apartments to go look at. Within a week I was moving my belongings into a studio flat about six blocks away. Janet dug out some cutlery, saucepans, plates and dishes, along with towels and linen, bedsheets and pillows. I was sorted.

My first night there and I had invited her over for dinner. I rustled up a modest meal, she brought over the wine, we listened to some music and talked about the good old days. It was the most fun we had had together in months. But despite this auspicious start to my new life living alone, the following year was going to end in abject failure.

With the greatest of respect to my very kind, helpful new landlord, the apartment was a bit of a dump. A rusty old iron-framed, stained mattress that pulled down from the wall, threadbare carpets and a cockroach infested kitchen, along with the shower head that kept coming unscrewed and a toilet that refused to flush made me think that I should have spent more time and attention finding my new home. This was one part of West Hollywood that had escaped the cultural renaissance.

But no matter. I had no intention of spending any more time than necessary there and I would soon be on my feet again. Except the ability to stand tall is severely restricted when you are spending increasing amounts of time legless. My daily diet had become one of beer for breakfast and cocaine for lunch. The mumblings into the tape machine had begun again in earnest. Most evenings were spent bar-hopping, driving, usually off my head to the houses of complete strangers to buy nasty, cheap, impure cut-cocaine. Trawl the streets of Hollywood looking for hookers, for more drink and drugs, more excitement.

The depths of my cocaine addiction reached new lows when I engineered some sessions at one studio out in the San Fernando Valley who, by mutual consent, paid for my services in grams of the white powder. Oblivious to the dangers, I was hitting the self-destruct button and it felt good. Until that is of course, the next day, waking up feeling like death. Grab a beer for breakfast -----

I was, over the course of the next twelve months, mugged and robbed three times, held up by gunpoint at a cash machine in the early hours of the morning and beaten within an inch of my life one late drunken night outside my apartment for telling a very big black guy to "fuck off!"

Not very clever.

It is with no degree of pride or even guilt that I recount these tales of woe, merely as an indication of the thinness of the veneer of respectability that separates the most fortunate of us from the hellish experiences that for others are the norm. I did manage to hold on to some degree of self-respectability and pull myself through this retched period, if only because of the love I knew I had from others. From Janet and her family, from my music industry friends, on and off the soccer field and, most importantly, my family back in England. How could I have let them down so badly? This had to stop, and it did, in 1984 when, for the sake of my health and sanity, I had to say goodbye to Hollywood, to Los Angeles, to California and the United States of America. Even then, it would take a few years of living back in London before I would finally shake off my demons.

The most significant single event that would shape my soon-to-be-found new happiness would be my meeting, in 1989, with an angel. Do they come down from heaven, or are they already here, simply waiting for us to find them? My angel, Kim, was living in west London, unaware that she held the future key to a very dark room that someone, six thousand miles away at the time, was locked in.

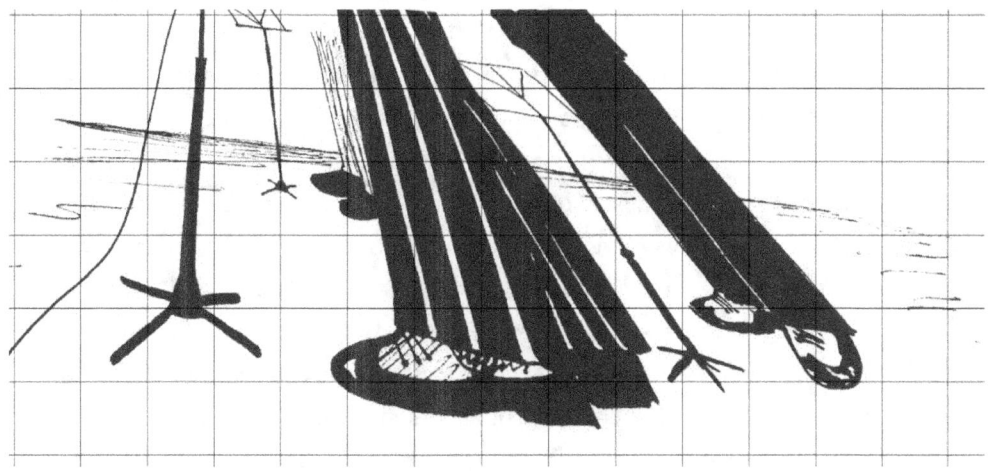

--- I got closer than most

Just Before She Fainted

John Helliwell had been a regular player in the ex-pats football team, and as the saxophonist with Supertramp, he was one of our much-loved, high-profile players, until he injured his knee and was unable to play anymore. He was a little upset and found comfort from Rod, who suggested that maybe he could come along next week and referee. Not the same as playing, but at least you would still be a part of our close-knit community of football lovers. The following week, we were out in the San Fernando Valley for our usual Sunday morning kick about and were all kitted up and ready to play. In the distance, I could make out John's Jeep approaching. He parked up, got out of the car and approached the pitch. He was wearing full battle dress. A complete referee's outfit: black top and shorts, a whistle, yellow and red cards, a notebook and a pencil. He called the two team captains to the centre circle and flipped a coin. Rod suggested that perhaps he was over doing this referee business and John looked at him and scowled. This disparagement probably contributed to Rod receiving the first yellow card and a stark warning that any more tackles like that Mr. Stewart and you will be taking an early bath. Oh, what fun we had out on the football field and John's antics contributed so much. Such a grand gesture of comedic clout and a true measure of the kind-hearted genius of the man.

There was another Sunday match that surely has to go down in the archives of all-time footballing classics. One of our regular goalkeepers was an English chap called Nick who, along with another English gent ran a bespoke limousine service. In a gesture of pet-owning extravagance, they turned up for the game driving one of their sleek, elongated black limousines, out of which jumped a pair of grown Cheetahs. With incredulous disbelief on the part of all the sporting participants, combined with the justifiable collective fear felt by twenty-two grown men, the whole of the match, both first and second half was played along one side of the pitch, the side away from where the big cats sat, basking in the warm sunshine.

Only in California.

During one of our Wednesday evening games, I mentioned to Rod that I wouldn't be around the following week as I was going to be in the U.K. for a while. Not to worry, he said, and in any event, he was going to be in London himself doing a gig at Earls Court. He very kindly invited me to the show and gave me a contact telephone number where he would be staying. He asked me to call him and he would sort out the tickets. I saw the London show and the next day was in Island's offices chatting with studio manager Trevor Wyatt. We were talking about football. "Can you play a game with us on Tuesday?" he asked. Of course I would, and at the same time Trevor asked if I knew of anyone else I could recruit for the match. The Island team were short on numbers and this was an important music business league match. I said I would have a think and see you next Tuesday.

I called Rod. Fancy a game on Tuesday night? Most definitely, came his reply. So on the evening of the match, I turned up at Rod's Chelsea retreat and climbed into the back of his Range Rover, squeezed in amongst the Adidas footballs. His driver took us to the astro-turf pitch in Kings Cross and Rod walked a couple of paces behind me. I entered the changing room and Trevor thanked me for making the effort and threw me some kit. Had I managed to find anybody else? Only one, I replied as Rod entered, right on cue.

Within a few months, Janet had a new love in her life. I still had keys to the apartment and had gone along to collect a few of my things. It was Paul's car I saw in the driveway where my car used to be parked. It was Paul's shoes in the hallway where once used to be my dusty footprints. In my old wardrobe hung his clothes. It's then that it hits you. Quite a strange feeling of having been supplanted, replaced and discarded. I hoped he was paying his share of the rent. I eventually got to meet Paul and oddly enough we got on really well. So imagine my surprise when, a few months later I had returned for a final visit to collect some of my boxes of stuff from the garage. Overwhelmed by the desire to take one last look at my old apartment I climbed the steps at the rear and made my entrance via the utility room behind the kitchen. I could make out the grunting and groaning of a couple making love in the bedroom. I recognised Janet's voice for obvious reasons; I had after all been in that, so to speak, position myself on many previous occasions. But who the hell was Mark??!! Yes, that was the name coming out of Janet's mouth as she begged for more. I couldn't believe my ears. Mark? My first thoughts were of my new friend Paul. Wait until I tell him, Janet. How dare you cheat on him. I then began to chuckle to myself as the ludicrous irony of the whole thing exploded before me. I slipped quietly away.

Strange how things turn out, how one's loyalties can shift.

When I look back now at my experiences of living in Los Angeles for those predominately happy, industrious and relatively successful nine years (well, at least the first eight, the last being a lost one) I find myself, probably because I am recalling the end of my time in California, remembering much additional detail. Like the night Janet and I went to The Roxy Theatre on Sunset Strip to enjoy a three-and-a-half-hour concert by Bruce Springsteen. The Paul Korda album launch just a few doors down at The Troubadour, where after his show a lone figure approached the unlit stage. The waiters and busboys were cleaning up as people were leaving. We waited around and were rewarded by an impromptu performance at the piano by Rickie Lee Jones, who at the time was achieving international success with her hit single *Chuck E.s in Love*. Through the smoky haze, you could just make out her tiny figure at the dimly lit piano. Someone placed a bottle of bourbon next to her, and it wouldn't have been out of place if Humphrey Bogart and Lauren Bacall had walked in.

My friend Phil Brown and his wife Jackie travelled out from Birmingham to holiday in California. When we met in the arrivals lounge at L.A.X., Jackie was so excited at the prospect of seeing many Hollywood stars and was convinced she would meet her favourite television idol, James Garner, of Rockford Files fame. On their last night before returning to England, there was no plan to go out anywhere, until a few beers later when the cry rang out for some live country music. We jumped in the car and drove along Lankershim Boulevard out into the valley to the hottest Country and Western bar in town, The Palomino. The band Canned Heat was already on stage playing, so we grabbed a few beers and found a table. Lo and behold, who was sitting just a few feet away from us? Jackie's jaw dropped. Without a moment's hesitation, she leapt out of her chair and went over and introduced herself to, yes, James Garner himself. "I told you I would see him" were her last words just before she fainted.

Living in and around Hollywood one could be forgiven for being a little blasé when it came to celebrity spotting. Like the time Janet and I were driving through Beverley Hills on our way to the beach when a white, convertible Rolls Royce swerved unexpectedly across our path, driven by the stunningly well turned out, albeit somewhat reckless Diana Ross. She waved her apologies.

There was an unannounced visit to our Wednesday evening kick-around at the running track in Beverley Hills by British journalist and television presenter Alan Whicker. He was filming his *Living with Uncle Sam* 1984/85 series for I.T.V.'s Whickers' World and the subject matter was expatriates living in California. He brought along his film crew and chatted with us all both pitch-side and at the customary post-match guzzle in the Cock and Bull on Sunset. An exquisitely charming man, he was understandably most interested in Rod. Sadly, these scenes remain on yet another cutting-room floor, quite possibly archived for later viewing.

Janet and I became good friends with musician Kim Gardner, who was a close neighbour in West Hollywood. He had found fame with the musical trio of Ashton, Gardner and Dyke and they had enjoyed a massive hit record with Capitol in 1971, called *Resurrection Shuffle*. Kim kept as a pet and unique conversation piece an extremely large, rather ferocious looking albino shark in a large, yet barely big enough fish tank in his living room. One afternoon Kim and I went to the local aquarium supplies shop in Hollywood to buy his shark something to eat. If I remember correctly he purchased two frogs, some crickets and a small water snake. Whilst Kim was standing at the check-out waiting to pay for his pet's lunch, I stood alone staring at some other large fish in a tank, mesmerised by the graceful swirl of the fish's tail, the hypnotic to-ing and fro-ing around its aquatic wonder world. The peace and tranquillity of the moment was destroyed when a man's large, black hand appeared next to my face, teasingly pointing and waving at the fish. The fish became agitated and the man's voice proclaimed victory over the entrapped species. I turned to look at and confront the protagonist of this unkind act, my eyes only to be met by the man's belted trouser waist. Okay, I thought, so he is taller than me, but words must be said. Except that when I raised my gaze to confront his towering face, I was speechless. It's not every day that you meet the Heavyweight Champion of the World in an aquarium shop and in the winter of 1978 that is exactly where Muhammad Ali was. Kim came over and all hands were shaking with this mighty man who had with him as his accomplice a small young black boy. His son, I thought? He kindly gave an autograph and as he walked away towards the door I heard him quietly preaching to the young boy about how scared he had made the fish feel and that was why you should be kind to all animals, treat all creatures with respect ------.

How about over-running your official finish time on a recording session at Crystal Sound Studios in Hollywood, only to be invaded by the next client who waltzes into the live room with his entourage of about a dozen young, beautiful and predominantly black musicians and singers. The main man, sunshades on, head rolling from side to side, led by the arm of a carer directly to the piano begins to play. Like a musical party-popper going off, the whole studio explodes with vocal harmonies and hand-clapping, foot-tapping rhythms. You are in the presence of greatness and of joy. You are in the recording studio with Stevie Wonder.

Oh Selfie, oh Selfie, were for art tho'? Not bloody invented yet!

Then there was the year when Hollywood was on fire. The Kirkwood Bowl/Laurel Canyon fire of 1979 destroyed twenty-three homes and the smoke and flames could be seen from Hollywood Boulevard. Driving to work with the hills ablaze.

Lenny's pool party. This was one of the guys I used to get my drugs from and he lived in an apartment block that had, as was commonplace, its own swimming pool. Janet and I were invited to the afternoon gathering and were somewhat startled to notice that everyone in the pool was naked. I was about to make my excuses and leave when I noticed that Janet had already stripped off and was jumping in. Oh well, I thought. What the heck. As it transpired, there was no orgy to follow. I couldn't have coped with that although I'm not so sure about Janet.

There was another party, a big industry splash and I can't remember for whom. You could find yourself getting invited to all manner of parties just from a contact at a record label or through a musician friend, especially if you were part of the "Hollywood Circle" which, albeit reluctantly, I was. But I do recall that this particular event was in an especially exclusive part of Beverley Hills. The house address was 10,100 Sunset Boulevard! A huge, detached mansion that used to belong to American actress and Hollywood sex symbol Jayne Mansfield. Nicknamed "The Pink Palace", there were Grecian statuettes in the landscaped gardens, a heart-shaped swimming pool and white suited butlers milling around the hundreds of guests, serving an unstoppable flow of Dom Perignon Champagne in cut-glass crystal and at each table endless mounds of cocaine on silver platters. I got completely hammered, which is why I can't remember very much else about this lavish affair.

The one magical Wednesday evening when I decided to walk the short distance to the Beverley Hills running track for our regular game of footy. I was met halfway by Mr Stewart who gave me a lift in his bright yellow, spanking new Lamborghini. Talk about making a grand entrance; I was teasingly whistled at and jeered pitch-side by some very jealous team-mates.

Breakfast at a musician's house up in the West Hollywood Hills, before going off together for our daily duties at the studio. (Which studio? Which musician? No diary! I think it might have been Michael Monarch, the guitarist from Detective.) The unforgettable sight of the lady of the house, as she appeared in her dressing gown and slippers, no make-up, hair in a mess, serving us up the bacon, hash browns, eggs and orange juice. No diary is required to vividly remember how absolutely stunning a young, as yet undiscovered Demi Moore looked that morning.

One moment of madness, after an all-night session with guitarist "Snuffy" Walden. I hope, Snuffy, that you will forgive my telling of this tale of lunacy. We are both older and wiser now (or at least older) and I know you have gone on to have a very successful and established career, both as a musician and songwriter, but we were both much younger and foolhardy. We can only gasp now at the youthful and reckless self-belief embodied in the following short story.

We had been on session all day, recording out in North Hollywood at Mama Joe's studio, with you on guitar and John "Rabbit" Bundrick on keyboards. We enjoyed somewhat of a party atmosphere throughout the afternoon and evening, culminating in the three of us emptying a bottle of the Mexican speciality drink, Mezcal. Made from the Agave cactus plant and referred to in pre-Spanish Mexican culture as the "elixir of the Gods", we left the studio in the early hours, as the sun came up, in a slightly hallucinated and extremely merry state of mind. Riding in Snuffy's bright, garishly red pickup truck we drove to the nearest Seven Eleven store to pick up a couple of six packs for breakfast. As we drove into the almost empty car park, at speed, giggling away like a couple of stoned teenagers, I noticed two "black and whites" (Los Angeles police cars) parked right by the store entrance, on either side of one vacant parking space. The policemen were sat in one of the cars enjoying a relaxed morning coffee. So where did Snuffy park his red pickup truck? Right in between the two cop cars. As the truck screeched to a halt, out stepped Snuffy and with a tip of his Stetson cowboy hat, bid the two incredulous officers good morning and waltzed straight into the store. He returned with the beers under his arm, wished the officers a further good day, stepped back into his red truck and accelerated away. Surely, I thought, the police would be in hot pursuit, but no. Snuffy had successfully used his Texan charm and bravado to good measure and we had unbelievably avoided the grim clutches of the L.A.P.D.

The wonderful array of restaurants:

Carney's, a converted railway carriage parked on Sunset at the start of the Strip, for the best chilli dog on the planet.

The Cock 'n' Bull restaurant/pub on the edge of Beverley Hills, a favourite haunt of us ex-pat footballers after a Wednesday night kick about. Hollywood movie-star Julie Christie flirted with me there after a game, who I'm sure was aware of my friendship with Rod.

El Coyote on Beverly Boulevard, the cheapest and the best Mexican food this side of the Rio Grande! Catch "Happy Hour" and enjoy the free Spanish hors d'oeurvres and litres of dangerously affordable Marguerites.

Fatburger on La Cienega Boulevard, North Hollywood. As the name suggests, it is the biggest, leanest, juiciest hamburger imaginable with all the trimmings. Janet had picked me up one time at LAX in a hired, vintage Rolls-Royce Silver Shadow and driven straight to Fatburger's for lunch. We sat in the car park stuffing our faces, ketchup all over the leather seats.

The original Barney's Beanery on Santa Monica Boulevard. Hard shell tacos with rice and cheesy beans, beers from all around the world and a dozen or more pool tables. One afternoon I put my quarter down on the table as was customary if you wanted to play next. The winner stays on the table. My opponent was a large, bearded truck-driver type with a huge belly and cowboy hat to match. I broke, hitting the triangle head-on, balls rolling everywhere, watching to see which, if any, goes down a pocket first. Only one ball did, the black ball. Truck-driver man slowly and somewhat menacingly came over to me and I felt for certain that I had done something terribly wrong. He held out his hand and congratulated me. "Ain't seen that in fifteen years, kid." Apparently, that is how you win at pool with one shot. He ran a tab for me at the bar and I got very drunk with him. Later that same evening, recovering at home I switched on the late-night news. There had been a gun fight at Barney's Beanery which had left one man dead, who was described as a rather large guy with a cowboy hat and a beard.

Glad I didn't overstay my welcome.

I telephoned my Island engineer friend Bob Potter and told him about my plans to return to England. He was living near Newbury, West Berkshire, with his new wife, and there was a room there for me if needed. He offered helpfully. It was all so anti-climactic. Packed a toothbrush and some underwear, a couple of T-shirts and a spare pair of shoes, grabbed my passport and the trusty "get out of jail free" T.W.A Getaway card, and I was off. Untypically, the flight from Los Angeles to London took a polar route and as we flew east over the southern tip of Iceland I gazed out of the left-hand side of the 'plane. A most beautiful sight to behold as the twisting, transparently colourful skirts of the Aurora Borealis hung spaciously in the night sky. From the ground, this is one of the most magical sights in the Universe. At 38,000 feet, near the top of the troposphere, it is infinitely more so. I had hoped this spectacle was an omen of magical things to come, but when I awoke the next morning in Bob's spare room looking out over the cold Berkshire countryside, I felt nothing but gloom. I had left behind all my friends, work associates, music business and studio connections.

I had left a marriage.

As I lie there, I imagine that I am back in the air-conditioning duct at United Western, staring up at Frank's legs. What to do

next? No point feeling sorry for yourself so, as Frank would say, "pick yourself up, dust yourself off and start all over again."
  Again.

Rod entered, right on cue.

Time Is Money, Mica

I am eternally grateful to Trevor Wyatt. He was at the time studio manager at Island Records' Fallout Shelter studios and head of production for the release of re-mixes and the re-mastering of the label's back catalogue. On my return to the U.K I had paid him a visit and he got me straight into work. Various compilation albums of all the reggae artists on the label, including Toots and The Maytals, Third World, Black Uhuru and of course Bob Marley and The Wailers were required to be assembled. Similarly, with the blues and rock artists: Free, Traffic and Spooky Tooth. The country and folk acts such as Fairport Convention, John Martyn and Nick Drake were being given the same treatment and Trevor gave much of the work to me. He also introduced me to Joe Boyd, the American record producer. Joe had been heavily involved with the careers of Pink Floyd, Fairport Convention, Nick Drake and John Martyn and thanks to Trevor, I found myself in the studio with him as his engineer.

Joe Boyd, along with Trevor Lucas, was producing a posthumous album of the work of English folk singer Sandy Denny, a beautiful boxset entitled *Who Knows Where The Time Goes*. We had found some un-released recordings of Sandy at the piano, playing and singing live, sessions that I, coincidently, had recorded many years earlier. We pieced them together as best we could, but I remember Joe commenting on how he would have liked to have re-recorded some of the vocals which, of course, we couldn't. Sandy had died in 1978, aged thirty-one, in a Wimbledon hospital from a brain haemorrhage.

Back in chapter two, I referred to the untimely loss of so many of the Island artists. Without wishing to simply provide a morbid list of the label's deceased, the following, along with Sandy Denny were all to die young and should be remembered. Blessedly in their wake, a fine body of work lives on:

Nick Drake, singer/songwriter, 1974, aged 26. Paul Kossoff, guitarist/songwriter, 1976, aged 25. Jim Capaldi, drummer with Traffic and solo artist in his own right, 2005, aged 60. Chris Wood, saxophonist with the same band, 1983, aged 39. John Martyn, folk singer/songwriter, 2009, aged 60. Robert Palmer, vocalist/songwriter, 2003, aged 54. Rebop Kwaku Baah, conga player, 1983, aged 38. Norman "Dinky" Diamond, drummer, 2004, aged 53. Andy Fraser, bass player/songwriter, 2015, aged 62. Dave Swarbrick, folk musician, 2016, aged 75. Robert Nesta Marley, Jamaican reggae singer, songwriter, musician, 1981, aged 36.

Others from the period, sadly missed, who were not part of the Island label, but with whom I had the greatest pleasure to work with:

John Bonham, 1980 aged 32.
David Byron, 1985, 38.
Steve Marriott, 1991, 44.
Harry Nilsson, 1994, 52.
Linda McCartney, 1998, 56.
George Harrison, 2001, 58.
Billy Preston, 2006, 59.
Boz Burrell, 2006, 60.
Arif Mardin, 2006, 74.
Donald "Duck" Dunn, 2012, 70.
Joe Cocker, 2014, 70.
Dallas Taylor, 2015, 66.
George Martin, 2016, 90.
Leon Russell, 2016, 74.

My sadness, sympathy and joy are in equal measure. To have known all of the above, to have shared wonderful times in the recording studio with them, to be in a position to say "look at my

C.V. Not bad, eh?!" is so much more than I could have ever imagined back in 1963, standing outside my sister Pat's bedroom door, daring to dream.

In the here and now as I write this section of the book in 2016, it seems that every day I am reading of yet another pop star's death. The year is but half-way through and regrettably another catalogue of lost creative souls is forthcoming:

David Bowie, aged 69; Natalie Cole, 65; Glen Frey, 67; Prince, 57; David Guest, 62.

In this age of mortal longevity, it seems that the good die relatively young. Perhaps their earlier youthful excesses have been brought home to bear, or is it more kindly to suggest that modern-day pressures of the media and social networking have taken their premature toll? Along with a myriad of other show-business celebrities who have, this year thus far, at an alarming rate, departed our world, it serves to remind us of the fleeting scarcity and fragility of talent.

But let us return to the more light-hearted, jovial experiences of my return to the U.K.

Trevor Wyatt had also put me forward to engineer a few sessions with Scottish-born songwriter Mike Scott and his band The Waterboys on their second album, *A Pagan Place*. Again, Trevor linked me up with a top producer, John Williams (Alison Moyet, Simple Minds) to engineer sessions with London Records' band Blancmange for their second album *Mange Tout*. Assisting me on these sessions at Island's Fallout Studio was a very talented and likeable young man, Stephen Street. He exhibited all the "right stuff" to go on to become a successful engineer/producer, working with Morrissey and The Smiths, Blur and The Kaiser Chiefs. The Blancmange record we worked on together went into the top-ten of the charts. Life was on the up for me, with plenty of studio work and it felt good to be back amongst the familiar sights, smells and sounds of London. Yet despite my outward appearance, sporting a robust California suntan, several years of the bodily abuse of drug taking and alcoholic excess had taken its toll. I was in need of a physical and mental re-build.

I rented a one-bedroom flat near Ealing Common, got my place back in the Island football team and made many new friends. Once again, it became Wednesday evenings for football, not in Beverley Hills this time but on Homefield Recreation ground in Hammersmith, a stone's throw from the Island offices in St. Peter's Square. After each game, we would retire to the nearby Cross Keys public house for some light refreshments. Some evenings not so light, but always good natured. "The Keys" as it was known was a central part of both the business and after-work social life of Island, as it had been when I had drunk there with John Martyn and Danny Thompson all those years ago. One evening I was introduced to a chap from the royalty department of the label and on hearing my name he suggested I call into his office the next day. Bring along some I.D. because I may have some good news for you. As we sipped our morning coffee he produced from a filing cabinet a stack of royalty statements going back several years. The artist name on the paperwork was the band Free and the album was *Heartbreaker*. He explained that there had been no forwarding address for me over the years and hence the amounts due to me, as the producer with a one percent of sales royalty, had been held on account. He handed me a cheque for just over two thousand seven hundred pounds which in 1984 was, for me, a substantial amount (about nine thousand pounds in today's money). We shook hands and he updated the account with my contact details. Before too long those details would need to be updated again because I used that money as a deposit on my first property, a one-bedroom flat in Chiswick. I was on the first step of what would prove to be a very lucrative housing market in 1980's London.

Another interesting encounter one evening at The Keys secured me many "brownie points" with Island staff members. Pint in hand I joined the busy table, where all the attention and conversation seemed to be focused on one particular gentleman, Peter. The talk was about forthcoming albums and single releases, tour dates, promotional activity and general music business gossip. I sat quietly listening. I was still in a Utopian bubble of excitement at being back in London and was enjoying the company and the banter. At a suitable interval, I introduced myself to Peter who I was conveniently sitting right next to. He showed genuine interest as I unravelled my tale to him, of my returning from having lived in Los Angeles and of my renewed association with Island records here in London. He told me he was a D.J. and I said something like "Oh, that must be interesting. How long have you been doing that for?" Quite a few years, was his reply. I asked him who he worked for, for example, did he do private functions, you know, like weddings, or did he work in pubs and night clubs. Mostly radio, he smiled. What a smashing bloke, I thought. We chatted some more, I got up to leave, shook his hand and wished him luck. The next day as I breezed into the Island offices I was greeted with cheers and soft applause. Trevor explained that the D.J. I had been chatting to was no less than B.B.C. Radio One's top presenter Peter Powell. His best remembered features are *5 45s at 5.45*, where Powell played five new singles, and the *Record Race*, in which listeners had to identify songs purely from their intros. Every Tuesday he ran through the new singles chart which had been revealed at lunchtime, the first chance many young listeners got to hear the new Top 40. He also featured the album chart on Wednesday evenings. Everyone who had sat at that table last night, except me, knew who this man was and how important it must be to have him on-side. His position of influence in radio was second to none and the fact that he was being spoken to by someone who didn't have a clue who he was, proved most refreshing for the Island team.

I suspect it was equally as refreshing for Peter Powell.

When I had first moved to London in 1970 there would have been no more than the three or four dozen recording studios that had been on my original list. By the mid-eighties, there would be more like a hundred. In those intervening years a large number of independent studios had opened up, so there was plenty of work for freelance studio engineers, as there had been in the States. Also, as in the States, work would come by word of mouth from musicians, studios and producers who you had worked with in the past. Today's modern producers/engineers will almost certainly have management representation whereas during my years in the U.K. and in the States, I always took care of my own business.

I walked into Flame studios, near Manor House in north London and introduced myself to Mel Simpson, the studio owner. We had a mutual friend in Brian Short, a songwriter and producer from Newcastle who I had met, worked and played football with, in Los Angeles. Flame had a decent sized live room and although the control room was compact Mel had kitted out the studio with all the latest equipment of the day: Emulator keyboard and sequencer, AKAI S950 sampler, Atari ST. 1040 midi sequencer with Cubase software. These were the early days of computerised studio systems and strangely enough I had not come across this advanced technology in the States, where the emphasis was still very much on analogue recording and live performance, undoubtedly driven by the fact that the level of musicianship in the States is so much higher. In America, it is not uncommon to hear top quality High School bands featuring twelve-year-old kids, reading and playing very sophisticated musical manuscripts. Out there they are taught to read music and achieve musical competence at a very early age. Conversely, here in the U.K., we teach children how to reluctantly generate annoyingly screechy sounds from violins and recorders. When my children were at school in the nineties, music was only taught during lunch break or after school. I always thought that was appalling and in my years as a co-opted parent/governor, I repeatedly made my feelings known. But sadly, it seems little has changed.

So, back in the U.K. with lots of new technical wizardry to get my head around I had a lot to learn and Mel was the perfect teacher. Although the early sessions that I worked on at Flame were mostly demos, it was bread and butter work and it paid the bills. Mel's guidance through the newly developing world of digital recording stood me in good stead for the technological changes that were on the way.

Mel had me working alongside gospel producer Nicky Brown who, as part of The London Gospel Community Choir, had introduced two of his vocalists to Flame. Lavine Hudson, with whom we recorded songs for her debut album *Intervention*, on Virgin records and tracks with the greatest of British gospel/soul singers, Mica Paris. At the time Mica was unsigned, but it was apparent very early on that this incredibly talented young lady was going places. Her temperament suggested a reluctance at times to perform in the studio and she certainly tested the patience of her manager, Viv Broughton as well as mine and Nicky's. "Don't feel like singing today" was her usual lament. "Time is money, Mica," was always Viv's response "so you've got no choice. Now do us all a favour and get a vocal on this track". It was all a bit of a teasing game, good natured and at times quite hilarious. Mica would sulk into the studio, pick up the headphones, stand at the microphone and completely blow us all away with her powerfully passionate singing. Perfect intonation, the clearest of enunciation and so much soul. The tracks we recorded at Flame contributed to Mica's first album deal, *So Good*, released in 1988 on Fourth and Broadway (a U.S. subsidiary of Island) and certified platinum by the British Phonographic Industry.

Before we leave Flame studios, I must just relate a short story told to me by Mel, the studio owner. A young band he had been recording at his studio were massive fans of The Shadows, Cliff Richard's former backing band and had in fact recorded a cover version of one of their hits, I forget which, but that is of no consequence. The band fantasised as to how wonderful it would be if they could get Hank Marvin, the lead guitarist with The Shadows, to play the guitar solo, just like on the original record. As it happened, Mel had worked with Hank, had a contact number and amazingly got him to agree to come to the studio and record the guitar solo. The guys in the band were delirious with excitement as Hank walked in, switched on his Fender amp, plugged in his Stratocaster guitar and started playing. Now according to Mel, this was a one take wonder. After all, Hank had been playing the song for years so knew his parts back to front. Into the control room for a playback and all is fine. Assuming complete satisfaction, Hank unplugged his guitar, switched off his amplifier and readied himself to leave. But hang on. One of the guys in the band had heard something. Play the solo back again. There, stop. Listen again. There's a tiny mistake, the faintest blip of a "funny" note. Er, Hank, before you go could you come and listen again. So embarrassing, having to point out to a Great Master that he's played a wrong note. Hank listened back and nodded his recognition of the suspect musical moment. That's fine, he said confidently, just like I played it on the original. You said you wanted it exactly the same. After Hank had gone someone dug out the original Shadows version and lo and behold, at exactly the same spot in the solo, was the same "funny" note. Genius.

Another big thank you goes out to Mike Finesilver, who co-founded Pathway Studios in Newington Green, north London. Mike had found fame and some small fortune from co-writing Arthur Brown's classic 1968 hit *Fire*. His studio was a small eight-track facility, noted for excellent drum sounds and big, warm analogue recordings, such that he attracted many influential bands to come and record there, including Madness, Nick Lowe, The Damned, The Police and Elvis Costello. Many of the scenes from the 1981 docudrama/comedy film featuring Madness, *Take it or Leave it* were shot at Pathway studios and although I was never to record any major projects there myself, Mike did provide me with much useful employment and I am happy to have been a small part of that studios important history.

One of my footballing team-mates in London, who I was to spend many happy hours with both on and off the pitch, was George Coulter. His Northern Irish humour became legendary in The Keys and I have always thought that George missed his vocation. No other person I have met could match his encyclopaedic depth of comedy. With a joke for every subject matter, for every occasion and eventuality, he could reduce me to tears at any point with his always perfectly timed deliveries. He ran his own printing business for a while on Acton Lane, near where I was now living in my second flat. One night in the Keys he described how an attractive young girl who was working in the same building had caught his eye. He brought her along to the Keys one night and we all thought the same. Very young, very attractive. No chance, George. In your dreams. But he persisted and twenty-nine years later he and Charmaine are still very happily in love and living together, as am I with Kim, my angel in waiting, the one with the key, whom Charmaine introduced me to about a month after she had met George.

In 1988, just prior to meeting Kim, I had moved up the property ladder into a two-bedroom ground floor garden flat in Chiswick. Kim moved in with me, we married and raised our two children in that most delightful part of west London. Nearby was Eden studios, a state-of-the-art professional recording facility used by many of the top artists of the day: Elvis Costello, Joe Jackson, Tom Jones, Kylie Minogue and George Michael to name but a few. Eden studios was the brainchild of three ex-B.B.C. employees, Philip Love, Mike Gardner and Piers Ford-Crush and with the studios almost literally on my doorstep, it was a convenient place for me to offer my freelance services. Unfortunately, I never found myself in that studio working with any major artists, but again, bread and butter projects kept the roof over our heads for a number of years. Besides which, I got to meet some interesting industry people there, including Boy George, who frequently manned the reception desk, answering the telephone, chatting to musicians and engineers. A very likeable, friendly and polite man. I also rubbed shoulders with Sinead O'Conner, the Irish singer/songwriter who had a massive global hit with the Prince composition *Nothing Compares 2 U* which I believe was mixed at Eden with producer/engineer Chris Birkett. A controversial character, Sinead was vociferous in her opinions on women's rights, politics and particularly child abuse in the Catholic Church, so there was no shortage of heated debates in the studio lounge.
Not sure what Boy George might have made of her.

Across the road from our garden flat in Chiswick lived Boz Burrell, bass player with English blues/rock supergroup Bad Company. That band, under the same management company as Led Zeppelin (with Peter Grant) had taken the music world by storm in the mid-seventies. Their debut album *Bad Company* reached number one on the U.S. Billboard charts and went on to be certified five times platinum. Other successful albums and singles followed and they remained at the top of the industry tree for several years. You can easily go check out the history of that band yourself, but what you may never know from any reference books or magazine articles is that the bass player was into remote controlled model aeroplanes.

Boz or his girlfriend Kath would often drop by our home to borrow a guitar lead, a music stand, or the obligatory cup of sugar and were always most generous in supplying us with a bottle of wine or a recreational smoke by way of thanks. The roles would often be reversed and myself or Kim would pop over to The Burrells, always and I repeat, always greeted by Boz at the door with his bass guitar umbilically attached to his person. In their front room was a baby grand piano and displayed on the top of this beautiful instrument were two petrol engine propeller driven models, both hand-built by Boz. One day he was sitting at his kitchen table, bass guitar on his lap, putting the final touches to another splendid model aeroplane. "Where" I asked "are you going to display that one?" "I will have to buy another piano" was the laughing response!

At the top of a hill in Richmond Park was where the model 'plane enthusiasts would congregate to show off their flying skills and it was on his return from one such outing that I spotted a very dissolute looking Boz. I had gazed out of our front room window and could see him walking towards his front gate with a carrier bag full of bits of a broken aeroplane. A piece of snapped wing protruded from the top and dirty brown oil was dripping out of the bottom of the bag. Boz walked slowly and sorrowfully, head bent down in the manner of a broken man. I went over to him and asked what had happened. He explained that he had been on the hill in the park flying his 'plane when a fellow hobbyist standing next to him had enquired as to his movements with the joystick and throttle controls. "I'm flying my 'plane, right?" said Boz. "Wrong," came the reply from the gentleman. "That's not your 'plane" he continued, pointing to a crash site in the bows of a nearby tree. "That's where your 'plane is."

After many happy years in Chiswick, we up-scaled to our first house in East Sheen, southwest London and lost touch with Boz and Kath. I drove past their house one day on my way to work at Eden, and I noticed two baby grand pianos in the front room.

In the early days, with a young family to support, I took a permanent studio position at Island's music publishing studios on King Street in Hammersmith. It was mostly demos for would be songwriters and bands looking to get signed to the label, so you could say a step down the career ladder for me. But I didn't let my ego get in the way of what were regular hours and a steady income, besides which, I got to work with some quality artists. One such talented singer/songwriter was Tim Freeman. Tim had enjoyed success with his band Frazier Chorus. Originally a four-piece, they signed to British indie record label 4AD and released the single *Sloppy Heart* in 1987. Shortly afterwards they moved to Virgin Records, and achieved reasonable chart success with a string of melodic pop songs about Dream Kitchens, Living Rooms, Happy Eaters and Little Chefs, all taken from their 1989 debut album, *Sue*. With the emergence of the indie-dance scene in the early 1990's the band changed tack. Singles from their second album *Ray* were remixed into indie-dance floor-fillers by a number of top re-mixers, including Paul Oakenfold, Chad Jackson and Youth.

I engineered and produced Tim's solo album *Wide Awake* at the Island Music studio and although we received little or no radio airplay the album exhibits Tim's song writing prowess as a thinking man's view of the world through the prism of pop. His sardonic lyrics and wistful melodies are most engaging and this will always be one of my favourite albums to have worked on. Should have played it to Peter Powell.

Richard Manners was the managing director of Island Music and he put me together with ex-Uriah Heep vocalist David Byron to produce his next E.P. I had already worked with David on the *Rough Diamond* album, with Steve Smith producing, so we had the required chemistry already in place. I put together a band featuring some of the most trustworthy and capable musicians around at the time: Alan Spenner (Joe Cocker) on bass, Neil Conteh (David Bowie/Mick Jagger) on drums, Tim Renwick (Sutherland Brothers, Al Stewart) on guitar and John Bundrick (Bob Marley, Johnny Nash, The Who) on keys. In addition, we engaged The Chanter Sisters, Irene and Doreen (Elton John, Roxy Music) for backing vocal duties. We checked into The Power Plant studios in northwest London and rattled off three tracks in as many days. Recorded, overdubbed and mixed. Great fun. You can always tell when you listen to a record what the vibe in the studio must have been like. If it sounds fresh, crisp and lively then that's how it would have been. Yes, pay attention to the details, be as meticulous as needed, but most importantly, let the musicians enjoy themselves and play their best. This is one such record and I still enjoy listening to it today. So sad that within less than a year after finishing the record the charming and very talented David Byron was dead.

On a lighter note, at the same time as we were recording David's album at The Power Plant, a young, attractive and up-and-coming female vocalist was working next door on her debut album. Sade's *Diamond Life* won the Brit Award for "Best British Album" in 1985 and went on to sell more than six million copies. I first met her in the reception area during a lunch break, and we chatted briefly. She needed fifty pence to make a 'phone call from the public telephone, so I obliged. Next time I see her -----.

Another album worthy of note that I recorded at the Island Music publishing studios was with ex-T'Pau guitarist supreme Dean Howard and his band The Herbs. *The Other Side* also featured Jim Riley vocals and guitar, Russ Kennedy on bass didgeridoo and Chapman Stick, and John Keeble on drums. One of the great "lost" albums of the period.

My time spent at the Island publishing studio helped re-establish my credentials as a freelance engineer/producer, and I was as busy as ever. Muff Winwood, who was now head of A&R for Sony/S2 Records, put me together with the Geordie band Prefab Sprout and, in 1985, sent me up to Lynx Studios in Newcastle to record an album of what was initially meant to be just demos. The band had enjoyed critically acclaimed success with their previous album, *Steve McQueen*, produced by English musician Thomas Dolby, and expectations were high for the next album. However, Paddy McAloon, the primary writer and vocalist, was determined that the recordings we made that year were to be released as an album in its own right and not as a demo of the next album. The *Protest Songs* album, as it was to be titled, was not released until 1989, and we enjoyed a hit with the song *Life of Surprises*.

The studio up in Newcastle was awkwardly positioned on the first floor above an industrial unit, where the noises of heavy machinery presented sound-proofing challenges hitherto unmet. But out of that adversity, we created a unique audio introduction to the last but one track on the album, *'til the Cows come Home* whereby a half dozen microphones were deployed around the factory floor, with unprecedented lengths of cable reaching back upstairs to the control room. The workers kindly agreed to start up all the machines, one after the other, with the increasing cacophony of whirring and humming been added to by the sound of clanging hammers hitting huge iron anvils. We recorded about five minutes of this din, edited together the "best" bits and stuck it to the front of the aforementioned song. One of, if not the most unique of song introductions.

The album that eventually followed *Steve McQueen* was recorded after *Protest Songs* and I contributed as an engineer, recording backing tracks for *King of Rock 'n' Roll*, *Cars and Girls* and *Hey, Manhattan*. The album, titled *From Langley Park to Memphis*, reached number five in the U.K. charts. If I may quote Jason Ankeny and part of his "AllMusic" review of the *Protest Songs* album:

"—*the stately grace and ingenious wit which remain the hallmark of every Prefab Sprout record*---"

One of my all-time favourite bands and the *Protest Songs* album is in my top five.

Creation Records was an independent label founded by Scotsman Alan McGhee. With artists such as Primal Scream and the hugely successful Oasis signed to the label, I was pleased to be asked to engineer and produce with another of their bands, Ride. Recorded at Matrix studios in Little Russell Street, near Tottenham Court Road, the album, titled *Tarantula* was not successful and Creation dropped the record from its roster after only one week! A record in itself.

But someone in Japan had bought a copy and must have loved it, because three months later, I was on a plane to Tokyo.

"I'm flying my 'plane, right?"

"Do You Smoke, Mr. Digby?"

The telephone call, as they often do, came one night completely out of the blue. The lady on the other end introduced herself. She explained to me that she represented Japanese artists' interests here in the U.K. We arranged a meeting and a few days later I was sitting in a coffee shop in Primrose Hill talking business with Mariko.

A typically petite, attractive and well-dressed Japanese lady, Mariko's first question caught me by complete surprise: "Do you smoke Mr Digby?" Well, I couldn't say no, because I did. Yet I was very aware of the increasing public disdain of the habit and so offered her two options. Yes, I do, but if required could place my dependency on hold. As it happens, she was pleased that I did smoke. She informed me that the last engineer who had worked with this band, despite being a smoker himself, had quit the sessions due to the chain-smoking habits of the Japanese musicians. We will be recording in Tokyo, she told me and there was at the time no ban in that city on smoking in public places so the control room will be, how shall we say, hazy. No problem, I assured her, thinking of my days spent in the studios in the early seventies in the fog of smoke, Rastafarian and otherwise.

In the months prior to taking on this project, I had been spending some considerable amount of time away from home. Residential, out of town studios were in abundance and I had found myself recording in a number of them. Wool Hall studios, near Bath had been home for a week when I worked there with Sony band Reef. I resided for a week in a studio on a small farm out in the Gloucestershire countryside recording tracks with Steve Winwood's wife, Nicole, for her recently formed publishing company, Winwood Songs. I had also been away out in Palm Springs, California for a couple of weeks (not delivering cakes!)

recording with my dear friend, band manager Don Tunnel, with his newly signed band U.S.K. So when the opportunity to travel to Japan arose, I wasn't sure how Kim would respond. We had two young children and I wasn't exactly spending a lot of time with them. But being the kind, understanding, intelligent and beautiful lady that she was (and still is) her take on it was simple. If it had been a residential studio in the U.K., or perhaps another trip to the States, she might have objected, but an opportunity to travel and work in Japan could not be refused.

The Japanese management company sent me glossy brochures of all the top studios in Tokyo, so Kim and I looked through them all together. There was nothing to choose between them. All were sumptuous, fully equipped state of the art facilities and I couldn't decide. So I let Kim pick the one. She liked the look of Bunkamura Studios so that's where we recorded.

On arrival at Narita International airport, at night and with Mariko at my side, I was greeted by the band's management team and after accepting a small welcoming gift from my hosts, was driven at speed to where the musicians were rehearsing. I was introduced to The Yellow Monkey (named sarcastically after the term used by British prisoners of war as an ethnic slur against their captors) and the tall lead singer Kazuya "Lovin" Yoshi made it clear that he wanted me to take a seat and listen to an album. I sat dutifully in front of the speakers and as Lovin removed the album from its sleeve and placed it on the turntable I, was somewhat surprised to see that it was the Ride album, *Tarantula*. After playing a couple of tracks he informed me that this was his favourite album of the moment and he wanted his next album to sound the same. That's why I was there.

I should mention the other band members: Hideaki "Emma" Kikuchi on guitar, Youichi "Heesey" Hirose on bass and Eiji "Annie" Kikuchi on drums. The use of female middle names dated back to their earlier days of performing on the Japanese, effeminate underground glam-rock circuit. This was to be their seventh album, the previous one, *Four Seasons*, having reached number one in the Far East charts. A more proficient, musically articulate group of musicians would be hard to find. So well-rehearsed and prepared, the recording went like clockwork, with time sheets for the day's schedule handed out to every band member and all the crew at the beginning of each session. For example, 12noon to 13.30hrs ---- guitar overdubs tracks 4, 6 and 9. 13.35hrs to 14.50hrs -----lead vocals tracks 2, 7 and 9. And so on for the whole eleven days, where the only problem would be if we should happen to get ahead of the schedule! Lots of scratching of perplexed heads and scribbling out times, moving overdubs around until order was restored. A bit mathematical, you might say, but from an engineer's perspective, it made life easier than the normal, often chaotic indecision experienced on most sessions. Another benefit was that you knew exactly what time you would start and finish.

On the subject of start times, I was to be reminded one morning of the importance of adhering to the meticulous requirements of punctuality when working with the Japanese. We were scheduled for an 11am start and at about two or three minutes past 11 my assistant and I casually glided into the control room with our cups of coffee, only to be greeted by the frown-like stare of Mr. Omoru, the executive producer. Somewhat puzzled and slightly intimidated, we proceeded to prepare the desk for the first overdub of the day. At a suitably discreet opportunity Mariko, my translator and chaperone, informed us both that Mr. Omoru would wish to have a meeting with the engineers at the end of the days recording. It was then pointed out to us, politely yet sternly, that an 11am start means 11am, not two minutes past. Sessions must be ready to commence at the specific allocated times. Point taken. Next day, also an 11am start and my assistant and I are sat at the desk, at exactly 11am, to the second, with our hands on the desk faders and machine remotes, ready to press "play". Mr. Omoru is sitting at the back of the control room, his wry smile suggesting he was suitably impressed. However, there was no sign of the band! They ankled into the studio about fifteen minutes later, all with armfuls of clothes shopping. I later heard Mariko say to one of the band members that Mr. Omoru would like to have a meeting with them all at the end of the session ----.

I wish I could say more about Tokyo. Didn't see much of the place other than the hotel, the inside of mini-cabs and the studio. This is always the case when you travel around the world to exciting, sometimes even exotic places as a recording engineer. A recording studio control room in Tokyo is as identical to one in London as to another in Los Angeles. All the band members get time to explore, go shopping and dine out ---- the engineer gets to sit for hours, trapped in front of the loudspeakers, move endless faders on a desk, adjust headphone balances and gaze longingly out of the window, that's if there are any windows. What does, however, stand out as exceptional about this particular project was the overwhelming display of charm, dignity and respect shown to me by the band and the whole entourage. I didn't open a door or carry a bag for the whole time I was there, was extremely well fed and watered, showered with gifts and what is more, had the most fun I have ever had in a recording studio, anywhere. It may not be common knowledge that the Japanese have the most wicked, sometimes very naughty, but rarely offensive sense of humour, not totally dissimilar to The Brits.

One example of a comic display was shown to me by lead singer Lovin on my birthday. I walked into a totally silent control room that morning, everyone sat around looking very serious and concerned. Lovin stood tall in the middle of the room, head and shoulders stiffly held high, hands clasped behind his back in the style of a military officer. He summoned me to stand in front of him, as if I was to receive an official dressing down. What on earth had I done wrong? There was a long pause as everyone looked on, stony-faced. The tension hung in the air and I admit to feeling quite intimidated. As I awaited my uncertain fate, it was with impeccable comic timing that Lovin presented me with a large gift-wrapped box and began singing, in perfect English, "Happy Birthday to You". The whole control room fell about laughing, entirely at my expense, and I loved all of them the more for it.

Let me tell you, working in the studio with the Japanese, well, I can't remember ever having laughed so much in all my life. Excellent company and great musicianship combined. It was a joy.

The final touches to the record were completed back in England, at Peter Gabriel's enchanting Real World studios in Box, near Bath, Wiltshire. Again, the red-carpet treatment from the band and from the studio staff. Peter was a perfect gentleman and would come down to dinner with us every night, always enquiring as to our well-being. In one of the live rooms, there is a part of the floor that is glass, beneath which runs the stream that once would have driven the mill wheel. It is lit up at night and you would often see kingfishers darting under your feet as you worked. What a fabulous place to work! Very close to the famous Box Hill railway tunnel, the high-speed Great Western trains rattle past the studios, but are unheard from inside. Built under the direction of Isambard Kingdom Brunel, at the time of its opening in 1841 Box Hill, at 1.83 miles in length was the longest railway tunnel in the world. The reason I mention this tunnel and this railway is because of where I stayed whilst working at Real World.

Accommodation at the studio was in short supply so I was given the keys to a nearby small cottage at the end of a short country lane. It was nighttime and after a long, industrious day in the studio, I was looking forward to a good night's sleep. I walked down the dark, unlit lane, found the cottage and put the key in the door. Upon entering I was struck by the abundance of miniature trains, tiny figures of railway workers and small water colour paintings of railway scenes that adorned the shelves and walls along the narrow hallway. As I climbed the steep stairs to my room, I noticed paintings of steam engines that featured cute, human like faces. Then the penny dropped. I was in the home of Thomas The Tank Engine. Built in 1876, Lorne House was, between 1920 and 1928 the childhood home of the Reverend W. J. Audrey, author of the famous tank engine tales. Every night I stayed there I would lie awake, listen to the trains rolling past, picture the Fat Controller and drift off into a childlike sleep.

A second album followed a year later, this time with the backing tracks being recorded from scratch at Real World, with overdubs completed at the legendary Air studios in Hampstead, north London. Associated Independent Recording studios had originally been located on Oxford Circus in the west end of London in 1970. The brainchild of a certain famous E.M.I./Parlophone record producer, Air studios moved to its present location in the former congregational church on Lyndhurst road, Hampstead in 1991 and it was here, working with The Yellow Monkey that I was privileged to meet the great man himself, Sir George Martin.

On our very first morning at Air, he quietly and politely entered the control room and introduced himself. He thanked us for choosing to work at his studio, wished us well and suggested we not hesitate to inform him or any of his staff of any requirements we may have in order to proceed smoothly with our project. Such a soft spoken, warm and sophisticated gentleman. Anybody who is reading this should be in no doubt of this man's single-handed, monumental contribution to the success of British popular music. His early work with Peter Sellers and The Goons; Flanders and Swan; Shirley Bassey; Charlie Drake; Matt Monro ------. Not forgetting, of course, the eleven albums he produced with that famous four-piece beat-combo from Liverpool who went on to conquer the World. John, Paul, George and Ringo always referred to George Martin as the "Fifth Beatle" and meeting him was for me, without comparison, the greatest single moment of my entire musical career.

The first Yellow Monkey album was oddly called *Sicks* and in 1997 it went to number one in the Japanese/Far East charts. At the same time, I was to have a number one album in the U.K. with Sony band Reef entitled *Glow*, which was to be recorded at the studios featured in my 1963 dreams. I was, finally, off to Abbey Road

..... 1963 dreams.

"You're No Geoff Emerick--."

I'm possibly spending too much time thanking the same people, but it just so happens that, over the years, certain people have repeatedly come to my assistance when I have been in need of a gig. So here I go again. Trevor Wyatt suggested to me (over a pint one evening in The Keys) that I give Muff Winwood a call. Sony had signed a band called Reef and they were about to go in the studio and record their second album, *Glow*. Trevor had thought their type of music would be right up my street and that I should put myself forward for engineering duties. Good tip-off Trev' so thanks again. Muff was almost apologetic when I spoke to him. "Of course, Digby, why didn't I think of calling you, this is perfect for you." Thanks Muff, genuinely.

I met up with producer George Drakoulias at one of the band's rehearsals and spent the evening listening to the songs we would be recording and forging the necessary relationships. George had been part of the successful American 90's hit label Def Jam, working on landmark singles by Beastie Boys, L.L. Cool and Public Enemy, so he was what you might call an industry heavyweight. As usually happens when you work with heavyweights you get to work at the top venues and in this case, at the very top: Abbey Road Studios.

On arrival for the first day of recording, I was greeted by a uniformed security guard at the top of the steps of the main entrance. I was certain this was the same man who had refused me entry back in October 1969, when I had turned up with my list of thirty-eight, only this time he pointed to my reserved car parking space and personally escorted me into studio two. I so desperately wanted to tell him that I had waited thirty-four years for this day, but I was too excited to even speak. I stood in the control room of studio two, looking down over the spacious, somewhat plain and functional studio, at the scuffed parquet flooring, the large movable beige sound screens and the ancient, rather drab acoustic tiles on the walls. The strength of this under-stated, utilitarian appearance only served to confirm that I was in the place of legends, of musical history, where a journey for me that had started in 1963, with the release of *Please, Please Me* was now, in 1997, complete. This was where Paul McCartney had counted in that first track on that first Beatles album and the sound of his voice had travelled all the way from this very space to my sister Pat's "Regentone" mono record player in her bedroom. Simply amazing.

Reef's drummer Dominic and I were walking around the corridors at Abbey Road one morning before starting the days recording. We were looking at the gallery of pictures on the walls: Yehudi Menuhin, Connie Francis, Glen Miller, Sir Edward Elgar, Cliff Richard, The Beatles, on and on. One picture caught our eyes at the same time. It was one of Ringo Starr sitting at the drums in studio two. Above the drums was a single pepper-pot shaped microphone, with no other microphones in sight. Is that how they recorded Ringo's drums, we both thought? We needed no further encouragement. Report to Lester in the microphone department and enquire as to the availability of the microphone in the picture. Yes, they still had it, so we signed the microphone release form and hurried back to studio two. Dom's drums had been set up in the middle of the room and every single drum and cymbal had a microphone on it, about twelve mics as I recall! Not my choice, I must say. Fewer mics the better was my experience, but George, the producer, had insisted. Anyway, George hadn't arrived as yet, so Dom and I wanted to experiment with drum sounds. We moved all the microphones away, dismantled the drums and re-assembled them in the same part of the room as where Ringo had been sitting in the photograph, the back left-hand corner. We put the pepper-pot mic on a stand and suspended it above the drums, just as in the photograph. Perfect. I ran up the stairs into the control room, lifted the microphone fader and put the machine into record. "Play your drums Dom" I shouted, all excited, down the talk-back. After two or three minutes of hitting the skins, Dom ran up the stairs into the control room and prepared himself for the playback. I hit the play button, and we listened and looked at each other. Dom said it sounded "like shit" and I concurred. What were we doing wrong? I jokingly said to Dom "Well, you're not Ringo Starr!" and with a swift repost he replied "Yeah, you're not Geoff Emerick either!" (Emerick had been The Beatles engineer since 1966, after Norman Smith). So we put the drums back to where they had been before and returned the pepper-pot mic to Lester. He smiled as he told us "Everyone who comes here looks at that picture and borrows that microphone and says that it sounds rubbish. You see, you need Ringo and his drums and Geoff Emerick as an engineer. (We were both right.) Also, he said, the old valve analogue E.M.I desk that used to be there".

Good try though.

When you are arriving for work every day at this "Temple of Sound", you can be forgiven for indulging in the obvious. I preferred to take the train from Chiswick to Swiss Cottage (the tube station nearest to the studios) rather than drive, if only because the walk from the tube station to the studio afforded me the opportunity to cross the most famous zebra crossing in the world, sometimes twice a day! Sad but true. Another regular pleasure for me was spending time in the evening with the security guys who manned the CCTV cameras, watching people standing outside in front of the studio wall. Visitors from around the world come to pay their musical respects by either writing some personal tribute on the wall, or simply standing in silent prayer. One evening a well-dressed Japanese man stood silently for several minutes, staring at the wall. He moved forward, head bowed and reached inside his coat. He removed the lid from a small copper urn and emptied the ashen contents across the wall. Then took two steps back, stopped and bowed his head one more time and disappeared into the night.

"Happens all the time" said the unsurprised security man.

In January 1997, the Reef album *Glow* made it to number one in the U.K. charts and at the same time The Yellow Monkey's album *Sicks* was number one in the Far East. For a brief two-week period I was the most successful recording engineer on the planet. Not my words, but those of my wife, Kim, who also wisely commented that the sun never sets on my hit records. But the music business is a cruel mistress, because at the same time as I was enjoying my global chart successes I was working on a building site cleaning out a cement mixer.

The way it works is like this. After an album is recorded it is usually many weeks, if not months before its release. There are matters relating to artwork, publicity and promotion that need to be put into place, so by the time both of these records were "in the shops" I had been through another of those self-employed rest periods. No phone calls, no Trevor or Muff, no work. I was wearing out the hall carpet, pacing up and down getting increasingly frustrated. What's more, the fridge was empty.

It was time to call Andy.

Andy Mould ran his own landscape gardening business in East Sheen, southwest London and I had worked with him before, doing general labouring, paving, fencing, brick laying and turfing. Being self-employed for so many years has encouraged me to develop many other skills and if there is no studio work then needs must when necessity compels. I rang Andy on the Friday night and he said to meet him at the usual place at seven on Monday morning. There was a driveway to repair in Kingston-upon-Thames and he could use some extra hands. Towards the end of the week, we had completed the work and I was a couple of hundred pounds better off. It was also the week that I had the two hit records at the top of the charts. So, last day and it was getting dark and starting to rain. Those heavenly words that you hear on a building site at the end of a hard day's graft came from Andy's mouth: "Clean out the mixer, beer time!" Except that Andy had one last request. "Got a bit of a shitty job for you Digby, sorry mate, but the drain in the street needs unblocking." We had been a bit lazy when cleaning out the mixer on previous days and the council had complained that the sand and cement had blocked the drain cover. Andy handed me a bolster and chisel and I set to work. I was on my hands and knees in the gutter, chiselling away in the dark, pouring with rain, covered in muck and soaked to the skin. I eventually got the drain cover to lift and was by now lying face-down in the gutter with my head and arms INSIDE the drain. Then the cruel, full head-on indignity of my position was exposed. Across the street from where we were working was a music college and four-thirty was home time for all the young students. Out they poured with their violin and guitar cases, folders of music manuscript paper, headphones plugged into mobile phones, no doubt listening to the latest hits. Nearly all of them glanced over at me and from the look of disapproval on their faces I knew exactly what they were thinking: "poor old sod, lying in the gutter covered in shit". I wanted to jump up and shout "This is not what it seems! I've got two, TWO number one records in the charts. You are probably listening to one of them now!!" But no point because appearances are everything and anyway, how were they to know. Besides which, I was happy; the fridge was full and the driveway looked good.

On the back of the success of those two albums, I was in a favourable position to approach a music publishing company for the finance to open my own recording studio. Francis Pettican had previously been managing director of Island Music, the publishing arm of the label and was at this time running his own company, Westbury Music. Amongst his clients were Cat Stevens (now known as Yusef Islam, after his conversion to Islam), David Bowie and Gerry Rafferty, so I was to be in good company. We found premises in the basement of an old industrial building in Chiswick, west London and made our plans. As it came to pass, Francis chose not to put his name to the lease, but I had developed a solid relationship with the owner of the building and he showed sufficient confidence in my business venture to offer the lease directly to me. Thus was born RDS Studios.

Westbury Music continued to provide financial support in the early years and the business grew. The model for the business was this: go across the road to the local B+Q builders' merchant, order many metres of timber, nails and screws, plasterboard, Rockwool insulation, electrical cable and paint. Sound-proof one of the many empty rooms and rent the space to an independent music production company. Use the deposit paid by the said client to go back to B+Q, order metres of timber, nails etc. and repeat the operation. Rent out sound-proofed space to an independent music production company, return to B+Q, -------. You get the picture.

Along with a lot of help from family and friends (especially musician/carpenter Steve Gould and electrician Chris Aylen) I constructed seven studios this way. I remember the telephone call from my accountant, Warren Weiss, when he told me that, after six years of submitting accounts and running at a loss, we had finally gone into profit. I think the margin was about three hundred and seventy-three pounds fifty-two pence, but we had got there! RDS Studios was a dream come true for me and my family and a lot of people had invested a tremendous amount of hard work, love and support in order for the business to become a reality.

We had some great successes at RDS: an album of exceptional musical integrity with Hamish Stuart (ex-Average White Band vocalist) titled *Sooner or Later*, an album with Lionel Blair, the dancer and entertainer, *Blair Sings Fred Astaire*, sessions with three-time Grammy Award nominee Joan Armatrading and music for the hit television series *Bob the Builder*. And what's more, we helped keep B+Q in business for quite a few years. In 2007 the business was sold on and I was ready for new musical challenges.

We all say it because, like most clichés, it is true: "My, oh my, how the years roll by." The kids grow up, you move to your first house, wrestle with the bills but somehow get through another year. If you have the support of a strong family and, most importantly, an extremely patient and understanding partner then life is a joy. And I am so pleased to be part of an industry that creates the joy that music brings to all mankind. I have witnessed the healing power of music a number of times, in care homes and hospitals as well as in the studio itself. Music is the great leveller and the great unifier. Music is my religion. Recording studios are my temples, my churches, my synagogues and my mosques. I have been on a musical crusade that has required little or no effort to impress so few non-believers. I preach to the converted. I am a music jihadist and I inhabit a global melodic and rhythmic caliphate. My religion pre-dates all others because it is born out of the primordial melodic whistle of the wind and the rhythmic pattern of rainfall; it speaks outward and listens inward and I have no competition from any other orthodoxy.

I wasn't sure where, if at all, to include this next paragraph in my book, but I have concluded that it would be remiss of me not to mention the passing of both my parents and so here it will be. We lost Dad unexpectedly and very suddenly. He had many of the common ailments of an eighty-one-year-old; failing eyesight, a little unsteady on his feet, but was otherwise generally fit and healthy. He would go for his regular morning walk to fetch the newspaper that he couldn't see well enough to read himself, was always interested in the world around him, liked to chat and enjoyed his cigarettes. On one of his early morning forays to the newsagent, he slipped and fell on the icy winter pavement, damaged his hip, went into hospital for a routine operation and died the next day from a heart attack. Mom lost the only man she had ever loved and over the following eight years slowly and painfully deteriorated. It was a few days before Christmas of 2010 when I and my two beautiful sisters became orphans. Even now, I occasionally indulge my sadness by crying myself to sleep with happy tears as I remember my wonderful parents.

In 2008, we moved the family to Devon, in search of perhaps quieter times. But no chance! I made contact with studio grandee Malcolm Toft (Trident studios, The Beatles, Queen), and his business partner at the time, BBC radio presenter Rick Ehringer. Both are well-established figures in the southwest of England and, at the time, were running a multi-media studio complex in Newton Abbot. Under the enthusiastic leadership of data-intelligence expert Mark "Lenny" McCoy and the marketing and management skills of his partner Allison Aitken, The Music Mill became a central creative hub for the region, and I enjoyed a fulfilling experience as chief engineer and producer at the studios for over seven years. My work there included mixing unreleased recordings of 80s rock superstars Bad Company and, at the complete opposite end of the studio spectrum, recording an audiobook with legendary radio presenter and political commentator Jonathan Dimbleby. The wide variety of musical talent that passed through the doors of The Music Mill included jazz quintets, school choirs, rock bands, rappers, retired ladies who work for the Macmillan cancer support group, the Purple Angel Dementia awareness charity, reggae and ska bands, solo singer/songwriters and even Morris Dancers!

Due to the changing nature of music production, with the growth in digital home recording having a massive negative impact on most professional recording studios' ability to survive commercially, we were all sad to see the business close in 2017.

Let me conclude with a fond memory of being in the Music Mill studio on a session with local singer/songwriter, the incredibly talented Sarah Yeo. I'm sat at the desk as I pause for a moment, remembering the early days at Basing Street. As so often happens, my mind drifts off, back in time, to the Old Kent Road and a wet October evening in 1969. A telephone box. A bedroom covered in egg-boxes, and an old mono record player. My sister Pat listening to the Beatles and practicing her jive steps with the wardrobe door. Dad off to a gig with his sax, Mom dancing in the kitchen with the radio on -----.

I snap out of my dream-like state because the musicians are waiting for the red light. Matt is on the drums, Sarah is singing, and Nick is playing guitar. We are ready to roll, so over to you, Matt; count us in:

"One, two, three, four ---------."

Music is my religion.

Epilogue

I must briefly thank a few musical friends from the past who I keep in touch with on Facebook: Henry Howard, Phil Payne, Mark Saxby, Greg Cobb and Jim Price. Love to you all and keep on rockin'! But let me apologise to all the many people I have met and worked with over the years, whom I haven't kept in touch with or have failed to mention. You know who you are, and I thank you for being part of my life and for allowing me to share some small part of yours.

Having arrived at this, for me, unique place and time (the conclusion of my first book), I feel it necessary to add some final thoughts. Most strikingly, the technological changes that have taken place over the last forty-eight years, both inside and outside of the recording studio, have been enormous. From when I first walked through the doors of Island Records' recording studios on Basing Street in 1969 to today, I have witnessed innovation and change beyond what could have been imagined. The emergence of digital technology has transformed many aspects of our daily lives, and nowhere more noticeably than in the world of music.

On the plus side, contemporary Digital Audio Workstations (DAWs) have placed affordable music production within reach of many more creatives, enabling songwriters, musicians, and producers to generate content on limited budgets. If there is a downside, then it is this: that the degree of forensic audio manipulation available throughout the modern production process has undoubtedly contributed to the lowering of standards of musicianship. Not entirely, it must be said; there are still those who have mastered their craft, and I have the pleasure of encountering them regularly. The other misguided, hopeful "musicians" are no longer required to play in time and tune; all can be "fixed in the mix" with software plug-ins that will auto-tune, pitch shift and correct timing issues. Total recall of mix-down settings allows for infinite, often microscopic and usually irrelevant adjustments that serve only to placate individual egos. These impostors should not be allowed to enter our "Temples of Sound" because they are devaluing the musical currency. Even amongst many of the proficient elite, the availability of these modern production procedures has, in no small measure, taken away much of the human soul of music. The flawed fragility of standing on the cliff-edge of musical expectation, the joy of free falling into melodic and rhythmic uncertainty, the freshness of spontaneity, for the most part, are all gone. Studio engineers have become "Mr. Fix-Its," and much of our time is spent creating perfect, often bland musical robotics.

Music has become, for better or worse, the property of the people. Go back to the nineteenth century, and the only time you could hear music would be when it was played live in front of you. If your tastes were of the classical or operatic variety, then the audio experience would be limited to a chosen elite. In contrast, folk music, as the name suggests, was available to even the humblest of enslaved persons or serfs. Man's inventiveness took us into the twentieth century with the introduction of the recording medium and the beginnings of the democratisation of music. From its crude beginnings, the format slowly developed over the next fifty years to the point when most people had in their homes what was called (for the benefit of my younger readers) a "record player". Music had arrived in our living rooms.

But of course, you had to purchase "discs", the sales of which generated income for newly formed record labels, musicians, songwriters and artists. Your television and radio licenses contributed to those same people receiving additional royalty income from the reproduction of their music. That aspect of the music industry is still relatively intact, whereas revenue from actual record, tape and CD sales has plummeted. Today's de facto view, especially amongst the younger generation, is that music should be available to all, at any time, on demand and for free.

I would refer my readers to a book written nearly forty years ago by French polymath Jacques Attali entitled "Noise: The Political Economy of Music". (Presses Universitaires de France 1977). A stunningly prophetic work, the premise of the book is as follows:

Attali believes that music has gone through four distinct cultural stages in its history: Sacrificing, Representing, Repeating, and a fourth cultural stage which could roughly be called Post-Repeating. These stages are each linked to a particular "mode of production"; that is to say, each of these stages carries with it a specific set of technologies for producing, recording and disseminating music, and also concomitant cultural structures that allow for music's transmission and reception. Sound complicated? Well, it isn't if you read the book!

Also, try to listen to the late, great David Bowie's 1999 interview with BBC Newsnight's Jeremy Paxman, where Bowie intuitively predicted the massive impact the internet would have on society, especially about the changing nature of the relationship between artists and the public in general. At the time, he described the implications as "unimaginable". Even the commonly over-persistent Paxman sat there mesmerised, almost silent in his disbelief. Bowie's last album was released two days before he died and contains tracks that allude to a self-epitaph. The first line of lyrics to the opening track, *Lazarus*, begins with the optimistic words: "Look up here, I'm in Heaven". Taking

Bowieism even further, it is glaringly apparent that this man prepared for his death with the internet in mind.

The need to embrace change is essential for our survival as a species. It is specifically crucial if you wish to survive today as a record producer, which is why I currently find myself making an album with a keyboard player who lives in Somerset, the bass player and drummer are in Texas, and the vocalist lives in Los Angeles. None of us has met or been in the same room together. All the audio files are transferred over the internet between the respective participants, and the album should be finished later this year.

Finally, it is with some sadness to hear news of the redevelopment of the iconic church that was once the home of Island Records/Basing Street and later, producer Trevor Horn's Sarm West studios. The birthplace of so many people's music careers and the creative Earth Spot for much of Britain's immeasurable contribution to popular musical history .... gone.

I will never forget my original 1969 list of thirty-eight London studios and the fact that Island's Basing Street studios were not amongst them.

R.I.P. number thirty-nine.

Glossary

Analogue – sound signals that correspond with variations in air pressure of the original sound.

Attack – speed at which compression occurs.

Attenuation – reduction in the strength of a signal.

A+R – artist and repertoire.

ARP – brand of American synthesiser keyboard.

Bouncing – combining several audio tracks into one audio track.

Cardioid – pattern of microphone sensitivity.

Channel – an audio signal communications path, usually found on a desk or console.

Chinagraph pencil – a waxy pencil used to make marks on magnetic tape.

Compression – reduction of the volume of loud sounds and the amplification of quiet sounds.

Condenser microphone – capacitance change, voltage-controlled microphone.

Control room – room where sound is monitored, recorded and manipulated.

Crystal microphone – a low-grade microphone that uses a piezoelectric crystal as its transducer.

DAW – digital audio workstation, or computer-based software system for

digitally recording and manipulating audio.

Delay – an audio effect reminiscent of an echo.

Demo – a demonstration of a song used as a reference.

Digital – audio signals converted into a sequence of discrete numbers.

Direct Injection Box (D.I.) –device to connect an electronic instrument to the console.

Dolby –noise reduction system for use with magnetic tape recordings.

Double tracked –layering of two versions of the same performance to thicken the sound.

Drop-in –to engage record whilst replacing/overwriting previous audio.

Echo –a reflection of sound, creating a sense of space.

Editing block – a metal block with angled slots used for splicing tape

E.Q. (Equalisation) –**alteration of the** frequency response of an audio signal.

Fader – a potentiometer that controls the volume of an audio signal.

Filtering –removal of unwanted frequencies.

Floating floor – construction technique designed to isolate a room from the main structure of a building.

Guides – part of tape transport on tape machine.

Hammond Organ –classic electric organ that creates sound using drawbars and electric current from a rotating metal tone wheel.

Head block –record or playback metal blocks that make contact with magnetic tape on an analogue tape machine

Heads out – winding magnetic tape onto the supply reel.

High pass filter – switching device used to remove unwanted low frequencies.

Insert switch –used as pathway to engage an external audio device on recording console channel strip.

Leader tape –a non-magnetic tape of paper or plastic used at the beginning, end or as a marker within the audio tape.

Leakage – also known as "spill" is the occurrence of sound being picked up by a microphone from a source other than that which is intended.

Leslie cabinet –rotating speaker, usually used with a Hammond organ.

Live room – room where instrumentalists and vocalists perform.

Master take –the final chosen version of a recording.

Master reel – collection of all master takes.

Microphone patterns –configuration of microphone sensitivity relative to sound direction.

Mix –stage at which multiple sounds are combined into one or more channels.

Monitoring section –part of console used for adjusting audio playback levels.

Moog –modular voltage-controlled analogue synthesiser.

Multi-sound –layering, or bouncing of audio onto a single or stereo track.

Multi-track –method of sound recording that allows for separate recording of multiple sound sources.

Overdubbing –simultaneous recording added to an existing recorded performance.

Overheads – microphones placed over or above the head of the performer and their instrument.

P.A – personal assistant.

p.a. –public address system.

Patch bay –a central audio connection area for outboard equipment.

Phase –the relationship between the same sound waves been recorded through multiple channels.

Phasing –an effect created by adding together two identical audio signals separated by a very short time delay.

Pinch wheel –rubberised free spinning wheel used to press magnetic tape against the head blocks.

Pop shield –protection filter for microphone to reduce "popping" sounds during recording of speech or singing.

Quarter inch –tape format which refers to the width of magnetic tape usually used on stereo mix down tape machines.

Ratio –specifies the amount of decibel reduction applied to the audio signal used during compression.

Reel to reel –form of magnetic audio recording where the magnetic tape is held on spools.

Release –determines how fast gain reduction resets during compression.

Reverb –persistence of sound after the sound is produced by the build-up of sound reflections.

Ribbon microphone –microphone that uses an electrically conductive ribbon, usually aluminium or nanofilm placed between magnetic poles to produce a voltage.

Rollers – part of tape transport on tape machine.

Sample –an audio value at a set point in time.

Schlieren photography – the photographing of air around objects.

Seperation –the avoidance of "spill" and leakage of sound between microphones.

Signal processing –the alteration of an audio signal through an audio effects unit.

Sixteen track – analogue tape or tape machine with sixteen individual audio tracks.

Soloing –the isolation of and individual microphone or audio signal.

Sound on sound – see "Multi-sound".

Spicing tape –adhesive tape used for joining together separate sections of magnetic tape.

Spill – sound leaking from one source to another.

Standing waves –undesirable frequency resonance between two opposite walls.

Stereo placement –positioning of individual sounds within the stereo field.

Synthesiser –an electronic musical instrument that generates electric signals that are converted to sound.

Tail out –tape has been stored after being played and must be rewound in order to play again.

Talk-back – microphone used for communicating between control room and live studio.

Tape alignment –record and playback configuration of tape machines to ensure repeatable and accurate sound quality.

Tape guides –part of the tape transport mechanism of a tape recorder.

Tape loop –sound recorded on a section of magnetic tape, cut and spliced end to end, creating a circle or loop which can be played continuously.

Tape operator –assistant to main engineer.

Tape phasing –see "Phasing".

Tape splicing –cutting of tape at a required point and rejoining it to another section of tape

Test pressing –first vinyl discs made at the factory for evaluation purposes before mass production.

Tie-line –connections between control room and live room and other studios and devises.

Track sheet –table or list of instruments recorded.

Valve microphone –a condenser microphone which uses a valve amplifier.

V.U. meter –volume unit meter which shows a representation of audio signal level.

Acknowledgements

After many years of relating anecdotes associated with my experiences of recording studio life, I was encouraged by family and friends to "write this all down", if only, I suspect, to bring to a halt the assault on them of my constant repetitions. I began to jot down my recollections about three years ago, with absolutely no idea what I was doing, or where I was going. But as is so often the case with the creative process, the writings began to take on a life of their own. It was as if the pen was taken out of my hand (or, more accurately, the mouse and keyboard) because I found it difficult to stop the flow, to not digress too far with add-ons of accumulative detail. So therefore, much has been omitted, perhaps to be included in any subsequent editions.

I will also undoubtedly omit to mention a few of the friends and colleagues who have assisted me along the way towards the realisation of this, my fist publication, but here, in no particular order, are some of the many.

Jayne Stroud, a leading figure in the South-West of England's business community, was the first non-family member to whom I dared to show an early draft of the book. She was instrumental in offering me an objective critique, a publishing industry contact and, most importantly, the encouragement to believe in myself as an author.

Caroline Davidson and Katharine Bratton at the Caroline Davidson Literary Agency, for their professional guidance and support. Caroline's were the first professional eyes to read my early text and I was both shocked and pleasantly surprised that she thought it was worthy of being published. More importantly, I was shown that the world of book publishing is inhabited by some genuinely creative, kind and helpful people and I will always be indebted to Caroline and her team at CDLA.

Neil Storey, former Island Records Press Officer, read a couple of my chapters and gave me some helpful suggestions in terms of embellishing some of the detail, and I look forward to the release of his latest work, the forthcoming definitive account of the history of Island, namely the Island Book of Records, due for release in late 2019.

Louise Jones, part of the management team at the Carlton Hotel in Torquay, Devon, has listened to an early draft of an audio version of this book and I was both flattered and encouraged by her compliments.

Laura Callwood's artistic contribution to the book with her exemplary and charmingly accurate illustrations is much appreciated. She has been waiting almost as patiently as I have for this work to be published.

www.ingramcontent.com/pod-product-compliance
Lightning Source LLC
Chambersburg PA
CBHW071150070526
44584CB00019B/2732